MW00462490

Roads ~ Less ~ Traveled Through the Coeur d'Alenes

Historical Driving Tours of Benewah, Kootenai and Shoshone Counties

Dorothy Dahlgren and Simone Kincaid

Published by
Museum of North Idaho
PO Box 812
Coeur d'Alene, ID 83816-0812
dd@museumni.org   www.museumni.org
208-664-3448

ISBN-13: 978-0-9723356-7-6
ISBN: 10-9723356-7-6

Copyright 2007
All rights reserved

Graphic Designer Grady Myers

Cover photograph: *It's springtime 1949, and some lucky folks have taken the top down on a brand new Mercury convertible for a scenic drive around Lake Coeur d'Alene, halting briefly overlooking Beauty Bay with Blue Creek Bay in the distance. (See driving tour four, page 4-5.)*

Photograph by Kyle Walker

~ Introduction ~

The beautiful valley and mountain landscapes found in the Coeur d'Alene region were formed by catastrophic floods, glacial advances, basalt flows, volcanic ash deposits and inland seas. Native Americans including the Coeur d'Alenes, Kutenai, Kalispel, and Nez Perces inhabited this landscape for thousand of years. They lived on the resources of the land by hunting, fishing, and gathering roots and berries as they moved across the area with the seasons.

The Lewis and Clark expedition through central Idaho in 1805 signaled the first recorded exploration by people of European descent into what was to become Idaho Territory. By 1809 David Thompson established the Kullyspell House trading post on Lake Pend Oreille. The hunters, trappers, traders and Iroquois guides who frequented the Kullyspell house brought with them stories of places in the far north and the east and of people who were teaching Christianity.

Coeur d'Alene tribal leader Circling Raven, had a vision and prophesized the coming of the Black Robes (Priests) in 1740. His son Twisted Earth stayed confident the prophecy would come to pass. It was not until 1842 that the prophecy was fulfilled when Father DeSmet met three Coeur d'Alene men at the "Headwaters", now the city of Coeur d'Alene. In 1843 the first Jesuit mission was established near St. Maries on the St. Joe River and then moved a short time later to its present Cataldo location. The Mission of the Sacred Heart (Cataldo Mission), on the Coeur d'Alene River, was completed in 1853 and is the oldest standing building in Idaho.

Shortly after the Cataldo Mission was established, the Mullan Military Road was built between 1858-1862 connecting Fort Benton, Montana and Fort Walla Walla, Washington. Camp Coeur d'Alene (later named Fort Sherman) was established in 1878, at the point where Lake Coeur d'Alene flows into the Spokane River, in order to keep peace between settlers and Native Americans. When the Fort was abandoned in 1901 there were 52 buildings including a sawmill, hospital, blacksmith shop, carpenter shop, and a chapel. The chapel, powder magazine and one officers' quarters remain standing.

Coeur d'Alene developed around the Fort, but it was not until the discovery of gold in 1883-1884 on Prichard Creek, on the North Fork of the Coeur d'Alene River, that many settlers arrived. Mining activity created an economic basis for future developments in lumbering, transportation and trade in Kootenai, Benewah and Shoshone Counties. The lasting wealth was not in gold but in lead, silver and zinc, all of which required large capital investments to mine and process.

In 1883 the Northern Pacific Railroad crossed Idaho Territory. Rathdrum developed as an agricultural center and supply point for the mining district and remained a railhead until 1886 when D.C. Corbin built a spur line from the Northern Pacific mainline, at Hauser Junction, to Coeur d'Alene. From Coeur d'Alene passengers traveled by steamboat up the Coeur d'Alene River, to the Cataldo Mission where they boarded the narrow gauge railroad which carried them to the mining districts.

As the railroads connected east to west and land was opened to homesteaders, settlers found their way into Idaho Territory. People from Northern European countries including Switzerland, Norway, Sweden and Finland settled in Kootenai, Shoshone and Benewah counties.

The 1889 launch of the Amelia Wheaton, built by the troops of Camp Coeur d'Alene, marked the beginning of the steamboat era on Lake Coeur d'Alene. By the turn of the century the Coeur d'Alene and Spokane Electric Line train made several trips a day from downtown Spokane to Coeur d'Alene where passengers boarded such steamers as the Boneta, Flyer, Georgie Oakes, Spokane, Colfax, or Idaho bound for St. Joe City, Harrison, or St. Maries. Sunday excursions on the Shadowy St. Joe River were popular as were other recreational activities associated with the many lakes and rivers of the area.

After 1900 large lumber companies from the east discovered the great stands of White Pine. The waterways provided cheap and effective transportation for the logs. In the spring logs were floated down swollen streams and rivers into sorting gaps on the lake and then towed to sawmills. Harrison, St. Maries, Rose Lake, Spirit Lake, Twin Lakes, Post Falls and Coeur d'Alene each boasted a large milling industry. By the mid 1920s the lumber industry began to slow down and many of the smaller mill towns disappeared. World War II saw improvement in the lumber industry; however, the days of accessible timber and cheap transportation were over.

As automobile travel increased, roads improved in North Idaho. By the mid 1910s the Yellowstone Trail connected east to west. Improvements were made and the highway was renamed U.S. Highway 10 in 1926. In the 1960s Interstate 90 replaced Highway 10. Highway 95 was completed in the mid-1920s followed by Highway 97 on the east shore of Lake Coeur d'Alene. These old byways still hold the colorful history of the Coeur d'Alene region. We hope you will enjoy these back roads and the communities found along the way as much as we have.

~ Table of contents ~

Introduction .... *i*
Foreword/Acknowledgements... *v*
How To Use This Self-guided Tour...................................... *viii*

TOUR ONE: Rathdrum Prairie... *1-1*
Post Falls...*1-2*
Pleasant View...*1-7*
Rathdrum...*1-11*
Twin Lakes... *1-17*
Spirit Lake.. *1-17*
Athol... *1-24*

TOUR TWO: Highway 95 North.. *2-1*
Farragut State Park... *2-2*
Bayview... *2-5*
Silverwood.. *2-10*
Chilco/Garwood.. *2-12*
Hayden Lake.. *2-13*
Dalton Gardens... *2-20*

TOUR THREE: Coeur d'Alene.. *3-1*

TOUR FOUR: Lake Coeur d'Alene Loop............................... *4-1*
Lake Coeur d'Alene... *4-2*
Wolf Lodge/Mineral Ridge.. *4-4*
East Shore of Lake Coeur d'Alene..................................... *4-5*
Harrison.. *4-7*
St. Maries.. *4-13*
Heyburn State Park.. *4-21*
Plummer.. *4-21*
Tensed/DeSmet... *4-23*
Worley... *4-24*

TOUR FIVE: Chain Lakes and St. Joe Country.................... *5-1*
Rose Lake... *5-2*
Lane.. *5-5*
Medimont... *5-7*
St. Joe River Road... *5-9*
Calder..*5-14*
Marble Creek..*5-17*
Avery...*5-22*
Moon Pass... *5-24*

St. Regis Side Trip.. *5-29*
Red Ives.. *5-31*

TOUR SIX: Historic Coeur d'Alene National Forest............................ *6-1*
Fernan Ranger Station & Village... *6-3*
Fernan Lake & Road.. *6-4*
Fernan Saddle, Windy Ridge, Spades Mountain.................... *6-7*
Delaney Splash Dam Site & Leiberg Creek............................ *6-11*
Magee Ranger Station.. *6-14*
McPherson Meadows.. *6-14*
Shoshone Work Center... *6-16*

TOUR SEVEN: Coeur d'Alene Mining District.................................. *7-1*
4th of July Pass.. *7-2*
Canyon Road.. *7-5*
Old Mission State Park.. *7-7*
Cataldo... *7-9*
Kingston... *7-11*
Pinehurst.. *7-14*
Smelterville.. *7-17*
Government Gulch... *7-19*
Kellogg... *7-22*
Wardner.. *7-26*
Sunnyside... *7-37*
Big Creek Area... *7-41*
Miner's Memorial Statue... *7-43*
Osburn.. *7-44*
Silverton... *7-48*
Wallace... *7-51*

TOUR EIGHT: Dobson Pass to the Coeur d'Alene River........................... *8-1*
Nine Mile Cemetery.. *8-3*
Dobson Pass... *8-6*
Delta... *8-7*
Kings Pass.. *8-9*
Murray.. *8-9*
Settler's Grove.. *8-13*
Eagle... *8-13*
Prichard.. *8-14*
Enaville.. *8-19*

Bibliography.. *B-1*
Index.. *I-1*

~ Forward ~

The Museum of North Idaho was established in 1968 as a non-profit organization. The Museum's purpose is to collect and preserve artifacts, photographs, archival materials and other information related to the history of the Coeur d'Alene Region and to educate the public about that history. The Museum is a regional repository for these materials.

The driving tour project began in the fall of 2000 when the Museum of North Idaho and area historical groups met to discuss how we could work together to preserve local history. The group decided to work on a driving tour of the region with members agreeing to select sites and supply information to the Museum of North Idaho. As the information came into the Museum and we drove the initial tours we discovered that there were many additional places that we wanted to include. What began as a pamphlet evolved into a book five years later. Because information on many of these sites was not readily available it took many hours of detective work to get even basic information such as dates built and owners. Sometimes we were unable to even find that. What we really wanted to include were the human-interest stories and information that bring these sites to life. Information was gathered from local residents, books, archival material and historical records. Much of the information is anecdotal for the reader's interest. Every effort was made to make this publication accurate and we appreciate any additions or corrections.

Our hope is that this project will give residents and visitors an awareness, understanding and appreciation of the area's cultural heritage and encourage involvement with and support of historical programs, projects and preservation.

Dorothy Dahlgren
Simone Kincaid

We would like to thank these funding sources:

Idaho Humanities Council, National Endowment for the Humanities
U.S. Department of Agriculture, Forest Service
U.S. Department of Transportation, Federal Highway Administration,
Western Federal Lands Highway Division in cooperation with the
Idaho State Historic Preservation Officer
Association for the Preservation & Commemoration of the Old Cataldo
Mission The H.F. Magnuson Family Foundation

~ Acknowledgments ~

This driving tour has been made possible by the many volunteer hours of the historical group members and other individuals. We apologize if we have overlooked anyone on the list. Many people canvassed their community for information for the tour book and relayed it back to the Museum of North Idaho through others. We give a special thanks to Joy Porter for the many hours she spent on research and proofreading.

Avery Citizens' Committee
Bayview Historical Society
Coeur d'Alene Tribe
Crane Historical Society (Harrison)
Northern Pacific Depot Railroad
Museum (Wallace)
Farragut State Park
Fort Sherman Historical Society
Heyburn State Park
Hughes House (St. Maries)
Kootenai County Historical
Preservation Committee

Museum of North Idaho
Old Mission State Park
Plummer Community
Post Falls Historical Society
Rose Lake Historical Society
Spirit Lake Historical Society
Spragpole Museum (Murray)
Staff House (Kellogg)
Wallace District Mining Museum
Wardner Gift Shop and Museum
Westwood Historical Society
Worley Community

Katherine Aiken
Bill & Diana
Albinola
Phyllis Allingson
Glenn Almquist
John Amonson
Barbara Anderson
Kathy Arneson
Francis Arnhold
Berti Arnzen
Everett & Lois
Arvidson
Fran Bahr
Fred Bardelli
Denise Best
Wade Bilbrey
Marcia Biotti
Brenda Blackmer
Clyde Blake
Sheryl Snyder Brandon
Kimberly Rice Brown
Tom & Sandy
Burnett
Darrel & Joann
Carlson
John Chapin

Ray Chapman
Gail Chatfield
Ray & Helen
Chatfield
Chris Christofferson
Denise Clark
Bill Cleveland
Gary Clizer
Lorene Cochran
Gerry Corbeil
Brad Corkle
Daniel & Spring
Cullum
Mr. & Mrs. Culver
George Currie
Darlene Curry
Monty Daner
Geri Daugherty
Debra Domy
Eileen DuHamel
Robert Dunsmore
Louisa Durkin
Alice Edwards
Loreen Ellersick
Marlo Faulkner
Lois Featherstone

Ellen Ferris
Jackie Fields
Tom Flanagan
David Fortier
Zella Goodwin
Jennifer
Gookstetter
Tracy Gravelle
Bob & Charlotte
Graves
Linda Hackbarth
Lela Hartley
Wendy Hei
Vivian Morbeck
Hogan
Bob Hopper
Jerry House
Roger Howard
Reese Hubbard
Lorelea Hudson
Pal Hughes
Archie Hulhizer
Jack Hull
Gene Hyde
Pauline Irvine
Butch Jacobsen

Mark & Judy Johnson
Wayne Johnson
Marian Jones
Elizabeth Keen
Terry Kincaid
Cindy Kirkley
Bev Klein
William Koetch
Myrtle Kramer
Dennis Kuisti
Marvin & Janet Lake
Ellen Larson
Harvey Legault
Richard Legault
Leigh LeGore
Leonard Lehtola
Al Leiser
Mr. & Mrs. Earl Lunceford
Richard Magnuson
Marie Marek
Mr. & Mrs. Hoyt McClain
Alice McGinnis
Deb Mellon
Barbara Milkovich

Jim & Dorothy Miller
Bob & Marge Moate
Bob & Joanne Monteith
Richard Mullen
Grady Myers
Evelyn Nordstrom
Leila Nordstrom
Northwest Archaeological Associates, Inc
Bill & Hazel Noyen
James Oderkirk
Marge & Ray Olin
Jim Oliver
Jan Patrick
Joe Peak
Al & Edie Peck
Chuck Peterson
Mildred Poland
Joy Porter
Jim Powers
John & Becky Powers
Kay Powers
Josephine Prophet

Art Randall
Nancy Renk
Carl Ritchie
Evelyn Rorie
Barbara Rossenberry
Phil Ruff
Marie Russell
Kay Sather
Mike Saunders
George & Katie Sayler
Joanne Schaller
Bob Schini
Bill Scudder
Billie Shewmaker
Shoshone County Assessor's Office
John Shovic
Cort Sims
Robert Singletary
Sharon Southerland
Philip Stanley
Shirley & Bill Stoller
Desiree Stuble
Terry Sverdsten
Mrs. Taylor
Janice Thompson
Ordella Triplett
Ed Vang
Calvin Vork
Jean Vosberg
Marilyn Wagenius
Delores Waide
Mary Waller
Sherman Watts
Bobbie Welch
Karl Wetter
Mary Etta White
Mike White
Connie White
Karen Hamer Williams
Ann Wilson
Patsy Wuolle
Roma Wuolle
Florence Wyberg
Dave Zabel
Kathy Zanetti

Stylish North Idaho motoring, circa 1914.

How to use this self-guided tour:

Welcome to *Roads Less Traveled: Historic Driving Tours of Benewah, Kootenai and Shoshone Counties*. There are eight tours and several of them take the better part of a day. Within each tour you can select areas of interest to focus on if time is limited. Physical addresses are used when practical, but milepost and mileage are also used. Please be aware that sites may have disappeared or changed since the publication of this book.

We encourage you to read more about this area's fascinating history (see bibliography) and to acquire supplemental tours and information from the organizations listed below. In most cases we have not included the verbiage from historical signage and exhibits along the road. We hope that you will stop and enjoy these sites.

Tours & Maps:

Idaho State Highway historical sign booklet for $5.00
Idaho Transportation Department, Office of Public Affairs
P.O. Box 7129, Boise, Idaho 83707
http://itd.idaho.gov/hmg/

For the Wallace tour:
Tourism Committee of the Historic Wallace Chamber of Commerce
P.O. Box 1167, Wallace, ID 83873
or call 208-753-7151
or www.historic-wallace.org.

For St. Maries information and the mural tour contact:
The Greater St. Joe Development Foundation
906 Main Ave. PO Box 338
St. Maries, ID 83861
or call 1-866-408-2456.

For Forest maps for $9 contact:
Panhandle National Forest
3815 Schreiber Way
Coeur d'Alene, ID 83815-8363
or call 208-765-7223

Checklist:

- Look over the tour prior to driving it
- Fill up on gas
- Check road conditions
- Check museums and other sites for hours
- Take road maps and Forest Service maps
- Take binoculars
- Take food and water
- Respect private property
- Please obey all traffic laws, pull completely off the road and do not block or slow other traffic

Abbreviations:

Drive... Dr.

Highway..................................Hwy

National Register Site............. 🄽🅁

Road...Rd.

Street...St.

Side Trip................................. ⭕

Rathdrum Prairie
~ TOUR ONE ~

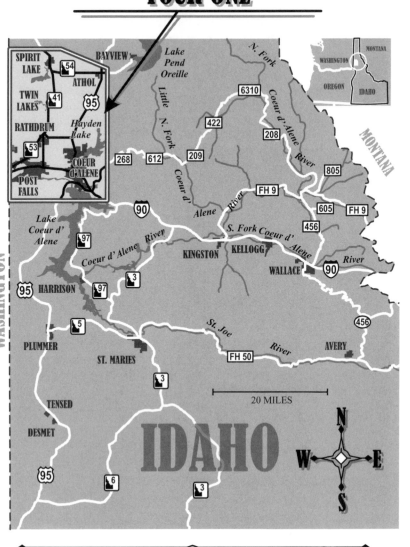

Beginning from Coeur d'Alene this tour covers about 90 miles and takes 3-4 hours. Take I-90 to Post Falls and take Exit 5, Spokane St., go left and get in the right lane to prepare to turn on 4th Ave.

~ POST FALLS ~

Once the site of the Coeur d'Alene Indian village *Q'emiln* meaning "throat of the river" the town of Post Falls grew from the early commercial lumbering efforts of German immigrant Frederick Post. Post came to the area from Illinois in 1871 and set up businesses in Rathdrum, Spokane and Post Falls, building the area's first gristmill at Spokane Falls in 1876. He returned to the "Little Falls" (Post Falls) of the Spokane River and used that falls to power the area's first commercial lumber mill. Several lumber mills operated in Post Falls over the years. Logs arrived by horse, water and later by rail and highway. Agricultural activities were also important to Post Falls' economy. Grass seed replaced earlier crops such as beans in the 1950s.

For information about the Post Falls Historical Society Museum call the City Library at 773-1506.

❶ Mullan Statue

106 E. 4th Ave. Just south of the freeway

This restored 14-foot marble statue honors Captain John Mullan's contribution to the construction of Idaho's first engineered road. The 624 mile military road extended northeast from Walla Walla, Washington, to Fort Benton, Montana. He not only brought the dry land route through the Post Falls area in 1861, but he and his crews were the first to map the topography and water flow at the "Little Falls" of the Spokane River.

Turn right (west) on 4th Ave. and go to the parking area

❷ Falls Park and the Corbin Ditch 🏞NR

This 22-acre park offers a great scenic view of the falls from accessible paved pathways. Interpretive signs provide an overview of Post Falls' stream flow from the Spokane River near the falls and provided irrigation for it's earliest economic history. The Corbin Ditch Head Gate, located here,

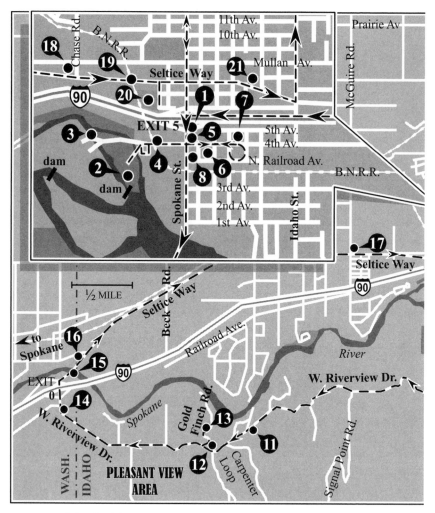

was part of the Corbin Ditch irrigation system which included 34 miles of canal. Portions of the canal are on the National Register. The headgate regulated farmland water east of Spokane.

➌ Washington Water Power Bridges 🏛

Visible from Falls Park, the open spandrel arched bridge was completed in 1930 at a cost of $24,000, including demolition of the original wooden bridge at the same location. The smaller bridge crossing the Spokane Irrigation Canal (Corbin Ditch) cost $4,215 and is used today as part of the road system leading to Avista's (Washington Water Power) hydroelectric

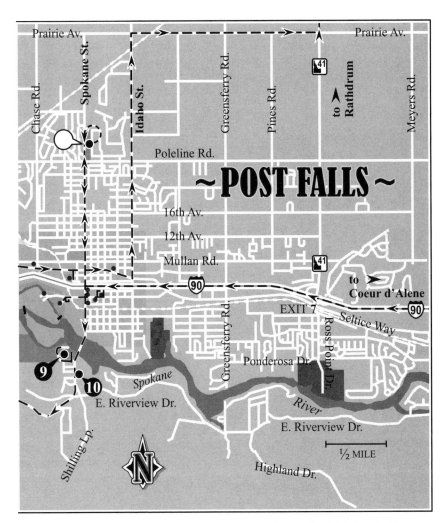

facility on the second channel of the Spokane River. The 221-foot bridge was one of the first reinforced concrete arched bridges in Idaho built for private use. It consists of 13 spans, each 17 feet long including the approaches, and spans the gorge 40 feet above the high-water mark. The bridges are closed to the public.

Turn around and go back toward Spokane St.

❹ North Idaho Centennial Trail

Commemorating the 1990 State Centennial celebrations of Idaho and

Washington, the *Centennial Trail* extends from Spokane to Higgens Point on Lake Coeur d'Alene. In Post Falls, the trail uses portions of the Coeur d' Alene & Spokane electric line railroad route, which once connected the Coeur d'Alene and Post Falls area with Spokane.

Go across Spokane St.

Looking southeast over the Post Falls Dam and Post Falls Lumber Company during the early 1960s.

❺ Chapin Drug
101 E. 4th St.
In 1922-23 Walter F. Chapin built this drug store. It housed a soda fountain and variety store with cosmetics, stationery and drugs. Chapin had an ice warehouse directly north of the old drugstore where ice was sold throughout the year. Crews sawed the ice on nearby Hauser Lake and stored it in sawdust. Dr. McCauley had an office in the back of the drug store. Chapin believed in the old adage, "location, location, location." His first drugstore was located in the old Advance building, near the railroad tracks. He then built a new brick building at this location, and when Hwy 10 was rerouted north, he moved his drugstore to the corner of Seltice Way and Spokane St.

Chapin Drug, on the corner of Spokane St. and 4th, in the early 1920s.

⑥ Samuel and Ann Young Home 🏛

120 E. 4th Ave. SW corner
Built around 1900 this Queen Anne house is one of Post Falls' oldest unaltered homes. English immigrants Samuel and Ann Young owned the home and nine lots in the area. Samuel Young was a hotel keeper, and one of his sons John owned a grocery store on Spokane St. In the 1920s Kate Peters, the town's postmistress, lived in the home. She married Oscar Reynolds, owner of the garage at the corner of Spokane St. and 4th Ave. The home is also known as the Reynolds House.

⑦ The Old Church 🏛

405 N. William St. (The Cultural Arts Center) NW corner of 4th Ave. and William St.
The "Old Church" is actually a combination of the town's oldest churches, the Methodist-Episcopal (1890) and the Presbyterian (1899). After a downturn in the economy following WWI, the churches were moved in 1921 from their original locations and united here. The Community Building Partners received an Orchid Award from the Idaho State Preservation Council for the restoration of the old church.

Turn around at the church, and go back to Spokane St. and turn left (south)

⑧ Seyforth's Grocery

312 Spokane St., left side (east) of the street (Handy Mart)
This is the oldest grocery store in Post Falls. It was originally owned by John Young, son of Samuel and Ann Young. As Young and Company, the

store was bought by William Seyforth in 1917. After his death, in 1948, his daughter, Evelyn Seyforth, ran the store until her retirement in 1972. Dale and Barbara James bought the store in 1980.

❾ Q'emiln Riverside Park
South side of the Spokane River
"Q'emiln", is pronounced *"ka-mee'-lin,"* meaning "throat of the river," by the Coeur d'Alene Tribe. The City of Post Falls named the park to recognize Native American heritage. The Coeur d'Alene's territorial homeland covered over 4 million square miles. Moses Seltice, father of Chief Andrew Seltice, lived in the area when German immigrant Frederick Post arrived in 1871. Due in part to white settlement, the Coeur d'Alene Indians left this area and other traditional villages in 1878 and settled south of Lake Coeur d'Alene near Desmet, Idaho. The park has a swimming beach, boat launch, picnic area and an adjacent trail system.

❿ Hughes' Florist Greenhouses
866 S. Spokane St., on the left side (east) of the street
This commercial flower growing operation began in Post Falls with Nancy Van Dorn's greenhouses south of the Spokane River in 1902. Ferrell and Lillian McCormick bought the operation in 1916. In 1945, two glass green houses were built on the north side and an aluminum, glass and steel green house was built on the south side in 1966. Eldred and Mary McCormick Hughes bought the operation in 1944. Third generation Howard and Marcia Hughes operate the greenhouses and floral shop with over 29 varieties of roses and market over 50,000 roses a year.

Continue south on Spokane Street, to the "Y," go right (west) along West Riverview Drive, approximately 5.5 miles from Post Falls
A great view of the Spokane River and the Rathdrum Prairie.

◆━━━━━━━ **~ Pleasant View ~** ━━━━━━━◆

Pleasant View was a farming area west of Post Falls named by German immigrant William Plonske for its "pleasant view." At one time, he and his family operated the Pleasant View store and garage.

⓫ Pleasant View School NR
18724 W. Riverview Dr.
Post Falls' oldest standing school was dedicated Thanksgiving 1910. In the beginning, the school had two teachers and a principal who doubled as a teacher. A large auditorium with a stage, a furnace room and a teacher's apartment was downstairs. The upstairs held two classrooms, a hallway and

his-and-her cloakrooms. Notice the bell tower and flagpole. Students and teachers shared a water bucket and dipper until March 1912 when a spring was donated to the school. Water was piped into the building for drinking only. The outhouse can be seen near the building. In 1937, the school closed its doors to regular classes and the building was donated to the Pleasant View Community Association to be used as a community center.

⑫ Pleasant View Church
19587 W. Riverview Dr.
The Pleasant View Missionary Baptist Church was organized in 1908 by Rev. Jesse Millsap. Rev. Millsap was known to give an excellent sermon but was sometimes long-winded. An old timer recalled that during one of his revved-up sermons Rev. Millsap's upper plate flew out. His son, sitting in the front seat, said "Pa, when you preach your teeth out, it's time to quit."

⑬ Pleasant View Cemetery
Go just past the Pleasant View Baptist Church and turn up Goldfinch Rd.
In Dec. 1899 a crew was cleaning the new cemetery when Arthur Mellville 'Mel' Benham commented "You know, I'll probably be the first one buried here." Mr. Benham died of small pox on Dec. 31, 1899, just one day short of his 35th birthday. The Cemetery contains about 360 burials.

Continue west on W. Riverview Dr. toward Stateline

⑭ Humphries House
3912 N. Idaho Rd. (Rockin' B Ranch) The first house after the yield sign on the right
This house, built in about 1905 by the Joseph Humphries' family, is the last building associated with the community of Spokane Bridge. Joseph lived here until his death in 1959. In 1992 Scott and Pam Brownlee purchased the property and operate the Rockin' B Ranch.

This area along the Spokane River was important for several reasons. As a natural river crossing it was first used as a crossing for a north-south Indian trail and in 1854 a Coeur d'Alene Indian named *Quin-Ne-Mo-See* operated a ferry with canoes and rafts. In 1858 Colonel George Wright ordered his men to kill 800 Indian horses and destroy the livelihood of local Indians. A monument remembering this sobering incident is located to the west. In 1864 the first white settlement in the Spokane-Coeur d'Alene vicinity developed around a toll bridge here. The town located where the I-90 overpass is had a population of 2,114 by 1918 with numerous businesses including a box factory and a sawmill. By 1970 the community had died and was buried under I-90.

Continue to Stateline

⑮ Spokane River Bridge

Although this bridge was completed in Dec. 1939 you couldn't drive over it then because the Washington side of the road to the bridge was not completed until May 1940. The four lane bridge cost $125,000 to build and was part of the four laneing of the Highway 10 between Spokane and Coeur d'Alene. The new bridge shortened the route between Coeur d'Alene and Spokane by a mile. Notice the inscription on the side of the bridge. The stretch of highway between McGuire and Stateline was the first four lane highway in the State of Idaho.

⑯ First and Last Chance

6911 W. Seltice Way

This building was moved from across the state line in the 1930s. As the name implies, it is either the traveler's first or last stop in the State of Idaho.

⑰ McGuire Wesleyan Church

2365 W. Seltice Way, NW corner of Seltice Way and McGuire Rd.

The church was designed by Dr. A.B. Robinson and built between 1910-1913 with the north side addition added in 1962. Local mason A.H. Rogers used field rock left by the Missoula Flood as construction material for buildings in the area. Not far from McGuire Rd. and Railroad Ave. was the passenger loading area for the Inland Empire electric line railroad, which ran hourly connecting Spokane and Coeur d'Alene.

⑱ Slab Inn

801 W. Seltice Way, NW corner of Seltice Way and Chase Rd.

The Slab Inn dates back to the 1930s. The building was originally sided with large log slabs. The Chase family operated the tavern for many years.

⑲ Railroad Overpass

The Burlington Northern Santa Fe Railroad overpass was part of D. C. Corbin's Spokane Falls & Idaho Railroad. It began in 1886 as a branch from the main line of the Northern Pacific Railroad at Hauser Junction and went to Coeur d'Alene. Corbin was a mining and railroad magnate influential in the development of the Inland Northwest. This overpass was completed in 1941 as part of the four-lane highway and the realignment of Hwy 10 through Post Falls. The highway used to run along West Mullan Ave.

The Northern Pacific took over the line and served Seiter's Cannery which operated on the south side of Seltice near this overpass. Edgar and Gladys Seiter owned and operated the cannery in Post Falls from 1935 to about 1973, serving growers from Spokane, McGuire, Dalton Gardens, Hayden Lake and Post Falls. They processed cherries, pumpkins, beans, tomatoes, apples and plums and made apple butter and cider vinegar products.

⑳ Treaty Rock Park

Turn right on Compton St. and follow the signs to Treaty Rock
The 4-acre park provides handicap accessible trails, interpretive signage and a picnic area. Native American pictographs on a large granite outcropping along with the petroglyph *Frederick Post June 1, 1871* are etched into the rock.

Go back to Seltice Way and turn right (east)

◯ Evergreen Cemetery Side Trip

At Spokane St. turn left (north) and go approximately 1.25 miles to the Evergreen Cemetery. It's on the east side of the street.
Frederick Post, founder of Post Falls, and his wife Margaret, as well as other family members are buried here. The cemetery was first known as the Post Cemetery. The oldest burial date is 1881. Sometime before 1894, a prairie fire destroyed the wooden markers as well as the record books that were kept in a wooden shed on the site. The Post family donated the cemetery to the City of Post Falls in 1917. The 7-acre cemetery has over 1,100 graves and includes a designated Veterans Memorial section.

Go back to Seltice Way and turn left (east)

㉑ The Falls Club

611 E. Seltice Way
A section of the Falls Club is a recycled Farragut Naval Base structure. Hwy 10 followed present day Seltice Way through Post Falls. The Frazey family operated the club for many years.

Turn left (north) on Idaho St., go to Prairie Ave. At Hwy 41 turn left and go 4.2 miles to Rathdrum

~ Rathdrum Prairie and Spokane Aquifer ~

The Spokane Aquifer is a geologic feature formed by the Glacial Lake Missoula and Spokane floods. Floodwaters deposited sediments ranging from fine clay particles to large cobbles and boulders, the heaviest being deposited first, thereby creating the aquifer. With the exception of the Spokane River, today almost no surface water flows on the Spokane Valley because it drains into the aquifer as soon as it reaches the vast gravel deposits. The aquifer deposits range from 150 feet to more than 600 feet deep and cover over 321 square miles from Athol to Spokane. The aquifer has one of the fastest flow rates in the nation, moving as much as 50 feet per day and provides the sole source of water for the area. In 1909, Spokane's water was proclaimed the purest in the world and remains of high quality today.

As you enter Rathdrum at 4. 2 miles turn left on Coeur d'Alene Ave.

~ Rathdrum ~

Fredrick Post's son-in-law Charles Wesley Wood, gave the town its first name of Westwood. In 1881 when the postmaster applied for a post office the U. S. Government would not accept the name Westwood. M.M. Crowley gave Postmaster Zach Lewis a list of potential names. Lewis chose Rathdrum which was Crowley's native home in Ireland. In 1881 Rathdrum became the first organized county seat of Kootenai County and remained so until the county seat was moved to Coeur d'Alene in 1908.

Rathdrum was a supply and jumping-off point for the Coeur d'Alene Mining District. Miners would leave the Northern Pacific train at Rathdrum, take a stage to Coeur d'Alene and then a steamboat up the Coeur d'Alene River to the Old Mission, continuing on the Mullan Road to the mines. In 1886 D.C. Corbin built a branch line from the Northern Pacific main line at the Hauser Junction to Coeur d'Alene, lessening Rathdrum's importance as a supply point.

Several fires damaged Rathdrum. In October of 1884, a fire consumed 55 buildings and six city blocks, destroying the business district. Losses were reported at $85,000 with only one business carrying insurance. The town was soon rebuilt. On Aug. 29 and 30, 1924, fire leveled two solid blocks, destroying 30 stores and residences in the business section. Half an hour after the fire was discovered, it was beyond control. The water reservoirs were nearly empty due to repairs.

Several of the buildings date from the town's establishment and when it prospered as the county seat. Many downtown buildings reflect the effects of the disastrous fire of 1924. Although the northwest side of Main Street did not burn, some business owners decided to replace older wood structures with fireproof brick or block. Many owners did not rebuild after the fire, leaving a number of vacant lots in the downtown district.

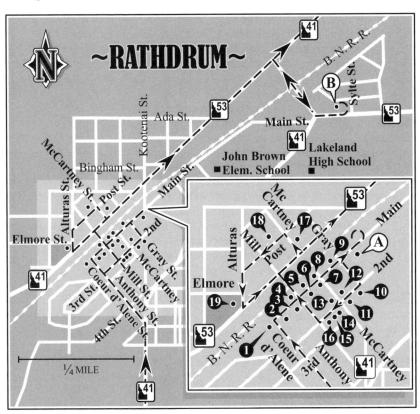

❶► The Cassedy Funeral Home

15291 Coeur d'Alene St.

Losing her undertaking business in the 1924 fire, Constance Cassedy built this fireproof funeral home with a separate morgue and supply building with the first story walls made of hollow-core brick. Her daughter Louise, also an undertaker along with her husband A. B. Nelson operated the business until about 1953. Both Louise and Constance were referred to in newspaper advertisements as "A Licensed Lady Embalmer". Louise's daughter Virginia married Dick Penman who later became an undertaker and they operated the business until the early 1960s. Virginia lived in the house until 1987.

❷ Interstate Utilities Telephone Building

8184 Main St., on the right (Chamber of Commerce)

Although the first telephone wires were strung to Rathdrum in 1895, the Interstate Utilities Company erected this building after the 1924 fire. The design is the same as other company buildings in Priest River, Spirit Lake and Mullan. The remodeled building served as the fire station for many years.

❸ The Hart Block

8162 Block of Main St., on the right (Westwood Inn)

Warren A. Hart lost his first store in the 1890 fire. He built a new brick structure in 1892 and added the north half between 1896 and 1908 at 832 Main. After the fire of 1924, he rebuilt using the original brick walls. Much of the upstairs was turned into a meeting room for the Moose Lodge. He added a new roof and a new floor in the upper story of his two-story building. During the supervision of the work Mr. Hart fell through a hole in the roof and fractured his pelvis. The *Rathdrum Tribune*, Oct. 3, 1924, notes "Mr. Hart, although 82 years of age and handicapped by poor eyesight, was supervising the work when the accident occurred". The Nov. 14, 1924, *Rathdrum Tribune* reported Mr. Hart received a pair of crutches and was recovering from his fracture.

❹ Stewart Skinner Service Station

Corner of 1st and Mill St., on the left

Stewart Skinner was in the midst of moving his garage from the Russell annex to his new garage building when the fire of 1924 destroyed the annex. He lost $1,000 in supplies, along with three old cars. He opened for business in this building in the fall of 1924. The following spring, he built the service station addition along the north wall.

Stewart Skinner's Service station in the late 1920s.

❺ Poleson Building
8065 Main St., on the left (Eagle Pawn)
Julia Poleson decided to replace two frame buildings on her lots with a fireproof one following the fire of 1924. Crews poured the foundation for 823 Main St. in early November, and the walls went up rapidly with the roof completed before the end of November. W.A. Poleson opened his barbershop in the east bay the day after Christmas. Less than a month later the Pioneer Market opened its doors in the west bay.

❻ Berges Block
8068 Main St. on the right
A.A. Berges purchased the property after the 1924 fire and built this one-story brick building. Divided into three bays, its first occupants were Wendler Brothers' confectionery, Henry Reiniger's hardware store and the post office.

❼ Wenz Drug Store
8016 Main St., on the right
Dr. Frank Wenz built a two-story brick drug store in 1902. He lost the store and his home in the fire of 1924. He rebuilt this one-story building and was back in business before Christmas of 1924.

❽ Crenshaw Block
Main St. and McCartney St. on the left
John Crenshaw purchased the Larsen Brothers' frame store building in 1905. Three years later he moved that building and constructed a concrete block building at Main and McCartney. Reiniger Brothers operated a bakery there for many years and in 1924 purchased the building.

❾ The Rathdrum Iron Works
Main St. on the left, with a sliding door
This building was constructed between 1908 and 1912. The façade originally had a stepped false gable made of concrete blocks. It was removed and windows added in 1925.

Ⓐ Rathdrum School Side Trip
Continue on Main St. to the Rathdrum School (Mtn. View Alternative High School) Rathdrum High School was built in 1937.

Turn right on Gray St. (if coming back from the school, turn left)

⑩ Kootenai County Jail
7940 2nd St.
Built in 1892 the Kootenai County Jail cost $2,500. The interior had offices for the sheriff and jailer on the first floor, a waiting room, kitchen, visitor's gallery and a small washroom. The second floor had two rooms, a bathroom and five small cells designed as holding cells and confinement for mentally unstable prisoners. The single-story rear section contained a double-tier set of eight steel cells. In 1908 voters elected to move the county seat to Coeur d'Alene. The City of Rathdrum purchased the building in 1910 from the county for $225. In 2005 the Westwood Historical Society was working on restoring the jail.

⑪ Masonic Hall
15190 N. McCartney St.
This is the lot where the old Kootenai County courthouse was located. W.H. Edelblute, active in the national guard, constructed a building between 1910 and 1912 for use as an armory for the Idaho National Guard. The Fraternal Benefit Association of Rathdrum purchased the property in 1928. The Loyal Order of Moose met there in 1932. The building houses the Rathdrum Masonic Lodge.

⑫ Harlan Fritzsche's House
15222 McCartney St. on the right
This bungalow-style home was built circa 1920. It was originally clapboard with stucco added later.

⑬ Wenz House
15225 McCartney St. on the right
Dr. Frank Wenz began construction on his home in 1925. Determined not to lose another home to fire, he had this one stuccoed on the exterior and shingled with asbestos on the roof. Wenz owned the drug store on Main St.

⑭ St. Stanislaus Catholic Church
8026 2nd St.
This Gothic-style church, built in 1900, is regarded by the diocese as the earliest brick church constructed in the State of Idaho. It is one of the finest churches for a town the size of Rathdrum.

⑮ Mark and Flora Belle Musgrove House
8050 2nd St. on the left
Built before 1892, this home originally had a porch that wrapped across the

front and down the right side. The present porch and second-story sleeping porch were added between 1896 and 1908. The house was scorched in the 1924 fire.

⓰ Warren Hart House

15152 Mill St. on the left
A well-known businessman, Mr. Hart built this Italianate-style house sometime before 1892. The house was moved to this location between 1901 and 1912.

Turn right on Mill St., drive 2 blocks, then right on Hwy 53, drive one block, and then left on McCartney St.

⓱ Rathdrum United Methodist Church

15468 McCartney St.
Frederick Post donated the land and Presbyterians began construction in 1905 at a cost of $3,200. The old church bell, cast in 1887, was placed in this new building where the first service was conducted Sept. 7, 1906. In 1918, the Presbyterians decided to discontinue services in Rathdrum and join with Post Falls as the Community Presbyterian Church. The Methodists took over this building. In late 2005 the church was sold to a private party.

⓲ Idaho & Washington Northern Railroad Depot

McCartney St. and Post St.
This Tudor-style depot built in 1908 was designed by famous Spokane architect Kirtland Cutter. Construction began in 1907 on the railroad, from McGuires west of Post Falls, to Metaline Falls. Owned by Frederick Blackwell and Associates, the railroad was built primarily to serve Blackwell's lumber company in Spirit Lake and the cement plant near Metaline Falls. It offered passenger services and connections with major railroads. The tracks were behind the depot. The Milwaukee Railroad took over the line in 1916.

Turn left on Post St. and then left on Alturas St. to the city park

⓳ City Park

This park dates close to the establishment of the town. Rathdrum Creek runs through the park and for many years filled a swimming pool. The fire bell located in the park was cast in 1897 and hung at the Interstate Utilities Telephone Building when it was the fire department. The Twentieth Century Reading Circle saved the bell and installed it in the park in 1971.

Continue north on Hwy 53 and then to Hwy 41 into Spirit Lake

Ⓑ⟩ Pine Grove Cemetery Side Trip

Turn right at Hwy 53 then left towards Sandpoint. The cemetery is on the left two-tenths of a miles east of Lakeland High School. *The cemetery has over 1,200 graves with many unmarked and unknown. The oldest date back to 1886. In 1999, 12 Chinese Union Pacific Railroad workers' graves were discovered under the Lions Club parking lot. Outside the cemetery's boundary, a fence was installed around these graves.*

Get back on Hwy 53 and return to Hwy 41 and go north towards Spirit Lake. On the west side of the highway the Idaho & Washington Northern (later the Milwaukee) railbed is visible almost all the way to Seasons Rd.

◯⟩ Twin Lakes Side Trip

Turn west at Twin Lakes Sportsman's Access Rd., and turn around at one of the sportsman's accesses.
Twin Lakes first was known as Sturgeon. The legend is that a large sturgeon swooping from one lake to the other formed the channel between the upper and lower lakes. The first settlers here were loggers and homesteaders. By 1910, Twin Lakes was a popular camping and recreational spot. The I&WN Railroad provided access from Spokane to Rathdrum and other communities for weekends and vacations. The depot was located where the Lightning Bar is. Hotels and resorts were built around the lake to accommodate the tourists. In the summer, commuter rates ran $1.50 for the one-hour round trip to Spokane, with up to six trains a day. Daily trips continued until about 1920.

The Icebox
Hwy 41
Continue to drive past the dip where there was a railroad overpass crossing Hwy 41. To the left was an old Greek cemetery. Open the window once you are on the top of Seasons Hill to feel the effect of the Icebox. The temperature is said to sink by10 degrees as you drop down the north side of Seasons Hill.

~ Spirit Lake ~

Spirit Lake was named from an Native American legend which explains the

Salish name *Tesemini*, meaning Lake of the Spirits. It is said that an Indian chief's daughter eloped with a young brave. The father pursued them and out of fear of being separated, the brave took the girl into his arms and jumped into the lake. Their bodies were never found. The tribe believed that *Tesemini* carried them away. Another version is that seven Indian braves were in a canoe that tipped. The bodies were never recovered and the accident was attributed to an evil spirit.

The development of the Panhandle Lumber Company by Frederick Blackwell and Associates was the beginning of the town of Spirit Lake. In 1907 the Spirit Lake Land Company formed to sell lots. Within two years the town had a business district, grade school, a high school, organized sports, churches and fraternal organizations. It also had electric lights, concrete walks, and telephones. Spirit Lake was promoted as an ideal place to live and visit.

Ⓒ Nautical Loop Side Trip
Off Hwy 41
After Seasons Hill and almost to the next hilltop, turn west (left) on Nautical Loop, and this will take you to the first public access and Rocky Beach.

Near here, in Pete Rhodebeck's Grocery, was Spirit Lake's first post office. Missoula Flood formed this cliff, providing a spectacular viewpoint. It is believed this is where the Indian maiden and her lover jumped to their deaths.

Keep right at the "Y" and continue back to Hwy 41Continue through town and turn east (right) on Jefferson St.

---

❶ St. Joseph's Catholic Church

SE corner of 5th (Hwy 41) & Jefferson St.
Built in 1909, it served the Catholics until 1966.

❷ Lutheran Church

6th Ave. and Jefferson St.
Built in 1909, the first pastor was Dr. A.M. Skindlov.

Turn left on 6th Ave., go 2 blocks and left on Madison St. and then south (left) on Hwy 41

❸ Spirit Lake Grade School

On the right (Woolen-Brown Civic Center)
Constructed in 1921, it was discontinued as a school in the late 1960s.

Turn right on Jefferson St.

❹ Presbyterian Church 4th Ave. and Jefferson St.

Built in about 1908, this church has a raised basement of cast stone and stained glass windows.

Turn left on 4th Ave., right on Adams St., left on Park Ave., right on Washington St. past the City Park

❺ Prindle Hospital

32318 N. 2nd Ave. and Washington St. (Whitehouse Apartments)
Dr. Earle S. Prindle, the company doctor for the Panhandle Lumber Company, opened this hospital March 14, 1909. It operated as a hospital into the 1960s.

Turn left on 2nd Ave. and notice several concrete block homes, built in the 1907 era for mill managers

Turn right on Maine St. and drive down the hill

Spirit Lake's Prindle Hospital in 1910.

⑥ Fireside Lodge
On the waterfront
Fireside Lodge was the Panhandle Lumber Company Office. The building was moved down the hill next to the millpond after the 1939 fire damaged the mill and burned down much of the timber in the yard.

Turn around and come up the hill

⑦ Real Estate Office
3rd Ave. and Maine St, on the right (Sondahl's Pottery)
This building served as the Panhandle Lumber Company real estate office in the early development of the city. It was moved from the east side of the old bank building on 4th Ave. and Maine St.

⑧ Historic Business District 🛡NR
Maine St.
Most of these buildings, of cast stone or rusticated concrete block, were built in the town's boom period from 1908 to 1910. A cement plant was set up nearby to provide the building material for a town that would have the appearance of a permanent and viable community. Several buildings were also built with brick.

⑨ White Horse Saloon
6248 Maine St.
The White Horse Saloon owns the longest continual liquor license in Idaho. An early Idaho law required that alcohol could only be served to persons renting a room in the establishment. Consequently, most bars had a second story with rooms for rent.

⑩ I.O.O.F. Building

6236 Maine St.

The round windows on the third floor signify that this was at one time the International Order of Odd Fellows Lodge.

A snow-choked winter scene along Spirit Lake's Maine St. in 1913.

⑪ Jo's Hole Bar

6228 Maine St.

Built in 1910 this establishment has a back bar with a mirror that was freighted west around "The Horn," then overland by wagon train to Spirit Lake.

⑫ Krech Building

6222 Maine St.

Henry Krech was involved in many ventures in Spirit Lake. Built in 1907 this building was the first mercantile store and brick building in town.

⑬ The Bank of Spirit Lake

SE corner of 4th Ave. and Maine St.

Built in 1907, the bank's major stockholder was F.A. Blackwell, president of the Panhandle Lumber Company. The building still has the original vault.

Turn right on Hwy 41 (south) and go one block

⑭ VFW Hall
Corner of New Hampshire St. and Hwy 41 (5th Ave.)
This was the funeral parlor. Where New Hampshire St. and 4th Ave. intersect is part of the original business district, built in the 1907 era when the town was established, but little remains today.

Turn right on New Hampshire St.

⑮ Episcopalian Church
3rd Ave. and New Hampshire St.
The Episcopalian Church was enlarged and used by the Seventh Day Adventists and then by the Baptists.

Continue onto the gravel road and go to the left

⑯ Three houses built for mill executives
Occupied by Panhandle Lumber Company executives these three homes were built in the 1907 era. They overlooked the former Panhandle Lumber Company mill, the I&WN Railroad depot and the former Railroad Depot Park.

⑰ F. A. Blackwell House
Vermont St. on the right
F.A. Blackwell formed the Panhandle Lumber Company and brought the railroad to Spirit Lake. He was said to be as honest as the day is long. His dream was to see a perfect town developed in Spirit Lake. An influential businessman in the region, he owned interests in several sawmills and railroads. Kirtland Cutter designed this home, as well as the former I&WN Railroad Depot.

Turn right on 3rd Ave., left on Vermont St. back to Hwy 41, and turn right (south). From Hwy 41 turn right at the St. Joseph's Church and Masonic Temple signs.

Park or turn around in the Catholic church parking lot to view these buildings.

⑱ Masonic Temple
D.J. Wright built this home, which has been the Masonic Temple since 1910. He was here when surveyors, sent by the owners of the coming sawmill, came to plat the town in 1904. Spirit Lake prided itself on having many social amenities, including several fraternal organizations and an opera house.

The Panhandle Lumber Company during the mid 1920s.

 Log cabin

This log cabin served as a way station for travelers and horses on the Seneacquoteen Trail from Oregon to Canada. It was the second Spirit Lake Post Office.

Go back to Hwy 41 and turn right then left on Hwy 54

~ Glacial Lake Missoula and Spokane Flood ~

A great flood created much of North Idaho's landscape. During the last ice age, some 15,000 years ago, a finger of the continental ice sheet dammed the Clark Fork River and formed a lake 2,000 feet deep, stretching 200 miles eastward. When the dam broke, some 500 cubic miles of water rushed southward at speeds approaching 60 miles per hour. The water shot out at a rate of 10 times the combined flow of all the rivers in the world. Geologists have documented as many as 42 separate flood episodes which make up the deposits of the Spokane Aquifer. Evidence of the flood is noted in Idaho and Washington in the form of huge sand waves and scablands. Notice the hills and dips along the highway. These are moraines left by the flood waters.

Mountain View Cemetery

Off of Hwy 54 left (north) at the top of the hill before you drop into Athol

Originally the Odd Fellows had all the records but they were lost when the Odd Fellows Hall burned. Of the approximately 258 burials, the earliest was in November 1902.

First known as Colton, the town was renamed Athol by a settler who came from Athol, Massachusetts. The Massachusetts' Athol was named after a town in Scotland named for the Duke of Atholl. A Northern Pacific Railroad station was built in Athol in 1882, and settlers hoped for a vast agricultural paradise. The jack pine forest first attracted early settlers to Athol, and logging, milling and agriculture created prosperity. By 1903 there were many businesses opened including the Pacific Hotel, a drugstore, blacksmith, jewelry store, restaurants, mercantile company and a saloon. The depression reduced Athol's importance and the community declined until the 1940s when Farragut Naval Training Station opened.

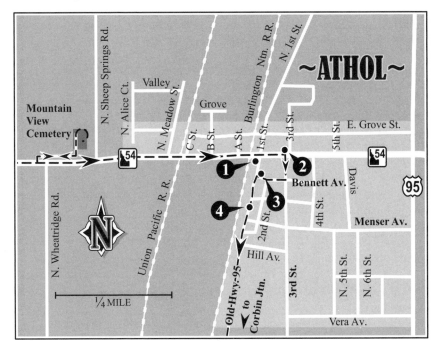

❶ Community Center/City Hall
Just over the second set of tracks on the right
This building served as the gym, cafeteria and music room for the Athol School from 1907 to 1972.

❷ The Little White Church
Hwy 54 & 3rd St. on the left
This church is a structure moved from Farragut Naval Training Station.

Turn right on 3rd St. and right on Bennett Ave. and go 1 block to 1st St. then left

❸▶ Johnson's Store and Post Office

30190 1st St.
Local lore has it that the grand opening in 1918 was celebrated with a big dance. The proprietors lived in the back and operated the Post Office and the store. In the 1930s the store included a service station. The Post Office moved in 1945 but the store continued to operate until the mid 1960s.

❹▶ Old Hwy 95

This segment of Old Highway 95 starts at Highway 54 in Athol and runs south for four miles to Corbin Junction. The Burlington Northern-Santa Fe tracks parallel the highway for 2.25 miles.

Although the Idaho legislature authorized the sale of $200,000 in bonds in 1914 for a north to south highway it wasn't until 1922 that the route between Coeur d'Alene and Sandpoint was selected. Much of the region was in a recession in the 1920s when the nationwide depression of the 1930s hit. Federal money provided Idaho with $15 million between 1934 and 1939 to work on 1,650 miles of roads. Hundreds of unemployed men were hired through the Works Progress Administration (WPA) to work on highway and bridge projects in the region including this stretch of highway. This section of highway retains its original setting and feeling from when it was built in the Depression.

Turn left (south) on 1st Ave. (Old Hwy 95) and continue south to Corbin Junction

Old Highway 95 Bridge

1. 5 miles
The five-span bridge is a good example of the many bridges constructed during the 1930s as federal public works projects. This bridge carries old Highway 95 across the Spokane International Railroad (later the Union Pacific Railroad) tracks. There is only a single track running under the bridge, but the extra guard rails through the pair of underpasses give the appearance of a double track. The rails pass under the bridge at an oblique angle to the roadway. The bridge design reflects this angle, with the eastern railing extending farther south than the western one, and conversely, the western railing extending farther north than the eastern one.

Northern Pacific Railroad Bridge
1.5 miles (Burlington Northern-Santa Fe Bridge)
This bridge carries the Burlington Northern-Santa Fe (originally Northern Pacific) Railroad tracks across the line of the Spokane International Railroad. It is located just west of the Old Highway 95 bridge over the same tracks. According to plans for this bridge, it was constructed in 1906, the year that the Spokane International Railroad was completed. The Northern Pacific probably elevated its track through this area at that time to allow for this crossing. The eastern side of the bridge retains most of the 1906 design. The western side was altered in 1964 during construction of the second set of tracks. The two sets of tracks cross at an oblique angle, and the design of the bridge abutments and wing walls reflects this angle. This is the only example of a short-span steel girder bridge remaining in northern Idaho. Other long-span steel girder bridges cross rivers in the region, but there are no other bridges like this one known.

At Corbin Junction turn right (south) on Highway 95 and return to Coeur d'Alene

Highway 95 North
~TOUR TWO~

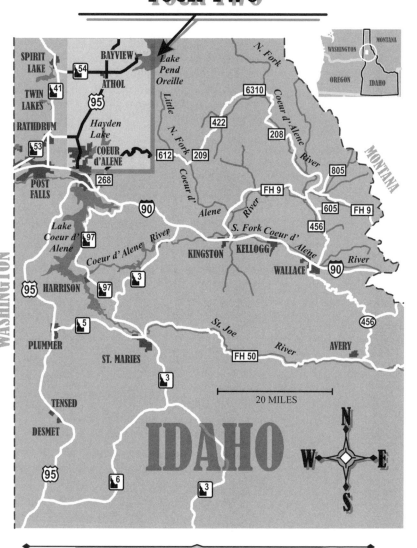

~ Farragut State Park ~

This tour covers about 75 miles if you begin in Coeur d'Alene and takes 2 to 3 hours. From the intersection of Hwy 95 and Hwy 54 at Athol take Hwy 54 east for 4 miles to Farragut State Park.

State Highway 54 holds the distinction of being the shortest state highway in Idaho at 15.5 miles long. In the mid-1960s it was widened to four lanes between Athol and Farragut State Park to accommodate the large National and International Scout Jamborees. The largest attracted 42,500 Boy Scouts.

Northern Idaho was still suffering from the Depression when Pearl Harbor was bombed December 7, 1941. In March of 1942, the government announced it would build a naval station at the southern end of Lake Pend Oreille. Building Farragut Naval Training Station, at a cost of $75 million, provided a great economic surge for this area. Many local residents recall that everyone got out of debt during "Farragut Days." At the peak of construction, the Walter Butler Construction Company employed almost 22,000 men on the project. The first recruits arrived in September of 1942

Farragut's Camp Waldron and its busy drill field sometime during WWII.

and in the first 15 months 293,381 men received training. President Franklin Roosevelt named the base for Admiral David Farragut who is known for his Civil War quote, "Damn the torpedoes! Full steam ahead!" during the Battle of Mobile Bay.

The base consisted of seven camps, each a small city in itself, designed to feed and train 5,000 men at one time. Some 98 million board feet of lumber were used to construct the 650 frame buildings on the site. Each training camp included a 14-acre drill field called "the grinder;" 22 two-story barracks; a mess hall; a recreation building, which included a soda fountain, merchandise area, two barber shops with eight chairs each, an eight-lane bowling alley in the basement, a library, a game room with pool table and table tennis and a drill hall.

In the spring of 1946, Farragut Naval Training Station was decommissioned. Farragut College & Technical Institute operated in its place from late 1946 to 1949 when funding cuts closed the doors. Many buildings were moved and put to new uses. In 1965, a 4,000-acre state park was created on Lake Pend Oreille.

❶ Visitors Center/Headquarters Building

This site provides historical and recreation information including a geology exhibit "Born of Ice and Flood" and photos of sailors who were stationed at Farragut. Pick up a map to find the brig, powder magazines, pump houses and a water tower from the naval training station days.

Park fees are paid here. If you do not want to pay the park fees continue on Hwy 54 to Bayview

❷ Pend d'Oreille City

Turn right onto South Rd. just beyond the Visitor Center/Headquarters Building. Follow South Rd. 1.6 miles, turn right on Buttonhook Rd. at the marker to Buttonhook Group Camp. (Park at the gate if closed; do not block it). Walk downhill to the second gate, at the lowest part of the loop, and take the trail down to the lake.

This area was an early gathering place for Native Americans. Established in the early 1860s in Idlewild Bay, Pend d'Oreille City, later known as Steamboat Landing, is North Idaho's second white settlement. A log store (believed to be located about where the restrooms are) supplied miners and homesteaders. This was an important supply point along the mail route crossing the Rathdrum Prairie. By the late 1860s several steamboats, including the *Mary Moody*, took miners, passengers and supplies across the lake to the Clark Fork River where they went on to points in Montana and to the north end of lake where they took the Wildhorse Trail to British Columbia. This harbor is sheltered and does not freeze in the winter. Pend d'Oreille City's heyday lasted only a short time.

❸ Jokulhlaup (yo-kull-loup) Point

Return to the South Rd. and turn right. Go 1.8 miles, passing the campgrounds, boat ramp and Sunrise Day Use areas

Here can be found a lake view and interpretive signs explaining the Ice Age floods, Rathdrum Aquifer and origin of the name *Jokulhlaup*. Water 300 feet below this point is recharging the Spokane/Rathdrum Aquifer.

❹ Brig Museum

Return on the South Rd. for 1.1 miles and turn right onto Kinglet Rd. Take a left at the "T" onto Locust Grove and turn left on Highway 54 and continue 1 mile. Look for the "Do Not Enter" sign on the left side of the divided road and turn left onto the road just before the sign. The Brig Museum is the yellow and brown building on the left and is open for visitors in the summer months and by special request.

Constructed in 1942 the brig housed 100 to 200 prisoners at a time. Each cell contained only a bunk, a mattress and a bedroll. Prisoners were kept busy during the day cutting firewood for the boiler or pounding rocks into gravel with sledgehammers. When not on work detail, they stood or paced in their cells. They were not allowed to sit and three times a day they were escorted to the bathroom. Prisoners in solitary confinement were stripped naked and placed in roughly 5-by-7 foot concrete cells. Meals for these prisoners consisted of bread and water and were served in isolation.

The U.S. Naval Training Center entrance during WW II.

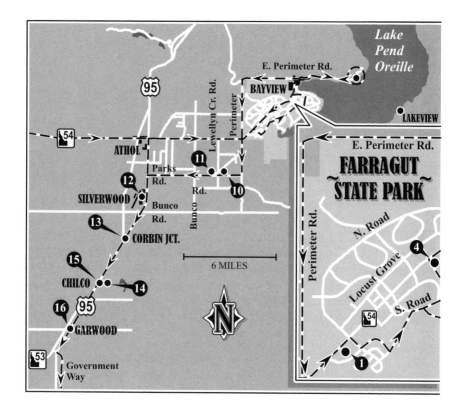

Most sailors were in the brig because of absence without leave issues. During operations at Farragut, only one woman was placed in the brig. She was the wife of one of the officers and had crossed a drill field to tell her husband that their baby had just died in the hospital. Since civilians were forbidden on the drill fields, she was escorted to the brig and quickly released once the commandant learned of her imprisonment.

When Lady Bird Johnson came through Farragut State Park in 1967, during her Beautify America campaign, she suggested the window bars be covered with slatted wooden screens and that the military green brig be painted a lemon yellow.

Turn right onto Hwy 54

~ Bayview ~

This logging, fishing and limestone mining community was first known as Squaw Bay. After 1900 the name was changed to Bayview. In 1910, a

FARRAGUT STATE PARK & BAYVIEW, IDAHO
Tour Route Maps

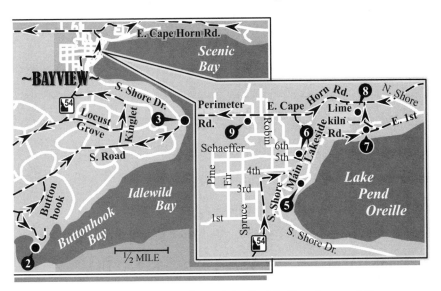

group of Spokane entrepreneurs formed the Prairie Development Company and platted a town site, hoping that the new town would attract tourists and residents. Bayview was laid out with 27 blocks of streets and avenues.

A Spokane International train at Bayview. The brick building in the center is the Bayview Inn, and the depot is in the upper right. The train is on the Washington, Brick & Lime Company spur. Circa 1920.

The Spokane International Railway (SI) provided transportation from Spokane. To serve the growing tourist industry, J. Grier Long, founder and longtime president of the Washington Trust Company in Spokane, built the Bayview Inn in 1910. The two-story brick building was located near the corner of Main Ave. and 5th St. It had hot and cold running water, 13 guestrooms on the second floor, a roof garden, and businesses on the first floor. Rates were $2 per day and up and $12 or more by the week. Sightseers took the train from Spokane, enjoyed a steamer ride on the lake and slept at the hotel. The Navy took over the hotel during WWII. After the war the hotel went into private hands and was demolished in the mid 1960s.

People are attracted to the area for the fishing, boating and a relaxed life-style. About 200 float homes are in Scenic Bay. People enjoy the proximity of wildlife, such as bald eagles, osprey, mountain goats, and deer.

❺ Acoustic Research Detachment
The Navy's entrance gate is at the start of Main Ave. entering Bayview and is not open for visitation
The Navy has maintained a presence in Bayview since WWII. The Acoustic Research Detachment conducts ongoing stealth research for U.S. Submarines. Lake Pend Oreille is perfect for acoustic testing due to its depth of 1,236 feet and low ambient noise levels. Two deep-water test platforms can be seen on the lake, one in the bay and another north of Cape Horn. Unmanned, scale-model submarines (some over 100 feet long) are tested and modifications are made before the Navy produces new designs.

❻ Spokane International Railroad Station
16601 5th St., turn left at 5th. St. The station is three houses west of Main Ave., on the right (north) side and is a private home
In 1910, the SI extended a branch, the Coeur d'Alene and Pend Oreille Railway, to Bayview. This line was primarily a freight service for the local lumber and mining industries with limited passenger service. The telegrapher sat at the bay window on the east side of the station. A water tower to the west provided water for the engines. One track led to the Washington Brick and Lime Company site, with a spur going to a dock where rail cars were loaded onto a barge for the trip to the Portland International Cement's cement crushing plants across the bay near Lakeview. The old cement foundations for the railroad dock are visible at low water. The other track went up the hillside to a wye, providing a way to turn the engines.

The Spokane International's Bayview Depot sometime during the early 1920s.

⑦ Washington Brick & Lime Company lime quarries and kilns

Go back to Main Ave., turn left (north), follow Main Ave. and stay right of the wye. Go to the end of the street, turn right, and follow the lower road along the north side of the bay and park along the road to look at the remains of the kilns, which are part of the Scenic Bay Resort

Limestone operations began in the 1880s and the Washington Brick and Lime Company acquired it in 1900. With a great demand for building materials in Spokane and the surrounding area, the business was believed to be at one time the second largest of its kind in the Northwest. The remains of five lime kilns are visible along the road. Lime was quarried from the adjacent hillside, brought to the crushing plant, and then placed into the kilns. The burned lime was extracted from the doors at the base of the kiln. Originally the processed lime was placed into barrels and taken north across the lake by steamer to the Northern Pacific railhead at Hope. Later, both raw and treated limestone were loaded onto railcars for the trip to Spokane. Limestone mining continued until the late 1930s.

Turn around and go back to Limekiln Rd.

⑧ Joseph Spear Home

Follow Limekiln Rd. uphill. Beyond the kilns and to the east, above Bitter End Marina, is the home, but it can't be seen from the road. This site is difficult to see, and the best view is from the Bitter End Marina Dock looking up to the right.

The Spokane International Railroad's Bayview dock and the steam tug "Rustler," circa 1906.

Joseph Spear, the president of the Washington Brick and Lime Company, built this two-story Craftsman style bungalow about 1910. A caretaker's house, cook house, gazebo and other original buildings remain. Five company employee homes are on the hillside above Limekiln Rd.

For a scenic view continue up Limekiln Rd. Off to the left are two of the five quarries. These were filled with rock from the Cape Horn slide in February of 2000. The other quarries were above Cape Horn Rd. Turn right off Limekiln Rd. onto Cape Horn Rd. and go one mile to a spectacular view of the lake where the slide took place. Originally just a trail, this road was built in the 1950s. There is a wide spot in the road at the far end of the slide to turn around.

From Limekiln Rd. turn left on Cape Horn Rd. Go 0.2 miles to the stop sign and turn right. Turn into the Community Center on the left (uphill) side. The Bayview Memorial Garden and bell are located here

❾ Bayview School Bell

20298 E. Perimeter Rd.
The bell is the only reminder of school days at Bayview School #34. Larry Bockstruck, who attended school there, built the foundation under the bell from bricks saved from the Bayview Inn when it was demolished in the 1960s. The strange stone and cement rock next to the bell came from the foundation of the school that was built in 1911 and operated until 1943. Despite efforts to save the building, which was a National Register site, it was demolished in 1988.

Turn left from the parking lot onto Perimeter Rd. After a few miles the road curves to the left. At 4.75 miles is a trail that was the Northern Pacific's spur operated by the SI from Athol to service the Naval Training Station. At 4.6 miles you are back to the roundabout entrance to Farragut; continue straight onto Good Hope Rd. for 1.5 miles and then turn right (west) on Parks Rd.

⑩ Cedar Mountain School #74 🔳

Go 1.1 miles along Parks Rd. to the school on the right side of the road and west of the intersection of Parks and Lewellyn Creek Roads.

The Cedar Mountain School was originally located on McCoy Rd., south of Bunco Rd. It is an example of one of the many one-room schoolhouses of Kootenai County, measuring approximately 18 by 24 feet, with a gabled roof and shiplap siding. The building was constructed in 1915 and operated until 1929. It is one of 14 rural Kootenai County schools placed on the National Register of Historic Places in 1986.

⑪ Belmont

Whitetail Road, which runs at a diagonal northeast from Parks Road, was the right-of-way for the Spokane International Railroad's branch line known as the Coeur d'Alene & Pend Oreille Railway that extended into Bayview. The railroad grade can be seen in several places in the area. Belmont was a small community and a stop along the route with the general store serving as the depot. By 1911-12, the population was listed as 20 and in 1913 the post office opened. Several homesteaders and ranchers raising cattle and hay kept the store in business.

One of the earliest homesteaders was Mr. Sage who settled in 1896 along the creek that now bears his name. Mr. Sage once climbed over Cedar Mountain to the head of Hayden Creek carrying a 5-gallon jug on his back in order to bring back trout to stock his creek. During the 1910 fires women and children were packed into wagons and taken to the clearing near Lewellyn Creek to gain shelter from the flames. The men fought the fire for several days before it took off over Bernard Peak to the east.

Continue on Parks Rd. heading west for 3 miles then turn left (south) onto Hwy 95

⑫ Silverwood Theme Park

Clay and Nadine Henley and Herb and Gladys Buroker bought and cleared 80 acres of land to make an airstrip at this site in 1972. Incorporated as Henley Aerodrome, it became a base for vintage airplanes. They built an airstrip, the Wingover Café, hangar, homes and a vintage aircraft museum. Air shows were held, featuring antique aircraft, hot air balloons and other attractions.

After Clay Henley died in 1977, Gary Norton purchased the aerodrome. His first big air show in 1981 drew 2,500 spectators and more than five dozen aircraft from the Northwest and Canada. That night a fire destroyed $650,000 in vintage airplanes, none of them insured. Norton estimated his loss at $1 million. As he began rebuilding his vintage squadron, brother Wayne Norton was killed in a stunt plane accident at the aerodrome in January of 1983. Ready to put the aerodrome up for sale, Norton changed his mind when he went to an auction in Reno, Nevada. Intending to look at a 1928 Ford Tri-Motor, an old narrow-gauge locomotive caught his eye. Gary bought the Tri-Motor (the most money ever paid for an antique airplane), three automobiles, and he outbid Disneyland for the 1915 Porter steam engine and three miles of track. At first he planned to lay the train track, add a restaurant and store at Henley. But what evolved over the next few years was Silverwood Theme Park, opening in 1989.

⑬ Corbin Junction and Rickel Ranch
South of Silverwood on the left

Corbin Junction was a stop on the railroad route just to the west of the ranch property owned by D.C. Corbin, owner of the Spokane International. Corbin Junction at its height included the depot, a store and five small section houses for SI railroad workers. The SI employed a section crew (at one time entirely Japanese) at Corbin Junction to maintain the rails. There was a wye to turn trains, a half mile spur track and the start of the branch line to Bayview. A portion of that branch-line railbed can still be seen south of the power lines to the east of U.S. Hwy 95, north of the ranch entrance.

The Corbin Ranch was established in 1905 with fruit orchards, grain and hay fields. For three years, sugar beets were raised on the property and hauled to Corbin's processing plant at Waverly, Washington. The sugar beet venture was given up because the soil contained many small rocks. These could not be separated from the beets, during processing, and caused the equipment to break down frequently.

Jerry Rickel, who was employed at the Waverly plant, managed the ranch for Corbin and then took over the ranch in 1943. His son Bob Rickel remembers how each year the family would cut and split 100 cords of wood on the ranch and haul it to Corbin's mansion in Spokane. The ranch remained in the Rickel family until 2004.

⑭ The Rimrock and Chilco Falls

Near Chilco to the east (left) is the rimrock that makes up the edge of the Rathdrum Prairie. It consists of Miocene age (20 million-year-old) Columbia River basalt (lava). The lava flow extended across the entire Rathdrum Prairie, and subsequent Lake Missoula floods cut down through the lava forming the rock cliffs. Impure opal can be found in holes occasionally. Just south of the Rimrock Golf Course, Chilco Falls is visible during spring run-off or heavy rainfalls and in winter as a frozen waterfall.

⑮ Chilco

Clarence S. Argo worked for the Milwaukee Railroad as an attorney in 1909 when he first came to North Idaho. He bought land around Chilco and made plans to develop an agricultural paradise. A promoter

Chilco Falls, circa 1910.

encouraged people from the east to buy his irrigated orchard tracts of land. In 1910 Argo built a dam at the head of Chilco Falls. The dam formed a pond, which provided fishing and boating as well as water for an irrigation system. The population was 65 when the post office opened in 1912. The landowners lost everything due to a killing frost, but the school stayed open for many years, and the SI railroad continued to stop to fill up at the water tank while they still ran steam engines.

⑯ Garwood

The Ohio Match Company named this spot Garwood from gar "spear" wood used to make matches. This is the junction where the Spokane International Railroad met the Ohio Match Railroad. The railroad followed much of what is now called Ohio Match Road. From the junction with the SI, it went eastward over a rugged range of mountains, past the north end of Hayden

Lake, dropping down the east side and reaching the headwaters of the North Fork of the Coeur d'Alene River. It operated for 20 years.

At the intersection of Hwy 95, Hwy 53 and Government Way turn left (south) onto Government Way
This road served as part of the old highway.

~ Hayden Lake ~

Rich with game, fish and berries, Hayden Lake, *Hnt'ꞵa'n*, was a favorite gathering place for the Coeur d'Alene Tribe. According to tribal legend, there came a time when the land stopped providing, and the medicine man advised them to leave, but no one wanted to go. One day a great whirlpool engulfed the chief as he fished from his canoe. Another version of this story tells of an Indian couple swept up by a whirlpool and drowning in the lake. Because of this, the tribe moved away from the lake.

In 1846, Father DeSmet was among the first white men to visit Hayden Lake. But it was not until the late 1870s that the first homesteaders, Mr. Strahorn and three soldiers from Fort Sherman (Mathew Hayden, John Hager and John Hickey) settled in the area. Legend has it that Mathew Hayden and John Hager, whose homestead was on the site of the present day Hayden Lake Country Club, played a card game of seven-up to determine who should name the lake. Hayden won the card game.

Hayden Lake's early economy was based on agriculture, lumbering and recreation. In 1906, a branch of the Inland Empire Railroad (the electric line) extended to the Bozanta Tavern. The post office was established at Hayden Lake in 1907, and businesses developed at the south end of the lake. The town shifted from this area to Government Way as automobiles replaced rails. In 1959, the post office moved to Hayden Village. The area around Government Way is now incorporated as Hayden. The area from the west shore of the lake to a short distance west of Strahorn Rd. is incorporated as Hayden Lake but does not have a post office.

⑰ Lacey Ave.

The area on the east side of Government Way between the Hayden Lake School and Dakota Ave. was mostly occupied by Lacey's Gardens. The avenue was named for the Laceys, who grew and sold flowers and vegetables.

Turn left at Miles Ave., continue east on Miles Ave. to the Avondale Golf and Tennis Club

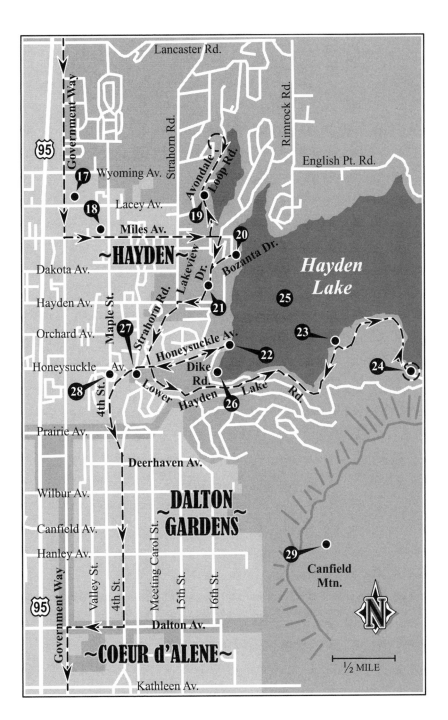

⑱ Miles House

587 Miles Ave., NW corner of Miles Ave. and Maple St.
Miles Ave. was named for a family who lived in this home. The golf course on the right is part of the Hayden Lake Country Club.

⑲ The Avondale Barn and Lake

10953 Avondale Loop Rd. Turn left on Avondale Loop and enter Avondale Golf and Tennis Club. The barn is from the Avondale Farms. Go past the barn and turn around
This lake, three-quarters of a mile long and a quarter-mile wide, has had many names. It was first called Fernwood Lake because of all the flowers and ferns growing around it. When John Hickey homesteaded in 1878, he named it for himself. Clement B. King acquired land from Hickey, Hayden and Hager, and by 1903 had 1,800 acres, which included the present day Avondale Golf and Tennis Club. King named Avondale Lake and stocked it with trout for family and guests to fish. The maid would go out in a boat, drop a line into the water and bring in enough trout for breakfast.

King built a three-story home on the southwest side of Avondale Lake with a large entrance hall, living room, billiard room, large dining room and seven fireplaces. There was a private school for his four children on the third floor. In 1903 King had nearly 50 head of fine horses and built a quarter-mile racetrack where guests would bring their horses and bet on the races. He built a big barn and carriage barn with quarters on the second floor for the men employed on the farm.

In 1907 King sold the property to M.D. Wright, including the house and the lake. Wright changed the name of Avondale Lake to Wrights Lake. In 1920 T.E. McBride bought the 650-acre ranch from Wright and changed the name of the lake to McBrides Lake. In 1967 Dr. Peterson proposed developing a golf course and residential area. The old King house was torn down in the 1970s and the lake was renamed Avondale. The Avondale Golf and Tennis Club occupies the site. The original barn has been remodeled.

At Miles Ave. turn left, then right for about two-tenths mile. By the crosswalk sign turn into the Hayden Lake Country Club on Bozanta Dr.

⑳ Hayden Lake Country Club

1800 Bozanta Dr.
John Hager took squatter's rights and eventually owned about 1,500 acres on this site. He built a one and a half story log cabin, which was later used by

the Bozanta Tavern and known as the Red House. In 1902 Homer King (his father had the big house on Avondale Lake) developed one-room log cabins known as Avondale Cottages. In December 1906 the Kings sold all the buildings, boats, docks, sheds, tents and personal property to the Hayden Lake Improvement Company for $12,000, which included $2,500 of Hayden Lake Improvement Company stock. Included on the list of property were three buildings of one and half stories, 12 log cabins, the Wigwam Club House, one rustic bridge, complete outfit of table china and glassware to serve 150 people, 259 towels, two nickel-in-slot machines, five steel boats and seven wood boats with oars.

The Bozanta Tavern Resort building in 1915.

J.C. Olmstead, of the distinguished Brookline, Massachusetts firm of landscape architects that designed New York's Central Park, was brought in to plan the grounds. Architect Kirtland Cutter designed the Bozanta Tavern Resort, built in 1907 with 35 guestrooms. The building to the left of the main building was the kitchen and dining rooms. It was built away from the guestrooms to avoid the kitchen noise and heat. The site also included 20 summer cottages, clubhouse, playground and dancing pavilion. The resort guests could occupy themselves with fishing, golf, tennis, ring quoits, croquet, box ball, brist and baseball. In 1907 a nine-hole golf course was added. By 1912 the golf course was enlarged to 18 holes, making this the first 18 hole golf course in the State of Idaho.

Turn around and go back to Lakeview Dr., and turn left

 Lakeview Dr.
The road in front of the Country Club

In 1906 the Inland Empire electric line railroad was extended from 12th St. and Mullan Ave. in Coeur d'Alene north to Hayden Lake. Stops were made at Pennsylvania Ave., 11th St. and Harrison Ave., 10th St. and Best Ave., Hanley and 4th St. and the Bozanta Tavern Depot, where the track looped around.

Bozanta Tavern golf course and grounds, 1933. Notice the electric line tracks and depot on the left. The Bozanta Tavern is by the waterfront.

This provided easy transportation for agricultural produce and timber out of the area. It also brought trainloads of tourists to the resort and transformed the rustic log cabin community into a resort of national repute. The winding road from Coeur d'Alene to Bozanta Tavern was straightened and oiled in 1929.

The road curves to the right at Hayden Ave. To take the side trip to Hayden Lake Elementary School, continue on Hayden Ave. to Government Way. To continue on the main tour turn left on Strahorn Rd. and go to the stop sign where Honeysuckle Ave. intersects. Turn left and proceed to Honeysuckle Beach.

Hayden Lake Elementary School Side Trip

9650 N. Government Way (NE corner of Hayden Ave. and Government Way)

The small wooden building facing Hayden Ave. is the first Hayden Lake School. The one-room schoolhouse, built in 1897, was moved from the SW corner of Government Way and Hayden Ave. to this site in 1911. The brick building, built in 1936 at a cost of about $30,000, housed nearly 200 students in its first year. C. E. Rodell was the first principal. Students from this school were transferred to the new Altas Elementary School in 2005.

To return to the tour, go south on Government Way and left on Honeysuckle Ave. Continue east to the beach

 ## Honeysuckle Beach

A sawmill was located at Honeysuckle Beach until 1909. This beach has long been a popular swimming area. After water for irrigation and the large pipeline toward Post Falls were discontinued, the lake rose and covered what was once a large beach and sand bar at Honeysuckle Beach.

Turn around and take a left onto Lower Hayden Lake Rd.

 ## Coopers Bay (Tobler Marina) 1.5 miles

Coopers Bay was named for Jake Cooper, an early settler.

Clark House 🏛

2.5 miles from intersection of Honeysuckle and Lower Hayden Lake Rd.

When Spokane millionaire F. Lewis Clark built his mansion in 1909, it was one of the largest and most expensive homes in the State of Idaho. Clark's summer mansion included 29 rooms, nine fireplaces, seven bathrooms, a billiard room, smoking rooms, a library and servant quarters. It had crystal chandeliers and hand-painted wallpaper. The 1,400-acre estate had a water system, three cottages, barn, garage, dairy with equipment and milk rooms, chicken run and dove cote, hothouse and heating plant, tennis court, retaining wall, garden tool house, ice house, blacksmith shop and wood house. Much of the estate was beautifully landscaped, including flowerbeds along the lakeshore. In 1914 the 51-year-old Clark took a trip to Santa Barbara, California, and mysteriously disappeared. Clark's wealth disappeared with him, and Mrs. Clark sold the estate at auction in 1917. The house passed through many owners and was used as a hotel, a convalescent center during

WWII, a youth home and a restaurant. When Monty Danner purchased the House in 1989, it was in disrepair. Through his massive renovation project, the Clark House is again part of the community.

Turn around and follow the Lower Hayden Rd. back to Honeysuckle Ave.

Clark House, Dec. 1972

㉕ Hayden Lake

Hayden Lake is 2,220 feet above sea level and at its deepest is 400 feet. It is three miles wide and seven miles long with 45 miles of shoreline. It has so many bays that its shoreline is five times longer than expected of a lake its size. The lake has no obvious outlet, but it is believed that an underground outlet exists on its southwest side. Matt Hayden, an early settler, used to dynamite this place every spring in order to keep the rocks loose and the mud from puddling, so water could run out.

㉖ The Dike

F. Lewis Clark built the dike in 1911 to save the land from being flooded each spring. Eighty big Swedes from the old country worked all summer on the big rock wall for the dike road. The rocks for this wall were barged across the lake from English Point, which Clark also owned.

Turn left (west) onto Honeysuckle Ave.

27 Finucane Ranch Barn and Manager's Home

826 E. Honeysuckle Ave. South side of the street near 4th St. and Honeysuckle Ave.

This barn was part of the F. Lewis Clark estate when George T. and Nellie Sims purchased 400 acres from the estate in 1918. Mr. and Mrs. Sims and their 12 children ran a dairy farm. George died in 1939 and his widow sold the property in 1948 to Charles and Marion Finucane. They developed Loch Haven Farm, stocking it with purebred black angus cattle from Scotland. The herd was sold in 1953 when Mr. Finucane served as Undersecretary of the Army in the Eisenhower administration. They later restocked the farm with black angus feeder stock. The Finucane home was located across Honeysuckle Ave. from the manager's home and barn. The housing development to the west was pasture for the cattle. The Finucane's were co-owners of the Davenport Hotel in Spokane from 1947 to 1953. Charles Finucane died in 1983. In 1987 Mrs. Finucane donated 10 acres of land for Finucane Park. She died later that year.

28 Honeysuckle Ave. and 4th St.

Mr. Justis opened the first store in Hayden Lake near Honeysuckle Ave. and 4th St. In 1907 this area was known as the town site of Monaghan, named after James Monaghan. F. Lewis Clark changed the name of Monaghan to Honeysuckle after Honeysuckle Hill, which was named for the large amount of honeysuckle that grew on it.

Continue south on 4th St.

~ Dalton Gardens ~

The City of Dalton Gardens was incorporated in 1960 and includes the area from Prairie Ave. south to Dalton Ave. and from Government Way to 17th St. However, the name and settlement date back to the time of Fort Sherman when Oscar F. Canfield settled in the area in 1878. It is unknown from where the name Dalton originated. Dalton Gardens and Hayden Lake were known for orchards and produce. In the 1920s, a large packing plant was built and the electric line railroad provided freight and passenger service. Temperatures below zero, beginning Oct. 31, 1935, killed all the cherry and many of the apple and pear trees (tons of apples were frozen on the trees). In a few days the weather warmed, and the apples began to ferment and drop to the ground. Only a few farmers managed to survive. In 1907 the Inland Empire Railroad (the electric line) built a small depot at 4th and Hanley. Passenger service was discontinued in 1929-1930 with freight service being discontinued in 1937.

29▶ Canfield Mountain

Look to the left (east)
Oscar Canfield came to the area in 1878 (the year Fort Sherman was established) and homesteaded land in Dalton Gardens. He contracted to supply beef to the fort and drove hundreds of cattle to the Coeur d'Alene area from Walla Walla, Washington, and Enterprise, Oregon. The cattle grazed at the foot of what is now known as Canfield Mountain. In 1880 Canfield built a two-story home on 17th St. It is believed to be the first home in Dalton Gardens. The Canfields and General Sherman were relatives, and when Sherman inspected military posts in 1883, he visited the Canfields and named the mountain near their homestead Canfield Mountain. Oscar Canfield was a survivor of the Whitman Massacre of November 29, 1847, at the Waiilatpu Mission in Washington. Nine-year old Oscar was taken prisoner along with his mother, two sisters and a brother. On January 1, 1848, the 51 prisoners were released for ransom paid by the Hudson Bay Company.

Much of Canfield Mountain is Forest Service land and offers a beautiful view of the area and trails for hiking, mountain biking and motorcycle riding. access is off 15th St. and Nettleton Gulch Rd. Nettleton Gulch was named for John Nettleton, who arrived in the area in 1889, logged, and farmed 160 acres until his death in 1952.

Turn right on Dalton Ave. and turn left (south) on Government Way to begin Tour Three

Historic Coeur d'Alene
~ TOUR THREE ~

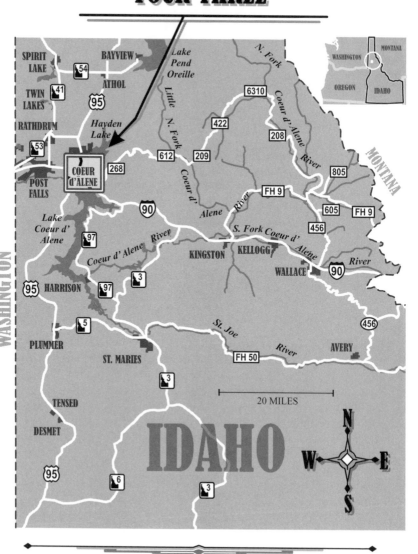

~ Coeur d'Alene ~

This tour of Coeur d'Alene is about 9.5 miles and takes less than an hour. At the intersection of Government Way and Dalton Ave. turn left (south).

The French name Coeur d'Alene can be traced back to the early 1800s when David Thompson, of the North West Fur Trading Company, encountered French speaking Iroquois Indians already living here. Since the Iroquois were familiar with the area, he hired them for guides and scouts. The words Coeur d'Alene (heart of awl) may have been the Iroquois' attempt to describe the sharp trading practices of the local Indians who called themselves *Schee-Chu-Umsh*. An awl is a pointed tool used to pierce leather.

With the establishment of Fort Coeur d'Alene in 1878, Coeur d'Alene City developed near the edge of the fort and within a few years, it became a supply point and navigation hub for the mining and timber industry. Coeur d'Alene's importance as Kootenai County's center was reinforced when voters moved the county seat to Coeur d'Alene in 1908. By 1910 the population was 8,000, with six large lumber mills in or near Coeur d'Alene, four banks, five hotels, nine churches, four grade schools and a high school, a movie theater and two telephone systems. Four railroads served the city, the Northern Pacific, Coeur d'Alene & Spokane electric line, the Milwaukee and the Spokane International. Coeur d'Alene's major industries were timber, tourism and agriculture.

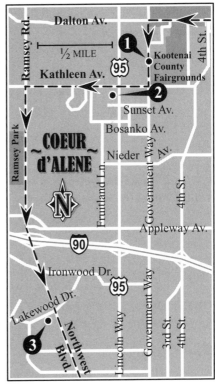

❶ Kootenai County Fairgrounds

Kathleen Ave. and Government Way, NE corner

About 1920 this site became the first municipally owned airport in the U.S. Weeks Field attracted hundreds of spectators to stunt flying, air derby, and parachuting events. During WWII, Gwin Hicks, and Herb and Gladys Buroker leased the airport to train pilots for the war, teaching over 400 students to fly. The large building along Government Way was built as a hangar during the war. In 1953 Weeks Field became the fairgrounds and the county built the grandstand in 1958.

Weeks Field with Canfield Mountain in the background in 1935.

Turn right (west) on Kathleen Ave. and go across Hwy 95

❷ The Schrieber Barn

On the hill to the left (south)

Although the barn was built in the last 60 years, the homesteading of this land goes back to 1897. This barn was part of a 160-acre dairy operation, owned or leased by several people over the years. As late as the 1970s Paul Zayer and his family sold milk by the gallon jar, which included several inches of cream on the top, for one dollar.

Go left (south) at Ramsey Rd. Once over the freeway, it becomes Northwest Blvd.

❸ Gibbs

Near Northwest Blvd. and Lakewood Dr.

The area from here south to the overpass was established about 1903.

Known as Gibbs it takes its name from one of the partners of the Stack-Gibbs Lumber Company. Gibbs was dependent on a succession of lumber companies that occupied the strip of land between the Spokane River and Northwest Blvd. The Winton Lumber Company operated the mill from 1918 to 1946. Northwest Timber Company bought the mill and operated it until it was removed in 1990.

Continue about 2 miles and turn right at Lincoln Way. There is a railroad crossing sign just before the turn, which only goes right. Then turn right at River Ave.

❹ Fort Grounds Tavern

705 W. River Ave.
Built in 1908 the building housed a drugstore and confectionery. Wyatt and Ruth Gray opened Gray's Grocery in the early 1940s. They added the west half to the building in 1959 for the grocery business and moved the tavern, run by Red Gray, to the east half. The grocery store closed and a kitchen was added in 1980. The Fort Grounds Tavern remained in the Gray Family until 2006.

❺ DeArmond Stud Mill

River Ave., on the right
This mill makes lumber for frame construction. The building on the right, seen often with steam coming out of it, is the dry kiln, which was built in 1960. Logs arrive at the mill at the Spokane River waterfront and by truck. The majority of lumber goes out by rail on the Burlington Northern Santa Fe and the remainder by truck. The mill will close in 2008.

Ⓐ Fort Sherman and North Idaho College Side Trip

Just before you go up the incline, turn left at College Dr. to see the three remaining Fort buildings. (North Idaho College Campus)
This area was the center of Fort Sherman, which occupied 999 acres and included 52 buildings. Before white settlement the Coeur d'Alene Indians called the confluence of Lake Coeur d'Alene and the Spokane River Yap-Keehn-um. The Coeur d'Alenes camped here with the Pend Oreille, Flathead and Kalispell Indians in the spring and fall to fish for salmon and socialize. In 1842 Jesuits came to provide religious teachings to the Indians.

In the summer of 1877, General William T. Sherman of Civil War fame selected this site for a fort. He established Camp Coeur d'Alene in the spring of 1878. The name was changed to Fort Sherman in 1887 to honor

General Sherman. *Soldiers left for the Spanish American War in 1898, and by 1900 the Fort was abandoned. The Fort Sherman grounds and buildings were sold at public auction in 1905. The Winton Lumber Company acquired a section of land and later donated 32 acres to Kootenai County for public use. Coeur d'Alene Junior College first opened as a private college in 1933 on the third floor of the Coeur d'Alene City Hall. In 1939 it became a public institution and changed its name to North Idaho Junior College. After WWII the number of returning veterans forced the college to expand. During the Christmas vacation of 1949 the college moved into the newly built classroom-administration building and gymnasium-auditorium. Along with academic courses the college offered vocational courses in aviation mechanics, watch making, radio and television repair, auto mechanics and forestry. In 1955 the enrollment was 200, in 1968 it was 800, and in 2005 it was over 4,500. Junior was dropped from the two-year college's name in 1972.*

(A1) Fort Sherman Powder Magazine

A small brick building set back from the street, on the left just before the Residence Hall (Ft. Sherman Museum)

The magazine was built in 1885 to store ammunition and spare weapons at Fort Sherman. It was used as a house for many years. In 1973 the Museum of North Idaho opened here and the site remained its headquarters until 1979 when it was moved to the Northwest Blvd. location. It now serves as the Fort Sherman branch of the Museum of North Idaho. Call 664-3448 for hours.

The Fort Sherman Gate and post guards circa 1900.

Turn left at W. Garden Ave.

(A2) Fort Sherman Officers' Quarters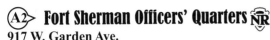
917 W. Garden Ave.
Built in 1878, this structure housed officers and their families. After the fort was abandoned, it became a home, then a boarding house. Acquired by North Idaho College about 1970, the building is used for faculty offices. In 1996, NIC remodeled the building and replaced the porch using historical photos to replicate the original design.

Turn right on Hubbard Ave.

(A3) Fort Sherman Chapel
332 Hubbard Ave.
Also known as the Little Red Chapel it was built in 1880, and served both military and civilians as the community's first church, school, and library. General Sherman worshipped here during his inspection tour in 1883. For information call 664-3448.

Turn around and take Hubbard Ave. back to River Ave., turn left and continue up the incline to Rosenberry Dr. for the main tour

❻ Rosenberry Dr. and the Dike
Rosenberry Dr. is named for the family who co-owned the Winton Lumber Company and donated the land on which North Idaho College sits. This raised road is part of a mile and a half-long dike built in 1941 by the U.S. War Department for flood control at the confluence of Lake Coeur d'Alene and the Spokane River. The first recorded flood occurred in 1894 when Fort Sherman was inundated. In December 1933 volunteers used 30,000 sandbags to hold back the flood waters. Other major floods occurred in January 1974, February 1996 and May 1997.

❼ The Fort Grounds Neighborhood
Between Hubbard Ave. and the City Park
When Fort Sherman was abandoned, the land and buildings were turned over to the Department of Interior and sold at public auction in 1905. Thomas T. Kerl and his partner David Ham, prominent land developers, traveled from Spokane by train and purchased the land, which became the Sherman Park Addition. Kerl brought a bodyguard with him to guard the gold he carried in his suitcase.

Homes in this National Register district were built from 1906 to the early 1920s. Styles include variations on the Craftsman/Bungalow style, Colonial

Revival, Dutch Colonial Revival and Tudor Revival, along with a number of vernacular style homes. These styles represent the architectural tastes of homebuilders during this period, not only in Coeur d'Alene, but also in other cities in northern Idaho and across the nation.

As Coeur d'Alene's earliest planned subdivision, this neighborhood features long, curving streets leading to the lake, uniform housing setbacks, and restrictive covenants, making the Sherman Park Addition probably the first area in the city to regulate the exclusive quality of a neighborhood. In 1908, the Sherman Park Addition had forty-six homes on its ninety-five lots. The neighborhood continued to grow rapidly and in 1921 only three vacant lots were left. These stayed empty until the owners built during the late 1950s and early 1960s.

❽ 701 W. Lake Shore Dr.

Mr. Olsen built this home in 1914 at 4th and Harrison for logging contractor J.M. Carey. In 1955 the house, built with virgin pine, was moved to its present location for Burl Hagadone, publisher of the *Coeur d'Alene Press*.

❾ 615 W. Lake Shore Dr.

Built in 1908 by Kate Newton, the home was sold in 1925 to Lars Tendall, a friend to J.C. Penney who made him manager of the first Penney's store in Coeur d'Alene in 1916.

❿ 613 W. Lake Shore Dr.

Anna Laurie Nevers built this home in 1907 and sold it to Mr. and Mrs. Eric Bjorklund in 1909. He owned IXL Clothing Store on Sherman Ave. for about 45 years and liked to be called "By Jork." The Edward Rutledge Timber Company (Potlatch Forest) purchased the house in 1927. In 1930 the Clarence O. Graue family moved into the house when he was purchasing agent for Rutledge Timber Company. He also served as president of the Red Collar Line. In 1932 he became general manager of Potlatch Forests, Inc. Clarence's wife Lulu established the first chapter of the American Association of University Women in Coeur d'Alene. Upon his retirement, the company gave him the house. The Graue family resided there until the mid-1970s. It was remodeled and the wrap-around porches were enclosed.

⓫ 607 W. Lake Shore Dr.

Judge James Beatty built this house in 1910. James Evenden, chief entomologist for the U.S. Bureau of Entomology, Dept. of Agriculture, bought the house in 1933. His wife Ella was instrumental in building the

Camp Fire Girls program in Kootenai County.

⑫ 205 Park Dr.

Charles Craik built this home between 1908-09. In the late 1910s J.W. and Grace Vollmeck moved into the home. By the 1930s he was the district manager for the Washington Water Power Company. Forrest Schini married Arlene Tendall, whose family home was just around the corner, and bought this house in the late 1930s. Forrest practiced dentistry in Coeur d'Alene for 36 years. His son Robert practiced for 35 years and his son took over the practice continuing to treat some of Forrest's patients. Schini's lived in the house until 1957 when Dr. Gedney Barclay's family purchased it. The Barclays lived here until 1991.

⑬ 207 Park Dr.

During the 1920s the Fort Grounds neighborhood was home to several young mill managers raising their families. David and Katherine (Kay) Winton moved into this 1910 house in about 1920. David's brother Charles and his wife Henrietta also lived on Park Dr. They co-owned the Winton Lumber Company with Walter Rosenberry. David and Kay often socialized with Phil and Helen Weyerhaeuser who lived at 319 Park Dr.

For almost a half-century it was the home of Capt. John and Thelma Finney. He ran the tour boats *Seeweewana* and *Dancewana* on the lake until retirement in 1984. Capt. Finney is credited with inventing water skiing. Finney's daughter extensively remodeled the house in 1997. A stained glass window depicts the original architecture.

⑭ 303 Park Dr.

Harry and Orene Knight built the house in 1907 and in March of 1911 died within 14 hours of each other. Mr. Knight, a successful attorney in the partnership of Gray & Knight, had been ill for several months, having contracted blood poisoning from a sliver beneath his skin. Upon the sudden death of his wife from ptomaine poisoning from eating peas, Mr. Knight died. After years of vacancy and renting, the house was in a state of disrepair when D.D. and Blanche Drennan bought it in 1918. John and Florence Shelton purchased the house in 1935. Their daughter, Susan Schrieber, and family moved into the home after Florence's death. The house was remodeled in 1952, 1980 and again in 1995.

⑮ 319 Park Dr.

J.P. "Phil" Jr. and Helen Weyerhaeuser lived here from 1920 to 1925. He came here as a sales manager representing the Weyerhaeuser family for

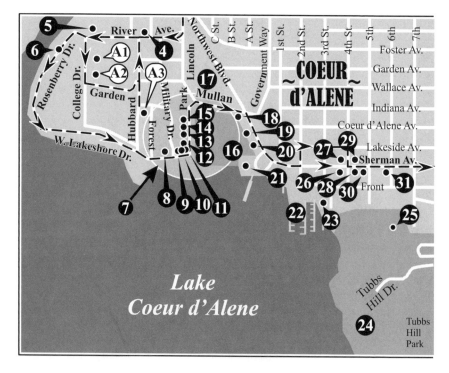

Coeur d'Alene's Edward Rutledge Mill. Phil started a Niscot Club in Coeur d'Alene composed of men between twenty-one and forty to serve as a medium through which the ideals and aspirations of the younger generation might find expression with the performance of civic duties. Several of his neighbors, including C. O. Graue and Dave Winton, were also in the club. When Phil and Helen moved to Lewiston in 1925 Glenn and Marguerite Powell purchased the home. Mr. Powell's family owned the Powell Building on Sherman Ave., but he preferred the outdoors to business affairs and ran a boat livery and provided a water taxi service in his motor boat the "Skippy." The home was restored in the early 1990s.

16 Coeur d'Alene City Park

In 1903 the Coeur d'Alene & Spokane Railway (Inland Empire electric line railroad) acquired a 200-foot right-of-way across the Fort Sherman Military Reservation. It also obtained 20 acres of land for a depot and park, which was named Blackwell Park after F.A. Blackwell, the company's president. The railroad spent $6,000 on improvements to attract tourists, including flower gardens, a bandstand, a dance pavilion, ball field and water fountains. This area became the Coeur d'Alene City Park in the 1910s.

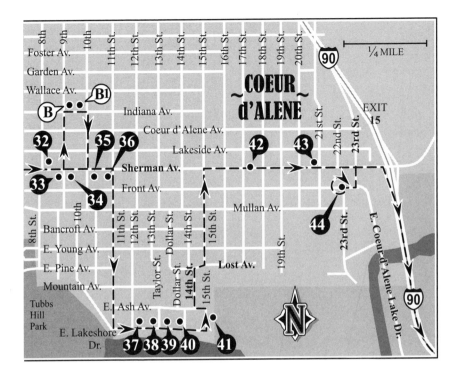

Turn right at the corner of the park onto Mullan Rd.

17 Memorial Field

On the left

Originally part of the Fort Sherman Military Reservation, most of Memorial Field was donated to the city by the U.S. Government. Thomas and Lola Kerl donated the land in the northwest corner of Memorial Field to the city in 1922. After WWII, "Blackie" Fortin of the American Legion Post 14, spearheaded an effort to bring baseball back to Coeur d'Alene. Fortin, with volunteer labor and donations, built this grandstand, complete with dugouts, press box and dressing rooms. It was dedicated in 1947 and later rededicated as Memorial Field in honor of Kootenai County men who died in both World Wars.

18 The Electric Line Railroad Substation NR

Mullan Rd. and Northwest Blvd. brick building on the right

Designed by Coeur d'Alene architect George Williams and built in 1904, this substation accommodated a configuration of five massive 300-cell storage batteries. It was fourth in a series of five electrical voltage transformer units, spaced at about 12-mile intervals along the Inland Empire electric line railroad between Spokane, Coeur d'Alene and Hayden Lake. The batteries prevented power interruptions on the electric railway and handled peak electricity demands. The passenger depot was located just south of here near Independence Point. From 1903 to 1939, the line provided passenger service.

Turn right on NW Blvd.

⑲ The Corliss Steam Engine
Museum Parking lot
The Corliss steam engine powered the Rutledge Sawmill (later the Potlatch Lumber Company) from 1916 to 1963. Edward Rutledge purchased the 50-ton engine and brought it from Butte, Montana, where it powered a light plant. The 16-foot-diameter flywheel turned 90 revolutions a minute and ran 24 hours a day. Over 100 cowhides made up the leather belt. Excess power generated by the Corliss was sold to the Washington Water Power Company. In 1988 Potlatch Corporation closed the mill and donated the Corliss engine to the Museum of North Idaho.

⑳ The Museum of North Idaho
115 NW Blvd., on the right
Cooperative Supply built this structure in 1966 and operated a feed store and gas station here until 1975. Museum volunteers remodeled the city-owned building and opened the museum in 1979. The Museum of North Idaho preserves and exhibits the history of Kootenai, Benewah and portions of Shoshone counties. For information call 664-3448.

㉑ Independence Point
In 1903 the Inland Empire electric line railroad depot was located in this parking lot. Passengers boarded steamboats at the pier for points around the lake and up the St. Joe and Coeur d'Alene Rivers. The depot was torn down in 1965. In 1941 the shoreline was extended into the lake to create the point and build the Playland Pier Amusement Park, featuring a midway, amusement rides and games. Fire destroyed Playland Pier in December 1975. In 1976 Independence Point Park was dedicated.

Stay in the right lane

㉒ The Coeur d'Alene Resort and Waterfront
In the early years, the focus of activities along the waterfront reflected the needs of industry such as transportation, logging, and boat building.

Beginning in the 1950s, the uses shifted to tourism. In 1965 Robert Templin built the North Shore Motel adjacent to Templin's Motor Inn and later added a convention center. Hagadone Hospitality expanded and remodeled the building, re-opening it as the Coeur d'Alene Resort in 1986.

Turn right on 2nd St.

㉓ The City Parking Lot and the 3rd St. Dock

The 3rd St. Dock, at the base of Tubbs Hill, has long been important as an access point to the water. In 1886 a dock was built into the water to transfer ore, brought by steamboats from the Coeur d'Alene Mining District, to rail cars. Goods were also loaded onto the steamboats to supply communities around the lake. As early as 1907 they began filling in the waterfront to accommodate industry and transportation. As roads and rail improved, the 3rd St. Dock was no longer needed as an industrial transportation hub and the use shifted to recreation. In the late 1950s, the railroad dock was removed, and over the years the Wildlife Federation, the Idaho Fish and Game Department and the city built this public boat launch.

Coeur d'Alene from Tubbs Hill, circa 1915. As early as 1909, the waterfront was filled in to accommodate industry and transportation. The diagonal boardwalk near center foreground of the photo was built by the Red Collar Line to connect passengers on the Electric Line Railroad, at Independence Point, with the Northern Pacific Line at the 3rd Street Dock. The Milwaukee depot is center near the waterfront and the new fill. The Northern Pacific depot is on the right. The Hotel Idaho is in the center and was built in 1903 and burned in 1972.

㉔ Tubbs Hill

Bordering McEuen Field

Tubbs Hill was named in the late 19th century after Tony Tubbs, who was granted a homestead in 1884. He owned a hotel at the base of the hill and planned to build homes on the hill. But Tubbs divided and platted his land on the hill as if it were flat ground. Consequently, the lots were unattractive to builders, because often the ground rose or fell away, making construction prohibitively expensive. Because of this quirk, the land remained undeveloped. In the 1960s preservationists successfully made Tubbs Hill part of the city's park system. The 2-mile trail around the hill provides spectacular views of the lake and native flora.

㉕ McEuen Field

Bordering Mullan Ave. between 3rd St. and 7th St.

From 1889 to 1929, the Saginaw and the Coeur d'Alene Lumber companies used the area at the base of Tubbs Hill for log and lumber storage. The city of Coeur d'Alene purchased 34 acres with the approval of a bond issue of $19,000 on Dec. 1, 1936. During the 1930s McEuen Field was known as Mullan Field and was used for rodeos, horse racing, Kootenai County Fairgrounds, carnivals and the circus. After WWII, the city acquired the property on the east side of the field in a trade with the County for the current fairgrounds. During WWII, low-cost housing known as Mullan Park was built to provide for the influx of workers that came to build Farragut Naval Training Station. The housing was demolished by 1956.

The Lakeshore Development Committee formed in the mid 1950s to stop commercial development and preserve the land for public uses. Service clubs contributed to the enhancement of Mullan Park Recreation Area and the development of the ball fields. The park's name was changed to McEuen Field in June 1965 in honor of Mae McEuen, who was a long-time member of the City Recreation Commission and active in local youth activities.

Turn left (north) on 4th St. and notice the four buildings on the corners of 4th St. and Sherman Ave., then turn right

㉖ Exchange National Bank Building

324 Sherman Ave., SW corner (Java)

William Dollar built the first Exchange National Bank in 1902. The City Library was housed on an upper floor from 1905 to 1909. The Hart Drug Store occupied the building from about 1930 to 1983.

㉗ Wiggett Building

325 Sherman Ave., NW corner

This block was known as the Merriam Block after Dr. Merriam, who built this building in 1890 as a two-story structure. J.W. Wiggett bought the building in 1898 and added a third story in 1912. Wiggett owned several buildings, and at one time was the richest man in Coeur d'Alene. The building housed the American Trust Bank and later the Idaho First National Bank until about 1965.

28▸ Dingle Building
402 Sherman Ave., SE corner
V.W. Sander built the Idaho Mercantile Company in 1891. After a fire destroyed the second floor in 1911, it was rebuilt as a four-story building and became the Morrow Department store. The Dingle family opened the city's biggest hardware store and mercantile in the mid 1930s. In Sept. of 1957, fire gutted the two top floors of Coeur d'Alene's tallest downtown building and destroyed two of the largest law libraries in the state. After the fire, this building stood just three stories. T. Hedley Dingle's grandchildren continue to own and manage the building. In 2002 his granddaughter Sandi Bloem was elected Coeur d'Alene's first woman mayor.

29▸ Wilson Drug
403 Sherman Ave., NE corner
James Carroll built this building in 1904 as the First National Bank and the Lakeside Pharmacy. After the bank closed in 1916, the Lakeside Drug and Book Company took over the first floor. It sold drugs, sporting goods, Victrolas, musical instruments, books, stationery and school supplies. In 1923, Clayton, Ralph and Victor Wilson purchased the Lakeside Drug and Book Company, and changed the name to Wilson's Pharmacy. Chuck and Lorna Sears and bought it in about 1961 and operated it until 1986.

30▸ Old City Hall 🏛NR
424 Sherman Ave.
In the fall of 1908, Kootenai County and Coeur d'Alene city officials were confident that voters would decide to move the county seat from Rathdrum to Coeur d'Alene, so they entered into a lease agreement to use part of the newly-built City Hall for county purposes. The City Hall, designed by George Williams and built at a cost of $40,000, housed the Kootenai County Courthouse until 1926, when the courthouse on Government Way was built. The jail was in the basement; city offices and the library were on the upper floors. North Idaho Junior College had its start on the third floor in 1933.

31▸ Masonic Temple 🏛NR
524 Sherman Ave.

George Williams, a 32nd degree mason, designed the Masonic Temple. Williams, who died in 1929, spent the last year and a half of his life as the custodian of the building he designed. Fire in 1938 destroyed many interior features, but the 1908 building continued to serve the Masons until they sold it in 1991. The original steps were replaced in 2004.

32 805 Sherman Ave.

J.C. White, president of the Red Collar Line, built this home in 1904. The White family lived in the carriage house while their home was being erected. E.W. Eller, president of the Red Collar Steamship Line, acquired the house about 10 years later. Phillip and Deborah McManam bought the house in 1924 and converted the back area of the house into two apartments during WWII. Phillip and Deborah McManam's daughter Mary Bjorklund, resided in the home until her death in the early 1990s.

33 The Blackwell House

820 Sherman Ave.

Frederick Blackwell, mill owner, promoter and co-founder of the Coeur d'Alene & Spokane Railway, built this Victorian house in 1904 for his son Russell and his new bride. The house featured a parlor, music room, maple floors, marble fireplace, crystal chandelier, native fir paneling and winding staircase. From 1919 to 1951 the Walter Rosenberry family lived here and made many additions, including an elevator and a garage turntable. Since then, the house has been apartments, offices and a bed and breakfast.

34 Major John O'Brien House

104 S. 9th St.

Major O'Brien came to Coeur d'Alene in 1886. He never married but built this large home upon his retirement in 1900. On holidays the Major gave local children new dimes. In January 1948 local attorney C.J. Hamilton and his family moved into the house. Fifty years later, to the month, his son Bill took over the home.

From Sherman Ave., turn left (north) on 9th St. then right on Indiana

B St. Thomas Catholic Church Side Trip 𝕟ℝ

9th St. and Indiana Ave.

Designed by Spokane architects Rooney and Stritesky, this church was finished in 1910 for $46,000 by E.M. Kreig. Unique in Idaho architecture as a Romanesque structure, mass-rendered in brick, the church features leaded *glass windows from G.C. Riordan of Cincinnati and an altar that is the only one of its kind in the United States. The church has a spire surfaced in painted galvanized iron and five crosses coated in gold flake.*

(B1) The Redemptorist Mission House
919 Indiana Ave.
In 1913 The Redemptorist Order from Missouri assumed title to St. Thomas Catholic Church to serve as a mission base for eastern Washington, Idaho and Montana. The Early American Colonial monastery, built in 1928, was originally connected to the church by a cloistered walk.

Turn right on 10th St., go back to Sherman Ave., and turn left to continue the main tour

35 1006 Sherman Ave.
Built in 1910, the house was first occupied by Edward and May McCarty. He was vice-president of the National Exchange Bank. After they moved out in the early 1940s the house served as apartments.

36 Thomson House
1028 Sherman Ave.
George C. Thomson, a well-known merchant and civic leader, purchased several lots in Coeur d'Alene, but decided to build here in 1903 because it was on the outskirts of town. In 1906 he died of pneumonia. In the 1930s the house was remodeled to rent rooms on the second floor. At various times George's three daughters, Margaret Wood, Mary Preston and Alice Potter, moved back to their childhood home after their husbands died. Robert and Connie Singletary worked on restoring the home from 1987 to 2006.

Turn right (south) on 11th St. and at East Lake Shore Dr. turn left (east)

37 The Barclay House
1203 E. Lake Shore Dr.
This Georgian house was built in 1925 for Dr. Alexander Barclay Sr. He owned the second hospital in Coeur d'Alene from 1917 to 1942.

38 Villa Glendalough
1221 E. Lake Shore Dr.
This house built in 1905 was named Villa Glendalough, after a famous villa in County Wicklow, Ireland, where Theresa Graham's mother was born.

Mrs. Graham was the National Democratic Committee woman for North Idaho from 1916-1936. Her niece, Ellen Healy, inherited the home and lived there until her death in 1989.

39➤ The Taylor House
1301 E. Lake Shore Dr.
Marshall and Edith Hubbard Taylor built this home between 1905-1908. This English Tudor has Italian marble fireplaces, original woodwork, and heavily leaded windows. On the second floor, a mural by Baron Feodar Von Luertzer depicts the construction of the home, the beach area, a sawmill and other scenes.

40➤ Stanly Easton House
1321 E. Lake Shore Dr.
Stanly Easton, general manager of the Bunker Hill Company in Kellogg moved into the house in 1923. The house had 19 rooms and large grounds with a tennis court behind the house.

41➤ The Jewett House
1501 E. Lake Shore Dr. and 15th St.
The Rutledge Timber Company built the house in 1915 to house its first manager Huntington Taylor. The Taylor's daughter started the first Polar Bear Club outing on New Year's Day in Coeur d'Alene. The Taylor family lived here until 1928. When George Frederick "Fritz" Jewett became President and General Manager of the Rutledge Mill in 1929 he and his family moved into the house. He moved to Spokane but used this home in the summer until the mid 1950s. In 1978 Potlatch Forest Industries donated the house to the city to be used as a senior recreation center.

The Jewett House in the early 1920s.

E. Lake Shore Dr. turns left, then left again, and on 14th take a right and a right on Lost Ave. then left on 15th back to Sherman Ave. and right on Sherman Ave.

42 U.S. Hwy 10 (Sherman Ave.)

Paving of the whole length of Sherman Ave. was completed in 1921. Before completion of I-90 in 1960, the avenue served as Hwy 10, also known as the Yellowstone Highway. Many motels and service stations were located along Sherman Ave. to serve travelers.

43 Hiway Ten Motel
2018 Sherman Ave. (Bates Motel)

Hiway Ten Motel opened in the early 1950s, using old barracks from Farragut Naval Training Station. After WWII, Frank Wester had the contract to sell the recycled buildings, and many of them are still visible throughout the area. About 1990 a group of men bought the property. When trying to decide on a name, they looked at all of their names and decided Randy Bates' name might raise the most interest in the motel by conjuring up visions from the movie Psycho.

44 St. Thomas Cemetery
Turn right on 21st St. and left on Front Ave. to enter the cemetery

This Catholic cemetery opened in 1900 on land donated by John J. Costello. Many prominent people in Coeur d'Alene's history are buried here, including Mathew Hayden, James and Theresa Graham and their niece Ellen Healy. James Graham bought the fort hospital and gave it to the IHM sisters for their convent and school. Father Thomas Purcell came to Coeur d'Alene in 1897 and helped build the St. Thomas Church. He brought the IHM sisters to Coeur d'Alene in 1903 to establish the first Catholic school. In 1925 he died at age 64 and is buried here. Sister Clement, the first principal of IHM academy, is also buried here. Local mason Frank Fruechtl built the shrine located in the cemetery. In 1960 Opal and Henry Hammrich became caretakers of the cemetery.

Lake Coeur d'Alene Loop
~ TOUR FOUR ~

This tour starts from Coeur d'Alene and goes around Lake Coeur d'Alene to Harrison, St. Maries, Plummer, Worley and back to Coeur d'Alene. It covers about 150 miles and takes about 5 hours. Enter I-90 east from Sherman Ave.

❶ Potlatch Lumber Company (Coeur d'Alene Resort Golf Course)
As you go up the hill look to the right
The Coeur d'Alene Resort Golf Course was the site of a sawmill, which operated from 1916 to 1988, first as the Rutledge Timber Company, and from 1933 as the Potlatch Lumber Company. The Hagadone Corporation bought the property in 1988 and developed the golf course and floating green.

❷ Veterans Memorial Centennial Bridge
Completed in 1991 as the Bennett Bay Centennial Bridge, a year later the bridge was renamed the Veterans Memorial Centennial Bridge. It is a segmental concrete box girder bridge nearly a third of a mile long and 300 feet above the valley floor. Howard, Needles, Tannem & Bergendoff of Bellevue, Washington designed the bridge which has received numerous awards.

Using the balanced cantilever method for the superstructure, the bridge was built from each of the three piers outward. Concrete was pumped to the top of each pier where crews poured each segment, until the roadway sections met in perfect alignment. Major repairs to the roadway slab are virtually impossible with this type of structure. Therefore the design included several features to help the bridge endure climactic extremes over the years. Concrete is kept in compression by post-tensioning in all principal directions, a dense concrete overlay for the riding surface, and all epoxy-coated reinforcing bars in the top slab. This was the first bridge in the United States with all post-tensioning strands in the top slab encased in polyethylene ducts, which will protect the strands from corrosion.

❸ Lake Coeur d'Alene
Glacier deposits formed this "T" shaped lake. It has about 100 miles of

shoreline, is 26 miles long and one to three miles wide. Steamboats made it possible for people to have easier access to towns and farmlands around Lake Coeur d'Alene and its interior in a time when there were few roads and no highways. Early steamboat captains named many of the bays. By 1910 more than 40 large steamboats operated on the lake. During the week they carried freight, mail, businessmen, miners and lumberjacks to communities, rail lines and mills around the lake and up the rivers. On Sundays excursion boats carried passengers on pleasure trips.

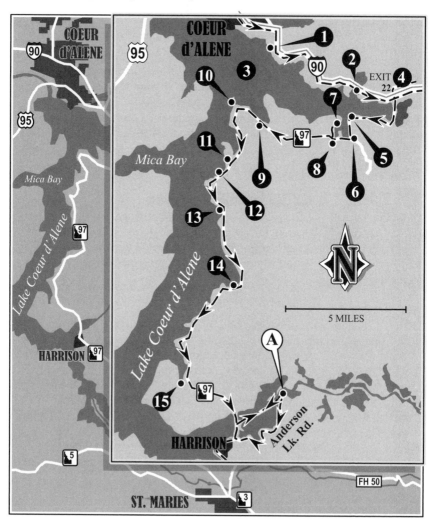

The Red Collar Line and the White Star Navigation Company controlled the steamboat business on Lake Coeur d'Alene. Steamboat transportation peaked in about 1915 when the automobile was gaining popularity and railroads were well established. Steamboats continued to operate into the late 1930s, but the grandeur of the early years was gone.

Take Exit 22, onto Hwy 97 turn right onto Hwy 97 to go to Harrison. Set odometer to 0

❹ Wolf Lodge

Known as Wolf Lodge Prairie in reports by Governor Stevens and John Mullan as early as 1853 it is unclear where the name came from. Eagles flying south for the winter stop in Wolf Lodge, Beauty and Blue Creek bays to fish for Kokanee Salmon, a land-locked sockeye salmon that spawn in Wolf Lodge Creek in the fall. They arrive in mid-November and leave in late January. Up to140 eagles have been sighted here.

❺ Mineral Ridge Scenic Trail

2.2 miles, parking area for the hiking trail
From this hiking trail a spectacular view of the lake can be seen, as well as the remains of mining prospects dating from 1891 into the 1930s. Prospectors built a log cabin in 1900 in what is now the parking lot. In 1963 when construction began, this was the first recreation site developed by the Bureau of Land Management in Idaho. Mineral Ridge is used for environmental education because of its plant and animal life including the observation of eagles from November to February.

❻ Forest Service Road to the Beauty Bay Campground

2.4 miles
In 1933, during the depression, President Franklin Roosevelt established the Civilian Conservation Corps (CCC) to provide young men with work. A CCC Camp was located here in 1937 with 150 men. They worked for $30 a month, of which $25 was sent home to the family, and were provided meals, a place to stay, clothing and medical care. One of their projects included building the road to Coeur d'Alene Mountain. The wood cook stove from the camp is used at the Harrison Grange Hall. The barracks at Beauty Bay were barged by Lafferty Transportation to the city dock in Coeur d'Alene and taken by a lowboy truck to the Coeur d'Alene Airport at Hayden Lake, where they served as an office and pilots ready room.

➐ Beauty Bay Viewpoint
At the top of the hill on the right
There is a picnic area and a handicapped accessible trail to a spectacular viewpoint of the bay. The trail is a 0.4 mile loop. Beauty Bay was a popular stop for steamboats and tourists in the early days.

➑ Beauty Bay Seed Orchard
On the left side at the top of the hill
This area is a seed orchard for growing blister rust resistant white pine trees. Planted in 1993, seeds will be used to reforest land. Blister rust is a disease that lives on currant and gooseberry plants, then attacks and kills white pine trees. A large number of Civilian Conservation Corp workers were involved in the enormous efforts of blister rust control (BRC). The host plants were dug out by hand, sprayed with insecticide or bulldozed. Although research began in 1949, it was not until the 1980s that the first disease-resistant seedlings were planted.

➒ Squaw Bay Resort Marina & Store
7.6 miles
Squaw Bay was a marine route mail delivery stop. The building along the highway has served as a gas station and general store since the 1940s.

➓ Arrow Point
At 9 miles park at the mail boxes and look behind you at Arrow Point.
This area was a Coeur d'Alene Indian Village. In the late 1800s, Joseph Boughton homesteaded the peninsula. A makeshift dance hall using tree limbs for a roof was built on top of the black rock at the end of the point. The hall, along with other facilities, was known as "Lake View." Soldiers from Fort Sherman and others came by steamboat to dance here. Later this point was the site of a private boys' camp, Arrow Camp, and a resort.

⓫ Camp Easton Boy Scout Camp
11.5 miles, 23513 S. Hwy 97
F.W. Fitze, a Coeur d'Alene businessman, gave a parcel of land to the Idaho Panhandle Council for use as a summer camp. Mr. Fitze suggested the new camp be called Camp Easton for Stanly Easton, president of the Bunker Hill Company and one of the organizers of the Shoshone County Council of Boy Scouts in 1916. Camp Easton opened in July 1929. In 1957, total camp acreage was 214.9. Service clubs, including the Lions Club of North Idaho, made many improvements over the years. Boy Scouts enjoy camping, swimming and other activities here.

⑫ Gotham Bay

The Gothams were early homesteaders here. Before the 1930s when the road was built, early homesteaders relied on steamboats for transportation and supplies. In the early 1900s, a steamboat delivered a pump organ to the dock here and a horse and wagon carried it up the steep hill to the Dahlgren homestead. This was also a marine route mail delivery stop.

⑬ Turner Bay

14.5 miles Burma Rd. and Hwy 97
The property above Turner Bay was homesteaded by a man named Turner. When he disappeared, the Andrew Fossum family took over the homestead. By 1900, Sherman Turner, not related to the first Turner, built a house up Burma Rd. and raised a family that lived in the area for many decades. A store was built in the 1940s, and the Ross Hall family ran it from 1947 to 1966. Later, when it included a restaurant, they featured warm homemade bread slices with strawberry jam.

⑭ Carlin Creek and Bay

17.7 miles Elk Rd. and Hwy 97
Colonel William Carlin served as Post Commander at Fort Sherman from 1886 until 1893. His son had a hunting lodge near the Bay, so Colonel Carlin named the bay for his son. A post office was established at Carlin Bay in 1903. When this area was logged in the early 1900s, there was a railroad up Carlin Creek. When the water is at low level, pilings are visible in the lake. A store also operated here.

⑮ Powderhorn Bay Rd.

24.1 miles
Logging railroads were built to the shores of many of the area's lakes. The Russell & Pugh Lumber Company had a narrow gauge railroad that followed the stream several miles to where they logged. Once the logs were dumped into the lake, they were contained in a log boom or brail.

Ⓐ Springston Side Trip

27.7 miles. Just before the bridge, turn left at Blue Lake Rd. (Sportsman Access) go approximately 3 miles and cross the Springston Bridge to the Trailhead for the *Trail of the Coeur d'Alenes.*
You will pass several osprey nests, an eagle's nest, and on the left, muskrat houses in the Thompson slough. Muskrat fur provided the warmest coats before the use of synthetic fabrics. On the right, crossing the Coeur d'Alene

River is the single lane Springston Bridge leading to the former site of the thriving lumber town of Springston. The first mill opened in 1901 and the town had a boarding house, homes, store, Oregon Railway & Navigation Company (later Union Pacific Railroad) depot and the Russell and Pugh Lumber Company's office, store and warehouse. Upriver a quarter-mile the Russell & Pugh sawmill employed approximately 100 people from 1917 to 1963. The Union Pacific railroad tracks, which once served the thriving town of Springston, are now the Trail of the Coeur d'Alenes.

Turn around and return to the Highway or for the more adventurous, continue on Anderson Lake Rd. until you come to the intersection with Bell Canyon Rd. and turn right to go back to Hwy 97 and turn left to return to the main tour

~ Harrison ~

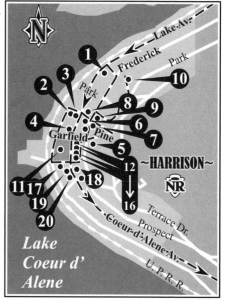

The Coeur d'Alene Indian name for the mouth of the Coeur d'Alene River is *Alkwari't*, meaning "Gold on the Water." When the Indians crossed the lake in their canoes at a certain time of day the water looked gold. The Crane family first settled here in 1890. Incorporated in 1899, Harrison is located on a one-mile strip carved out of the Coeur d'Alene Indian Reservation by a bill signed by President Harrison on the night of his last day in office, March 4, 1891. Passengers arrived on the Oregon Railway and Navigation Company Railroad and by steamboat. Harrison prospered as a gateway to the Coeur d'Alene mining district and the development of timber and farming interests up the St. Joe and St. Maries rivers. The 1911 city directory reports a population of 1,250, with lumber, farming and mining as the main industries, and lists four churches, numerous fraternal organizations, two hotels, weekly newspaper, high school and grade school. Numerous sawmills turning out lumber, stull, shingles and material for boxes lined the waterfront. Sparks drifting uphill from the mills were common. Early Saturday morning on July 24, 1917, a fire broke out at the Grant Lumber Company. The fire, driven by high winds, burned for two days and destroyed about 30 residences, sawmills and the business district. Much of the town was never rebuilt.

❶ The Osprey Inn
134 Frederick Ave., on the left side of Hwy 97
This building served as a boarding house for a nearby mill and for a short time in the 1950s as a hospital. It was apartments for many years before becoming a bed and breakfast inn.

❷ E.C. Hay and Sons Grain Elevator
107 N. Lake Ave. the Armstrong Garage building, the metal building on the right behind the Armstrong Garage building
Built in 1955 the grain elevator had storage for nearly 59,000 bushels. The quonset building, added in 1967, had a capacity of over 89,000 bushels. The Union Pacific Railroad right-of-way is located on Lake St.

❸ Theater/Armstrong Garage
104 N. Coeur d'Alene Ave.
The Princess Theater burned in the 1917 fire. John Nitkey's new theatre opened in 1918 but had difficulty making a profit, and the property's ownership changed several times. In the early 1930s it was turned into an automotive garage and the stage, balcony and projection booth were removed.

Miss Spokane at the Red Collar Line Dock at Harrison, after 1917.

❹ Masonic Temple/Export Building
100 N. Coeur d'Alene Ave.
The Masons built this building in 1918 and maintained a reception and meeting room on the second floor for many years. The Export Lumber Company, located on the main floor, sold groceries, hardware and clothing and in the basement portion sold salt, hay and grain. The Masonic Lodge

was unable to keep up the taxes during the late 1930s and in 1945 Russell & Pugh Lumber Company purchased the building.

Turn left up Garfield Ave.

❺ The Methodist Church
101 N. Garfield Ave. on the corner of Garfield & Prospect Ave. (Masonic Temple)
The Methodist Church was rebuilt shortly after the 1917 fire, and the building later became the Masonic Temple.

Turn left on Frederick Ave.

❻ City Hall
100 Frederick Ave. on the left
The building, originally located on Hwy 97, housed the City Hall and library.

❼ Senior Citizen's Building
Serving as the I.O.O.F. hall for many years, this building was moved from another location and may have first served as the Presbyterian Church. The Harrison Senior Citizen's group started in 1972 and met in the Grange Hall until they finished remodeling.

❽ Harrison Community Baptist Church
W. 101 Pine St. on the left side of Frederick Ave.
The Baptist Church, rebuilt in 1921, has exceptionally good acoustics. The outside is natural cedar.

❾ Our Lady of Perpetual Help Catholic Church
Frederick Ave. on the right
In 1924, Father T.A. Daly bought a house and remodeled it for use as a church on the site of the present church parking lot. That church was torn down and a new church erected in 1957, inspired by Father Martin Hughes. He and his twin brother, a priest in Boise, were born in Ireland. In 1994 a talented group of volunteers remodeled the church adding a social room, a steeple and landscaping.

❿ Harrison School
Frederick Ave. on the right
The school was built in 1909 for grades 1 through 12. In 1928-29 a

gymnasium was added to accommodate basketball and boxing events as well as drama club programs. From 1952 to 1980 several different organizations sponsored dances, talent shows and little theater performances, which benefitted community projects.

Pull into the school, turn around, go back to Hwy 97 and turn left to continue down the main street

 ## Harrison Cemetery Side Trip
Continue on Prospect Dr. up the hill about 1 mile
There are about 682 graves here with the oldest dating to 1895.

Loop around the cemetery, go back to downtown and turn left on Coeur d'Alene Ave.

 ## Harrison City Park

One whole block was not rebuilt after the 1917 fire and remained a pile of rocks and cement rubble for many years. With the intention of bringing the Harrison Old Time Picnic back from Coeur d'Alene, where it had been held for many years, a committee cleaned the rubble, planted grass and trees and built a barbecue pit. The last Sunday in July was selected for the picnic because rain had not been recorded on that day for fifty years. The first picnic and celebration, with a dance and crowning of a queen on Saturday night and a parade, races and contests was held on Sunday July 26, 1953, attracting 4,000 people. For more than fifty years it has never rained on the picnic.

105-109 S. Coeur d'Alene Ave. (Hwy 97) on the left

All the buildings in this block were destroyed by the 1917 fire and rebuilt in 1918.

The Bridgeman Building

Wayne Bridgeman operated a hardware and furniture store here until he sold to H.D. Brownawell in 1938. Brownawell added groceries and operated the store for four more years.

The Corskie Building

John A. Corskie was a druggist with one of the first two pharmacy licenses in Idaho. When there was no longer a doctor in town he was everyone's first-aid station, caring for every type of wound, even cutting out fishing lures.

Captain Billy's Whiz Bang, a risqué magazine of the 1930s, could be purchased from under the counter. Near the wood heater were a pair of chairs with a small table and a checkerboard ready to challenge anyone for a game. The glass case near the entrance had glass jars on top, which held peppermint and wintergreen candies, two for one cent. This building has been a cafe, gift shop and post office.

15 Marler and Brass Meat Market

Completed in 1918 this building housed the Paulsen Grocery Store and F.E. Marler and his partner, Gustav Brass's meat market and sausage factory.

16 Harrison Grange

The Harrison Grange #422 was formed in 1942 and in 1944 purchased this building from Anna Sala. She used it to store salt and feed for livestock and sold groceries and meat in the adjoining building. Before the 1917 fire, Burleigh's store with its *Rip-Proof Overalls* sign stood in place of the Grange building.

17 The I.O.O.F. Hall

200 N. Coeur d'Alene Ave. across from the park
The International Order of Odd Fellows' Hall was the first substantial building competed after the 1917 fire. The Odd Fellows had a difficult time making the payments, and in 1924, the property was foreclosed. Since that time the main floor has held groceries, a meat locker, post office, barbershop and café. The upper floor has been occupied by a dentist, a theater and in the 1950s a restaurant. The basement has been home to One Shot Charlie's for many years.

18 Crane House

201 Coeur d'Alene Ave. (Crane Historical Society)
Built in 1891 by Silas W. Crane, this was the first home in Harrison. Mr. Crane died in 1908. Before Mrs. Crane died in 1911, she deeded the house to their bachelor son, William, a jeweler. He sold it in 1923 to his brother Edwin Crane, who fell behind on his taxes and was forced to redeem the property from the county in 1931. He sold in 1936 to F.W. and Constance Wendt, who then sold to Howard and Evelyn, "Bubs & Jerry" Russell in 1945. They retained ownership until 1984 when they gave the building to the Crane Historical Society for use as a museum. Call 689-3111 for hours.

Set odometer to 0

⑲ Star Lodging
204 S. Coeur d'Alene Ave. on the right
After the 1917 fire this was the Star Lodging House. Several cafes have operated here.

⑳ First Bank of Harrison
206 S. Coeur d'Alene Ave.
The First Bank of Harrison was locally owned and in later years it moved to St. Maries and became the First Bank of St. Maries. The building was a beer parlor for a short time.

0.8 miles turn right on O'Gara Rd.

The Union Pacific Railroad, right-of-way, now the *Trail of the Coeur d'Alenes,* is visible along the Lake Coeur d'Alene waterfront.

Lacon
2.6 miles at O'Gara & Russell Rd. (Lacon Tracts)
A Union Pacific Railroad siding called Lacon was located here. Several section houses next to the railroad track were used to house the maintenance crew, but are gone. Dr. John Finney's dairy is also gone. Bert and Marie Russell bought the property in 1962 from Elma Cerny and subdivided it.

Log Chute 1917-1921
3.3 miles, on the left of O'Gara Rd.
Logs "whizzed" down a wooden chute built by Russell & Pugh Lumber Company as they logged the Harrison Flats above, creating the present day farmland. Once the logs splashed into the lake, they were captured into log booms. From here, the logs were transported by tugboat to area sawmills. Homesteader Winfield Addington's cow stepped across the chute and was killed by the first log to come down the chute.

O'Gara Bay
About 5 miles, at Benewah Rd.
This site was once an active steamboat landing, railroad stop and ferry crossing to Conklin Park. Annie O'Gara's store and house was near this bay in 1910. Approximately a quarter of a mile up the hill was "Shorty" Archer's cabin, where he was shot and killed by a gun concealed and fired from within a wicker suitcase.

O'Gara Rd Junction
8.5 miles, turn right onto Hwy 97 and continue to St. Maries

Potlatch Corp. St. Maries Complex

18.7 miles

St. Maries Lumber Company was built on this site in 1913. St. Maries' largest mills were located here and produced over 1 billion board feet of lumber. After several owners, depressions, floods and fires, the current mill was built in 1964 to make plywood. In 1975 the sawmill was added.

~ St. Maries ~

One of the most populated Coeur d'Alene Indian villages known as *Hnch'emtsn*, "Inner Mouth," was located where the St. Joe and St. Maries rivers join. On the north side of the St. Joe River, below rock cliffs, was another campsite known as *Hnmlmullsh, "*in the Cottonwoods."

The town of St. Maries (pronounced St. Marys) was founded in 1889, when the Fisher brothers, William, John, and Jesse built a sawmill. The largest body of white pine timber in the world grew near St. Maries. The St. Joe River is the highest navigable river in the world. By 1900, the business district along the waterfront bustled with steamboats arriving with passengers and goods. In 1917 St. Maries had a population of 3,000 with three sawmills, two shingle mills, two hospitals and five hotels. Its economy thrived on lumber, agriculture, livestock and dairy. The Milwaukee Railroad was constructed through St. Maries in 1909, providing transportation for lumber, passengers and agricultural goods. The business district shifted from the waterfront to its present location.

❶ James Warren House

3rd St. and College Ave. look across the street up on the hill

A huge furnace in the basement burned a cord of wood a day in this home built in 1910 by James Warren. In the 1950s the home was converted to apartments. In the 1970s it served as the VFW hall.

Ⓐ Side Trip

Turn left (south) on College Ave. Then left on 1st. St. to read the interpretive sign

Occupation of 1918 (interpretive sign)

The Industrial Workers of the World (IWW) hall was located in this area. In the spring of 1917, lumberjacks and millworkers in North Idaho joined a strike of 50,000 Pacific Northwest woodsworkers lead by the IWW. They demanded the 8-hour day, no work on Sundays and improved sanitation and living conditions in the camps. The strike paralyzed the timber industry in

North Idaho for several months as whole camps slowed down, or stopped work altogether. By fall of 1917 the timber companies, unwilling to grant demands, and unable to continue work, petitioned Governor Alexander to call out the National Guard. Troops destroyed IWW halls in Spirit Lake, Sandpoint, Bonners Ferry, St. Maries and Spokane. In St. Maries and other towns Wobblies (IWW members) were put in "bullpens," makeshift jails, where they were held on charges of "Criminal Syndicalism." Despite the arrests, the strikes went on until the early spring of 1918.

Turn around and continue west towards city center

---

❷► Bennett's Photo Studio
331 College Ave.
While Dr. Owen D. Platt was away during WWI, his wife built the square portion of this building as his doctor's office and hospital. A garage provided direct access into the building for his patients. In 1940, Art and Georgene Bennett Shamel purchased the building. They lived upstairs, and the Bennett family operated the photo studio on the street level. The Shamels added the concrete addition and the business frontage.

Turn right (north) on 4th St.

❸► Hughes House Historical Museum
538 Main Ave. on the right
Built in 1902 from hand-hewn logs, the building started out as a men's club. G.S. "Doc" Thompson bought the house in 1906 and used part of it as his office and treatment center. In the 1920s, Thompson lost the building to the Lumberman's State Bank of Kootenai County. In 1926 Raleigh Hughes purchased the home and began years of restoration and improvements including the porches. In 1989 the Centennial Committee purchased the home from the Hughes family and in 1990 opened it as the Hughes House Historical Museum. For information call 245-1501.

❹► City Hall
602 College Ave.
Originally built circa 1900 as the town's second schoolhouse, the structure was moved to this location for use as the town hall in 1909. A concrete foundation was added in 1913, including concrete cross-walls, permitting use of the basement as a jail. The original steel jail doors are still in place.

Turn left (south) on 6th St. and right (west) on College Ave.

⑤ Benewah County Courthouse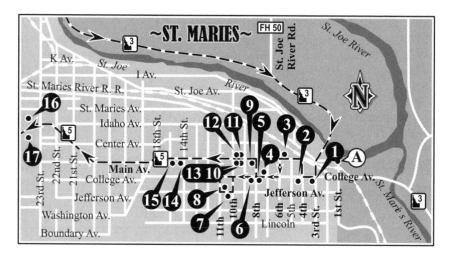

701 College Ave.

St. Maries became the county seat in 1915, when Benewah County split from Kootenai County. This Classical Revival building, built in 1924, conveys a sense of the post World War I period. The top floor houses the county jail with cells that were originally a brig mounted in a naval ship. At one time, there was an electrical switch line, controlling a single light bulb, that ran from the Sheriff's office to the corner of 8th and Main Ave. If the dispatcher/jailer needed the officer on duty who was often on Main Ave., he would flip the light on, alerting the patrolman to return to the Sheriff's office.

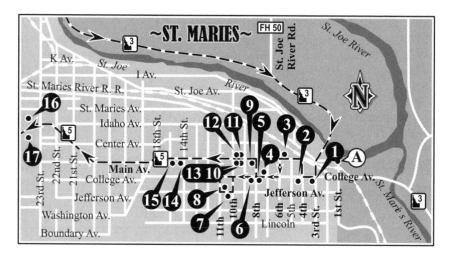

⑥ Masonic Temple

8th St. and College Ave.

A formal dedication ceremony, with a banquet and dancing, was held here on May 24, 1917. The lodge was still active in 2004.

Turn left (south) on 10th St. and right on Jefferson Ave.

⑦ Fort Hemenway Manor

1001 Jefferson Ave. on the SW corner of 10th St. on the hill

Frank Hemenway built this house in 1913 to outshine his neighbor Ernest Clark, who told him that he was not worth much. To disprove Clark,

Hemenway built this 4,500 square foot, sixteen-room house overlooking Clark's. Craftsman John Thompson included a built-in buffet and bookcase, oak floors with walnut inlaid designs, and handpicked vertical grain fir trim. The chandeliers were custom handmade, imported from England, and featured camphor glass globes. Hemenway lived with his sister Lucinda in the house. In 1951 it was sold to Iola Ellett.

St. Maries waterfront when it was the center of town, circa 1910.

❽ Clark House

240 11th St. on the right (Alternative School)
Lillian and Ernest Clark bought the property in May 1912 from Eli Laird, Captain of the *S.S. Flyer,* and built the house. They sold to Frank Noble in 1919. In 1921 Anna McMillan ran a boarding house for Fred Herrick's Milwaukee Mill workers. She sold to the St. Gertrude Sisters in 1922, who used the lower rooms for classrooms and converted the upper rooms to living quarters and a chapel. Two additional classrooms were added to the front of the house. The last eighth grade class graduated in 1968. The St. Maries School District purchased St. Mary's Academy in 1971. It was used for kindergarten classrooms for a short time, then for administrative offices and school board meeting rooms.

Turn right on 11th St. and right on College to 8th St. and then left (north) to Main Ave. (Hwy 5) turn left (west)

Looking east on Main Street, St. Maries, circa 1945.

❾ Red Cross Drug Building

801 Main Ave. (A.B. Annis Building/Gem State Bar and Café)
This building was built during the 1910s when "uptown" St. Maries was in a construction boom. At the corner was located the Red Cross Drug store, owned and operated by A.B. Annis. Note the crosses that were built into the walls at the upper corners. An early 1910 photo indicates an entirely different configuration for this building than what now exists. It is unknown if the upper floor and face brick were later added or if this is even that original building at all. Early newspaper accounts listed the local surgeon as having offices upstairs from the drug store.

❿ Lumberman's Bank Building

905 Main Ave.
Built in 1908, the face brick used was of such tight dimensions and quality that the mason allowed only 1/8th inch for the head and bed joints. This made it very difficult to maintain wall plumb and level, but with great skill, he did it. The top floor housed a large meeting room and numerous office suites. The Modern Woodmen of America rented it as a lodge hall in 1908. The bank was located on the corner. Next door within the same building was the US Post office.

⓫ 902 Main Ave.

Built between 1908 and 1910 this building housed O'Dwyer's Hardware. Remnants of an iron face piece, built by the Spokane Iron Works, remain on the Main Ave. side. The east wall has a very decorative recessed brick header bonding method that adds an artistic touch to a common brick wall.

⑫ Greater St. Joe Development Foundation

906 Main Ave.

Learn more about local history by picking up a map of St. Maries' Murals, a guide to St. Maries Outdoor Art Gallery. The murals are located on various buildings around town.

⑬ The Heimark Building

913 Main Ave.

Built circa 1910, the building originally housed Western Rooming House and C Sly Meat Company and possibly the Heimark Jewelry store.

⑭ Heyburn Elementary School

1405 Main Ave.

The first building on this site was the St. Maries Brick Works, which opened on April 17, 1908. They made a soft brick, which was only made during the no frost period of the year. Many of the brick buildings on Main Ave. were backed with bricks made here. The school was built in 1924 for $100,000 and the gymnasium was added in 1938, at a cost of $41,000. Although it has been remodeled extensively, the main building is intact. Notice the entry doors BOYS on one entrance, GIRLS on the other. The architect insisted that the entries be designated this way.

⑮ The Paul Bunyan Statue

The Paul Bunyan statue was a promotional item for an oil company. The local Lumberjack Booster Club obtained it and painted it to look like a lumberjack. Washington Water Power poured the legs full of concrete so it wouldn't blow over. The local high school teams are known as the Lumberjacks.

⑯ The John Mullan Statue and Steam Donkey

Mullan Trail Park on Hwy 5 across from the cemetery

Interpretive signs are located in the visitors' pavilion. The marble statue of Captain John Mullan was originally put up at the intersection of 9th St. and Main Ave. on July 26, 1918. It was later moved here. The three-spool, Williamette steam donkey engine was used until 1928 on Hobo Creek, a tributary of the St. Joe River. In 1958 it was skidded out to a lowboy and brought to town.

⑰ Woodlawn Cemetery Historical Fire Ring 🏛NR

SW corner of the cemetery, watch for one-way roads when entering

In 1912, 57 corpses from the 1910 Fire were exhumed from the St Joe River drainage and reburied in this circle. In 1924 the U.S. Forest Service appropriated $500.00 to mark the graves. These men were killed while employed (for twenty-five cents an hour) by the U.S. Forest Service as firefighters.

At one time, the cemetery was located near 6th St. and Lincoln Ave. (now the Vic Camm Park). The townspeople decided the cemetery was too close to town and needed to be moved. The sons-in-law of Joe Fisher, Alfred Lindstrom and Oscar Brown, volunteered to move the corpses as they had the teams and large wagons needed to do the job. It was a difficult task, taking about a week, made worse by the stench of the decay. At the conclusion, Lindstrom and Brown said that their families deserved the choice spot in the new cemetery. Their wish was granted.

Set odometer to 0 and continue on Hwy 5 to Plummer

⓲ Big Meadow Ranch

2.5 miles near the small grain elevators

This siding now sits next to a lake, on what used to be the Big Meadow Ranch. In the 1940s Fulton Cook owned it, then his son Charles, then it sold to Leinwebber, who farmed for years. It was called Leinwebber Spur when he owned it, and an occasional car of grain was shipped from here. Bob Wilson held the lease when the dike broke in 1997. It is now all wetlands and a wildlife preserve.

⓳ Benawah Lake and the Chatcolet Trestle

Can be seen at about 6.8 miles

One of the Coeur d'Alene Indian names for Benewah Lake is *Q'ele'ip*

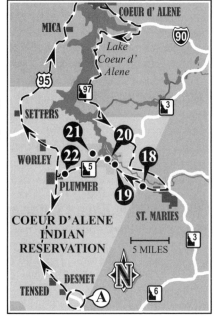

meaning "Bottom of the Lake." The surrounding area is called *Sbiinwạhu'lumkhw*, meaning "Benewah Country" after a Coeur d'Alene named Biinwạ, who lived in this area. Benewah is the Coeur d'Alene version of the French name *Benoit*.

The Milwaukee Railroad built this 2,200 foot trestle across Lake Benewah with over 120 wooden pile spans, except for a single 50-foot steel girder section. In 2006 a portion of the trestle collapsed and was rebuilt.

At 8.8 miles there is a viewpoint of the St. Joe River running between Round Lake on the right and Chatcolet Lake on the left. The Coeur d'Alene Indian name for Chatcolet Lake is *Chatqele'*, which means "Lake" or "On The Lake."

As you drive along the highway, the Milwaukee Railroad tracks are visible along the shore

The St. Maries Railroad uses the tracks to haul logs, finished lumber and plywood.

View eastward of the Union Pacific Railroad trestle and a steamboat passing the swing bridge over the St. Joe River at Chatcolet, circa 1925.

⍜ Union Pacific Swing Bridge

At about 10 miles look across the lake at the bridge
The swing bridge, a section of the railroad track crossing the St. Joe River at Chatcolet, was built in 1889 to allow boat traffic to pass. It was rebuilt in 1921. The bridge, now part of the *Trail of the Coeur d'Alenes,* was raised and no longer swings.

㉑ Heyburn State Park 🏞NR

10.8 miles turn right at the Rocky Point Loop Rd. entrance

Rocky Point was known to the Coeur d'Alene Tribe by the Spokane name of *Ch'omaqs* meaning "rock on a spur." Heyburn State Park is the oldest and largest (5,500 acres of land and 2,300 acres of water) state park in Idaho. It was created from the Coeur d'Alene Indian Reservation in 1908 and named in honor of Weldon B. Heyburn, a US Senator from Idaho. The park includes part of the St. Joe River, which flows between Benewah, Hidden and Chatcolet Lakes. This is home to one of the largest nesting osprey populations in North America. Wild rice grows in the shallow waters of the lakes and provides habitat for numerous waterfowl.

At Rocky Point the Civilian Conservation Corp constructed a lodge, restrooms, picnic shelter and a residence. The lodge and restroom are constructed of local stone. The park residence, which is on the National Register of Historic Places, originally served as living quarters for the park superintendent. It is located behind the lodge among 1920s era vacation cottages. Call 686-1308 for information.

Return to Hwy 5 and go right (west)

㉒ Culvert at Little Plummer Creek

15.6 miles

As you cross Little Plummer Creek notice the culvert and fill as it is said to be the largest of its type in Idaho. It is a 12-foot diameter corrugated steel culvert made of 3/8-inch plate. The fill is 106 feet deep and the culvert is over one-tenth of a mile long. It takes the place of the original bridge, which burned in 1967.

The Schmidt Brothers had a sawmill here that provided electricity for the streetlights in Plummer beginning in about 1912. The steam engine burned wood and when the tender fell asleep, the lights dimmed in Plummer, and someone would have to ride a horse out and wake up the tender.

~ Plummer ~

Plummer is located in the center of the Coeur d'Alene Indian Reservation and called *Hnt'achqn* by the tribe meaning "Dry Treetop." The city's name is thought to have come from a railroad construction camp run by a man named Plummer. The town was built near the junction of the Oregon Washington Railway and Navigation Company, which came through the area in 1890, and the Milwaukee Railroad, which came through in 1909. For a time, the site was called Plummer Junction. The post office was opened in 1910 after the opening of the reservation lands. Until Hwy 95 went through, C St. was the main street.

The huge Little Plummer Creek culvert under construction., about 1970.

School
Hwy 5 on the right of C & 6th, NE corner (Community Center)
Built in 1910 after reservation lands were opened to homesteaders, this served as the third Plummer school. The first was a tent, the second a one-room building later used by the Catholic Church. When the brick school was built in 1913, this building became a community building. It has filled many community needs over the years including supplemental classrooms in 1937 and 1938 and apartments during WWII. The basement served as a gun range for the gun club.

I.O.O.F. Hall
C & 6th, NW corner
Built in about 1914 as a church, it was soon taken over by the Odd Fellows.

American Legion Hall
Hwy 5 on the left on C & 8th, SE corner (Bobbie's Bar)
Built in 1911 as the MacAsslin Store, it became the American Legion Hall in the 1950s.

McMillen's Store
C & 8th, NW corner (Ernie Broulier Apartment Building)
Built in about 1912 as the McMillen's Grocery Store this building housed the post office for many years. It was a hardware store in the 1950s.

American Legion and Senior Citizens
888 C St.
The post office was housed in this building for a time. McFadden's law office was here in the 1950s and 60s.

Ⓐ Coeur d'Alene Tribe Reservation Side Trip
Turn left (south) on Hwy 95 (about 30 miles round trip)

Ⓐ1 Fairgrounds
(Plummer Forest Products Mill)
A professional horse racing track and fairground, complete with a large grandstand building, baseball field and dance pavilion stood here. In the 1910s, when the annual July week-long fair was at its heyday, it drew thousands of spectators including Indians who set up a village for the event. The celebration included band concerts, foot races, Indian parade, baseball games with neighboring towns, professional horse races, evening dances, wrestling matches, fancy shooting exhibition, bucking contest, native handiwork exhibits and farm and home exhibits.

Ⓐ2 Tensed
The Coeur d'Alenes met in the area west of Tensed, known as Ni'lukhwalqw meaning "Hole in the Woods," every summer to camp, dig camas, play stick games and race horses. The site had available water and was flat and sheltered by the ridge on the southwest. Springs in the area were called Hn(os(oskwe', "Lost Waters," also known as Andrews Spring and Ts'ts'p'qhwi'lus, "Punch in the Forehead with Sharp Instrument."

Tensed was called DeSmet, until it applied for a post office. Since a DeSmet post office already existed at the DeSmet Mission, the citizens turned the name around and requested their post office be named Temsed, but the US Postal Department misprinted it as Tensed.

Ⓐ3 DeSmet
The Coeur d'Alene name for DeSmet is 'L'khwi'lus, meaning "Little Hole in the Forehead," which was taken from the name of a small spring on DeSmet Hill. At Cataldo Mission long discussions occurred between the young men, who wanted to move to the camas prairie and begin their own farms, and the elders, who wanted to stay at their ancestral home on the Coeur d'Alene River. In 1876 Father Diomedi established the third and last Sacred Heart

Mission, naming it after Father DeSmet. This town included a three-story boys' boarding school, three-story girls' boarding school, rectory, a gothic church, Jesuit Seminary building, and housing. The Coeur d'Alenes built fine farmhouses, establishing big farms raising wheat and cattle. Others raised family gardens while continuing to hunt and gather in the old way. DeSmet served as tribal headquarters after the reservation was established by treaty in 1891.

The Sisters' Building
On the west hillside at DeSmet
The convent of Mary Immaculate was established in 1878. The grade school for girls was partially destroyed by fire in 1881. The convent was rebuilt and the dedication of the new Providence Academy of Sacred Heart marked the combining of the "girls and boys" schools. The Providence Academy closed in 1978 after 96 years.

Turn around and continue on Hwy 95 north for the main tour

<hr>

Turn right (north) on Hwy 95

State Hwy 95
Highway 95 was built in about 1926 and remains the only highway connecting the northern and southern parts of the state.

~ Worley ~
In 1909 a million acres of farm and timberland in the Spokane, Coeur d'Alene and Flathead Indian Reservations were opened up for homesteading. The town sites of Plummer and Worley were established on former reservation lands. Worley, platted in 1908, was named after Charles Worley, the first Indian Agent. The Coeur d'Alenes referred to Worley as *Tsenp'uytsn*, meaning "wrinkled neck" because Mr. Worley had a double chin. Early homesteaders cleared the land of timber making it suitable for agriculture. Homesteaders leased farmlands from Coeur d'Alene tribal members, and others made their living by making and selling hand-hewn railroad ties.

Grain Elevator
On the right (east) side
Worley was a large grain storage and shipping area. In the 1920s Worley

Grain Growers built wooden grain elevators. The Milwaukee Railroad depot and loading station were once located next to the grain elevators. These concrete grain elevators were built in the 1960s.

Interior of the Worley Post Office. Charles H. Hoag, Postmaster, Cecil Akers and Roy Holt (standing) both rural mail carriers, 1932.

Worley School
S. 29900 1st Hwy 95 on the left (Lakeside Elementary School)
Built in 1935-36 by the WPA using concrete, additions were made in 1950 and 1977. It served as a high school until 1989, when the classes were moved to Plummer. It now serves as an elementary school.

Two Yay Yays Grocery Store
9714 W. F St. SW corner of Hwy 95 and Cave Bay Rd.
The original building burned and this one was built in about 1957. It has served as a grocery store and post office with fraternal organizations meeting upstairs. A Coeur d'Alene calls his grandmother Yay Yay.

Service Station
9717 W. F St. NW corner of Hwy 95 and Cave Bay Rd. on the right
Built in the 1920s, this was one of the first service stations in Worley. Bert Folkins owned it for many years.

Meredith's Repair
W. 9814 F St. SW corner of 2nd and Hwy 95
Built in 1926 as a service station.

Worley Meat and Grocery Store
W. 9815 F St. right (west) side of 2nd and Hwy 95 (State Liquor Store)
Built in about 1910, it was owned and operated by Marge Lagow, a long time resident of Worley. Her husband was Worley's first mayor when it became a city in 1956.

Worley Grange and Co-op
W. 9825 F St. on the right
The original part was a service station built in 1922. It was gutted by fire in 1950 and rebuilt with additions in 1952 and 1962. With an economy based on agriculture, the grange provided important services such as a co-op store.

Parsons Building
W. 9820 F St. (repair shop)
Built in 1917 as a blacksmith shop, it served as a repair shop.

Service Station
W. 9705 F St.
Built in 1919.

School Gymnasium
F St. and 3rd St. on the left (west) (Jimmie's)
This site was the second school in Worley. The gym, built in 1922, is all that remains of the two-story building that served as the grade and high school until December 1939.

In 1952 Leo and Shirley Fleming purchased the building and opened the bar, naming it Leo's. They also built a motel on the south side of the building using Farragut Naval Training Station buildings. The following year they opened a small restaurant with a Saturday night smorgasbord. This was so popular they made the addition in the front in 1958. For a short time, a rollerrink operated in the old upstairs gym, but the noise was too much for the downstairs patrons. Leo's operated 24 hours a day seven days a week, except Christmas, from 1952 to the late 1980s when Leo died.

The Tree
On the left (west) side of Hwy 95

The tree on the curve outside Worley is a Coeur d'Alene medicine site with spiritual significance. When settlers cleared the area they left the tree as a landmark and place with shade to rest while doing fieldwork Willard "Wid" Parsons owned and farmed the land for years. Overhead utility lines once ran parallel to the highway. One day in the 1960s, as Wid was driving by, he saw a GTE crew parked near the tree. He stopped and asked what they were doing; they said they were going to cut down the tree because it was a danger to their telephone line. He said "No, you won't! That's my tree, and you can't cut it down." They said, "What's going to happen when it falls on our line?" Wid said, " I guess you'll just have to come fix it." Above ground lines have been gone for years, Wid is gone now, and GTE no longer exists, but the tree still stands in spite of fire, drought and mankind.

Milwaukee Railroad tracks are visible along the highway

Setters

Anne Setters served as the first postmaster from 1916 to 1918 and the community was named for her family. The grain elevators were serviced by the Milwaukee Railroad.

Lake Creek

The highway drops down into a "valley" formed by Lake Creek flowing into Lake Coeur d'Alene. This is the site of a community called Ford. Here the road crosses the location of the Oregon Rail & Navigation Company branch line that went down to the lake at the head of Windy Bay and on to Amwaco where passengers boarded steamboats to go across the lake to Harrison. The highway follows much of the old B.R. Lewis/Blackwell logging railroad that ended at Mica Bay.

Fighting Creek
23181 S. Hwy 95
One version of the story about how Fighting Creek got its name is that after a party at nearby Dance Hall Flat, where whisky was flowing freely, one thing led to another and fists flew and knives were drawn, resulting in one death and several injuries. Another version is that two women got into a fight and decided to call the place Fighting Creek. In 1910 "Swede" Emil Modine homesteaded in the Fighting Creek District. He built a store in about 1925. Originally, the B.R. Lewis/Blackwell logging railroad passed in front of the store. The old roadbed for the railroad became the highway. The wagon road behind the store was more like a dirt trail than a road. Most people found it much easier to drive to Rockford Bay and take the boat to Coeur d'Alene.

A hand-cranked gasoline pump established the store as one of the first Texaco gas stations in the Northwest.

Mica Flats Grange

7465 W. Kidd Island Bay Rd. Kidd Island Rd. and Hwy. 95, on the right (east) side

The Mica Flats school was built in 1901 and started with six students. In the 1920s the building was picked up and turned to face south instead of west. When schools were consolidated, the Mica Flats Grange #436 took over the building in about 1946. The grange has provided a voting, meeting and socializing place. It was expanded in 1954. Dances featuring local fiddle players and callers have long been popular at the Mica Flats Grange.

Cougar Gulch

Coming down Mica Hill look to the left

Native Americans knew this area to be a haven for cougars. When homesteaders settled in the area in the late 1890s, they were watchful of cougars. Mrs. James O'Reilly, who lived in Cougar Gulch until 1924, recalled: "Mr. O'Reilly killed a 'big fella,' 12 feet long or more. We skinned him and made a cougar rug." Children on their way to the schoolhouse were warned to watch for cougar tracks.

Chain Lakes and St. Joe Country Tour
~ TOUR FIVE ~

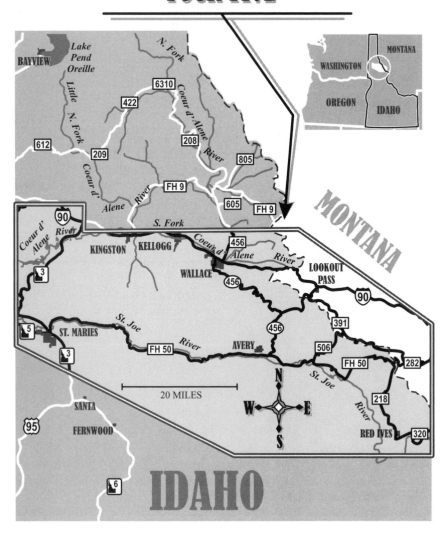

The trip from Coeur d'Alene to Avery and over Moon Pass is about 200 miles and can take a full day. The St. Joe River Rd., Avery and Moon Pass to Wallace, as well as the St. Regis route, can only be taken after the snow is gone. Check with the Forest Service for road conditions as well as camping and fishing opportunities.

From I-90 take Exit 34, Rose Lake/St. Maries and turn south on Hwy 3 and set your odometer to 0

❶ Rose Lake Cemetery
1.4 miles, turn right on Doyle Rd. The cemetery road makes a loop.
There are about 170 graves in this cemetery. The oldest marked grave is from 1906, although some of the many unmarked graves may be older.

Return to Hwy 3 and turn right and drive about 2 miles to the town of Rose Lake.

~Rose Lake~

Rose Creek and Rose Lake were named by a family who homesteaded on Cougar Creek, for their daughter Rose Brown. The Rose Lake Post Office was established in 1905, and by 1916 the population was 500. The town was primarily a company town for the Rose Lake Lumber Company, which was then known as the Winton Lumber Company.

Along the Coeur d'Alene River, which flows into Lake Coeur d'Alene there are 11 small lakes (in order: Rose, Porter, Bull Run, Killarney, Hidden, Medicine, Cave, Black, Anderson, Thompson and Blue). Most of the present camping sites along this river system were used since time immemorial by the Coeur d'Alene Tribe for winter village sites or seasonal camps.

❷ Rose Lake School
14901 S. Queen St. 3.2 miles, turn into the pullout
The Winton Lumber Company built this school in 1913 for first through eighth grades. High school students took the Oregon Washington Railway

and Navigation Company trains (OWR&N) later called the Union Pacific (UP) to Harrison High School until the WPA built the the high school classrooms and the gymnasium here in the 1930s. An addition on the left side of the school was added to accommodate first to third grades. The last high school class graduated in 1956. The school closed in 1985. Despite its proximity to the Coeur d'Alene River, the school has never flooded, even in the devastating 1933 flood. The building serves as a Community Center, Rose Lake Historical Society and library.

❸► Rose Lake Bridge
Hwy 3 and Bull Run Rd. (across from the school)
Several floods over the years have washed out the one-lane bridge crossing the river. In 1917 the ice jam flood took out the Dudley Bridge and other bridges down river including the one here. The December 1933 flood swept the bridge away, almost killing seven boys. The next bridge was rebuilt with scrap iron found after the flood.

◆──────────────────────────────────◆

Ⓐ► Bull Run Side Trip
At Bull Run Rd. cross the bridge and turn right

Winton Mill site
Charles and David Winton and Walter S. Rosenberry began operating the Rose Lake Lumber Company in 1911. The mill provided the basis for a thriving community that included a YMCA, employee housing and a store. The mill closed in 1928. Concrete remnants of the Winton Mill are visible along the road.

Rose Lake Lumber Company Office Building
15408 S. Bull Run Rd. house on the right
After the mill closed, the lumber company's office building housed the post office and served as the Masonic meeting hall. It had a vault in the basement and on the main floor. The Rories bought it in 1975 and remodeled it for a home.

Union Pacific Railroad *(Trail of the Coeur d'Alenes)*
Dec. 23, 1889, the first train took passengers from Wallace to Spokane Falls. The line was important to all the communities in this area providing access to the Coeur d'Alene Mining District, passenger service, shipment of produce and lumber and mail service. Before 1930 the train stopped here twice a day for mail delivery at the post office and delivery of freight to the Winton Store. Concrete remnants of the depot are visible on the shore of Bull Run Lake,

which was a hay field in earlier years. In 1910 the OWR&N was reorganized and the locomotives were lettered for the UP with small initials OWR&N on the cab. This right-of-way is the Trail of the Coeur d'Alenes.

View from the hillside across Bull Run Lake of the Winton Lumber Co., Rose Lake, 1912.

Winton Mansion
Look across Bull Run Lake and up the hill to the left
The Rose Lake Lumber Company built the home for its general manager Walter Rosenberry in about 1914. The Rosenberry's came to the house with two sons and two more were born here. Mrs. Rosenberry felt isolated here and was concerned when the doctor had to travel from Wallace to deliver her sons. The home included servants' quarters on the third floor. In 1919 the Rosenberry's moved to Coeur d'Alene. Bert and Sylvia Sellers bought the house after the mill closed and boarded schoolteachers in the 1930s and 1940s.

Turn around in the parking lot, return to Hwy 3 and turn left

Set odometer to 0 at the bridge

❹ Strobel Mill
1.4 miles from the bridge on the left
The millpond and the main sawmill building are located between the road and the river. John W. Strobel built the mill in 1956 and sold it in 1967. The mill cut mine timbers and lagging used in the Coeur d'Alene Mining District. After Strobel sold the mill, it ran sporadically for several years.

❺ Triplett Ranch Site

1.9 miles, park in the turnout. Walk to the Coeur d'Alene River and look across the river at the large meadow where the Triplett Ranch was located.

This fertile flood plain along the Coeur d'Alene River provided agricultural products to the mining district. The Kay and Allen Triplett Ranch was very productive. The ranch had a large orchard with apples that were shipped to the East Coast. Six-foot-tall oats were harvested along with blackberries and other produce. It was prone to flooding, and the 1917 flood caused the death of livestock due to arsenic in the soil.

❻ Winton Row House

2.1 miles, Hwy 3 and Killarney Lake Rd. look up to the right near the big barn. This site is better viewed coming from the other direction, traveling north, on the highway.

At one time, the Winton Lumber Company owned approximately 20 houses for its employees. All of the houses were flooded in the 1933 flood. This house was floated down the Coeur d'Alene River on a barge and pulled up the hill with horses to the location near the barn.

❼ Blue Lagoon Saloon

3.8 miles, 22090 S. Hwy 3, on the left

Harry and Wilma Chatfield built the Blue Lagoon Saloon in about 1939 and sold it in 1946. It was a popular tavern for locals and tourists.

❽ Lane and the Lane School 🏫NR

4.8 miles, milepost 110, look to the left up on the hill at the old school. It is about a 1/4-mile up Lane Rd. and is a residence

The Lane school was built in 1914 and closed in 1947 when the students went to the Rose Lake School. Like many country schools it was used as a community center. Old-timers recall that the bands often came from Plummer by the OWR&N train to play for the dances.

W.J. Johnson and A.W. Crawford built the Rose Lake Lumber Company Number 1 at Lane in 1903. A town sprang up with a population of 100, two general stores, a hotel, two churches and a school. The mill was destroyed by fire in 1904, rebuilt 3 miles east of here in 1905, and then burned in 1909. The Lane Cemetery is on E. Lane Rd., but it is not in use today. The oldest known gravesite is 1904.

ROSE LAKE
to the
SHADOWY ST. JOE RIVER
TOUR

EXIT 34

90

ROSE LAKE

1

2

A

3

5

Killarney Lake

6

3

4

River

8

7

N

Coeur d'Alene

B

3

Swan Lake
Cave Lake

Medicine Lake

Black Lake

9

3

10

97

11

12

2 MILES

St. Joe

St. Joe River Rd.

to Avery

FH 50

St. Joe River

5

River

3

ST. MARIES

3

The Klein homestead on Medicine Lake, about 2000. House and silo on the right.

❾ Klein Homestead

14683 S. Klein's Medicine Trail, between milepost 107 and 106
Joseph and Melissa Moe homesteaded on the shores of Medicine Lake in 1890. Melissa Anderson Moe was Medimont's first white woman. The farm still consists of 100 acres and is farmed by the fourth generation of the family. Seven generations have lived part-time on the property over the years. Joseph Moe and his father Iver Moe built the house in 1894. In the early 1900s the house was added onto and the ice house and silo were built. Fruit trees planted before 1900 still bear fruit. The Farm is recognized by the State of Idaho as a Centennial Farm (1890-1990).

◆━━━━━━━━━━━━━━━━━━━━━━━━━━━━━━━━━━━━━━━◆

Ⓑ Medimont Side Trip

9.6 miles, turn right at the Medimont sign and go about 1.5 miles. Keep to the left

Medimont

Coeur d'Alene Indians called this place Smag̱'wqn which, means "Bodies Lying on the Mount." Sometime between 1780 and 1850 many Coeur d'Alenes died of smallpox and were buried near here. Long before the missionaries arrived, a Coeur d'Alene Tribal Leader thought that immoral dancing caused the smallpox.

Settlers came to the area as early as 1890 for the fertile farm land. Several mines were also located in the area. When Joe Moe requested a post office for the town it was known as Medicine Mountain, but was changed to Medimont by the Postal Department. A small cemetery is located behind the homes on the hillside.

Medimont Mercantile

The OWR&N came through Medimont, and an early ferry took people across the Coeur d'Alene River to homestead sites. Built about 1910, the Medimont Mercantile provided a general store, animal feed, cold storage lockers, and ice. The icehouse is to the right of the store building. There is parking for the Trail of the Coeur d'Alenes.

---

⑩ Indian Springs School NR

About 0.8 miles past milepost 100 on the left on the hillside. Better viewed coming from the other direction

This one-room schoolhouse was built in 1915 and served grades one through eight until it closed in 1952. It served as a church and a community center hosting dances and community gatherings.

⑪ Remnant Basalt

After the highway intersection near milepost 95 as you drive downhill

Massive basalt flows of 17 million years ago, covered the broad region between Boise and Spokane. The St. Joe River is carved through Precambrian sedimentary rock and metamorphic rock from the Cretaceous period. During the Miocene period, 17 million years ago, the rocks of the mountain slopes along the St. Joe River had much the same look as today. The lava flows, which originated in Oregon and Washington, filled the lower valley, eventually creating a basalt plain over which the river then flowed. Some basalt was eroded away, but evidence of the basalt plain and ancient riverbeds can be found on some of the lower ridges of today's river breaks. Basalt bedrock is perched atop sedimentary and metamorphic rock, and outcrops are visible to the north of the St. Joe River between Trout Creek and Big Creek. Rounded river pebbles can be found alongside this basalt bedrock, evidence that the St. Joe riverbed was 1,000 feet above its current level.

⑫ St. Joseph Indian Mission (interpretive sign)

Hwy 3 and Mission Point Lane

Native Americans inhabited this area because of the coldwater spring, which flowed from the basalt cliffs at the north end of the bench. They built fish traps about 400 feet long and 18 inches high in the vicinity of Hell's Gulch

Creek, Goose Heaven Lake and the surrounding marshlands. As early as 1811 trappers and mountain men knew the importance of this site by the cold spring that didn't freeze. The first Catholic mission site in 1841-42 was known by the Coeur d'Alenes as *St'uts'te'wes*, "fish traps" or "Mission Point." Captain John Mullan established temporary headquarters here in 1859. His crew built a corduroy road across the marshland. This southern route was abandoned due to flooding. The road was rerouted through Coeur d'Alene and over the 4th of July Pass.

Take the St. Joe River Road to Avery. Set odometer to 0. Avery is 47 miles up the St. Joe River.

⑬ Omega Gospel & Hall
Mile 6, on the right
Located on the Emile Ducommun homestead, the church was built in 1909 by Henri Rochat to serve the Swiss families living in the Valley. It has been enlarged 3 times and flooded several times including in 1974 when 55 inches of water inundated the building.

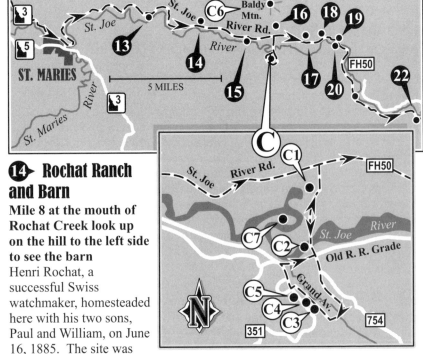

⑭ Rochat Ranch and Barn
Mile 8 at the mouth of Rochat Creek look up on the hill to the left side to see the barn
Henri Rochat, a successful Swiss watchmaker, homesteaded here with his two sons, Paul and William, on June 16, 1885. The site was selected because of the vast meadowlands along the St. Joe Valley which

reminded him of Switzerland. This barn with its distinctive cupola was built in 1887 of hewn logs and split cedar. The Rochat homestead marked the beginning of a small Swiss community in the valley, which included the Montandon, Ducommun, Jacots, Porrett and Stauffer families.

⓯ Camas Fields

Between mile 12 and Falls Cr. on the floodplain between the road and St. Joe River

The camas bulb was a staple of the Coeur d'Alene Indian diet. In the spring, fields of light to medium blue camas blooms can be seen in the river bottom. The bulbs were dug up, and if not used immediately, were dried, ground into flour and made into cakes. Bulbs intended for storage were baked in pits and then transported by canoe to raised pole platforms located at the winter villages.

ⓒ St. Joe City Side Trip

At mile 13 turn right on the St. Joe City Rd. This is about a 3-mile loop on a gravel road that leads to the sites of Ferrell and across the river and up the hill to St. Joe City and back down to the mill site.

ⓒ₁ Ferrell Site

Once located on the flat between the highway and the river

William Ferrell came to this area in 1884, acquired over a thousand acres in the valley, and established the town of Ferrell. During its heyday, there were three hotels, three stores, two drugstores, a bank, a lawyer, a floating hospital and many saloons and bawdyhouses to serve railroad construction workers, loggers and prospectors. In 1908 a two-room school was constructed serving 68 children in eight grades. The Chicago Milwaukee and Puget Sound Railway (Milwaukee Road) had plans to bring its route through Ferrell, but did not because Mr. Ferrell wanted $100,000. Instead the railroad built on the south side of the river where St. Joe City sprang up. This was the beginning of Ferrell's decline, and the December 1933 flood washed away the remaining houses except one, which remained until about 1948.

ⓒ₂ The End of Navigable Water

As you cross the bridge notice the river. This was the furthest practical point for steamboats to bring homesteaders, lumberjacks, wild women and tourists up the river. The Shadowy St. Joe ends near here and the Swiftwater begins. From Ferrell, pack strings and pole canoes hauled supplies to homesteads and mines until the Milwaukee Railroad was completed in 1909. This bridge was built in 1976, replacing the bridge that collapsed with the weight of a loaded log truck in January 1975.

Continue across the intersection of the old Milwaukee Road railbed
The road crosses Bond Creek which was named for brothers Walter and Lewis Bond. By 1908 there was a logging railroad up Bond Creek.

 St. Joe City
Turn right on Grand Ave.
With the Milwaukee Road going through St. Joe City, the community prospered. Located on the slopes above Flewelling's mill (Milwaukee Land Company) the city became the banking point for all the upriver communities and even had a newspaper, The Budget. *St. Joe City declined when the sawmill closed in 1926.*

ⓒ4 St. Joe City Photo Display
Grand Ave. on the left
The grandchildren and great-grandchildren of Henry and Mamie Dittman maintain the display.

ⓒ5 Bank Vault
On the left in the hillside
This is the St. Joe City Bank vault.

The Milwaukee Land Company Mill from St. Joe City, circa 1920.

ⓒ₆ St. Joe Baldy and Reeds Baldy

As you pass through St. Joe and before you go down the hill look to the north. The mountains and the ridges were important hunting and gathering areas for the Coeur d'Alenes. Tch'mutpkwe' peak (one who sits by the water) also served as a sacred portal for those practicing traditional religion.

ⓒ₇ Milwaukee Land Company Sawmill Site

As you near the bottom of the hill look over the bank on the right and see an old foundation from the sawmill

The largest body of white pine timber in the world was located in the St. Joe Country. Located in the flat below St. Joe City, the Monarch Timber Company was built in 1906 by A.L. Flewelling to cut ties for the railroad. The Milwaukee Land Company bought the mill and in 1909 opened a large mill. Winton-Rosenberry Lumber Company bought the mill in 1920 but closed it in 1926. The mill burned in 1928.

◆──◆

Continue to the Railroad Grade Rd. (the old Milwaukee rail bed) turn right and go back across the river via the St. Joe City Rd.

The Hanging Gardens on the side of the hill near the St. Joe River, circa 1935.

ⓖ Hanging Gardens

From the St. Joe City Rd. Look at the north slope in front of you

Although nothing can be seen today, tourists came to see Lyman Sperry's Hanging Garden, which was promoted by the Milwaukee Road as far away as Chicago. The garden had dirt steps up the center of this hillside where Sperry grew all kinds of fruits and vegetables that were used in the finest Milwaukee Road dining cars.

Turn right and continue on the St. Joe River Rd.

⑰ Scott Homestead
Mile 14

The Scott family came here in 1885 and was one of the first three families to settle on the St. Joe. The Scotts originally homesteaded in the St. Maries area and were among the surge of settlers here and farther upriver along the St. Joe River. Some 20 years later, Frank Scott bought up the homesteads of Dighton, Newcomb, part of the Ferrell ranch and later the Brown place. Walter Scott eventually owned and operated the former George Newcomb ranch. In 2005, members of the Scott family still lived here.

⑱ Falls Creek, Honey Jones' Homestead and Grave
Mile 15.8

Born Thomas Jones, on December 31, 1836, "Honey Jones" was one of the oldest pioneers and owner of the Little Falls. His nickname came from raising bees and selling honey. His well-kept cabin welcomed visitors where he discussed philosophy or recited poetry. As an amateur botanist, he grew a magnificent garden. Foxgloves from his garden continue to bloom here. His beard was so long he braided it and wore it in his shirt. He died in 1927 and is buried here.

⑲ Railroad Bridge over the St. Joe River
Mile 16.05

By October 1908, construction of the Milwaukee Railroad along the St. Joe River was complete from the Columbia River to St. Paul Pass on the Bitterroot Divide (Montana state line). The temporary bridge at this site was washed out by an ice flow in January 1909, while the permanent bridge here was still under construction. The bridge was completed later in 1909.

⑳ St. Joe River Rd. and bridge
Mile 16.4

The road from here to the curve before the Calder turnoff was not paved until 1968. The Civilian Conservation Corps (CCC) built the previous bridge in the 1930s. This bridge was damaged structurally when hit by oversized logging equipment and replaced in the 1970s.

㉑ Huckleberry Lookout
Mile 18.5, look straight up the road

Looking directly up the road and to the southeast is Huckleberry Mountain, elevation 5662 feet. A 20-foot, 14' x 14' frame pre-cut lookout cabin (called an L-4 tower) was built in 1933 and was replaced by a 20-foot TT flat tower in 1975.

㉒ Big Eddy Bar and Restaurant
Mile 19
Locals called the swirling pool of water here the Big Eddy. The Milwaukee Railroad named its siding near here Zane. In 1958 Rodney Wolfe built a bar and grill. In a few years, Erling Moe acquired the building and built this structure onto it. Elk feed seasonally in this area.

㉓ 1929 Fire
Mile 23.6 turnout on left side of road
Three miles north of here is the western edge of the 1929 Fire, which burned almost 20,000 acres. It burned a strip of timber north of Lemonade Peak and another strip of timber east of Slate Peak.

Ⓓ Calder Side Trip
Mile 24, turn left
The railroad signals on either side of the turnoff to Calder are from the Milwaukee Road siding at Calder.

Calder
Originally called Elk Prairie, its current name came from a Milwaukee Road engineer named Calder, who helped plat the town in 1909. Mrs. Goodrow was a homesteader and first postmaster of Calder in 1916. Calder was a large distribution point for Forest Service supplies to the fire lookouts and CCC camps located at Big Creek (Herrick townsite), Marble Creek and Ahrs Creek. Town population has remained steady at 60 to 100.

Calder School
As you approach Calder look across the river up on the hill to see the school
The Calder School was built in 1917, and it served grades one through eight.

Lloyd F. Buell Memorial Bridge
Constructed in 1990, the Lloyd F. Buell Memorial Bridge commemorates Mr. Buell's contributions to the St. Joe Valley and Calder area. He lived in the valley all of his life, attended the Calder School, farmed and lived just south of the bridge, and owned and operated a sawmill in Calder during

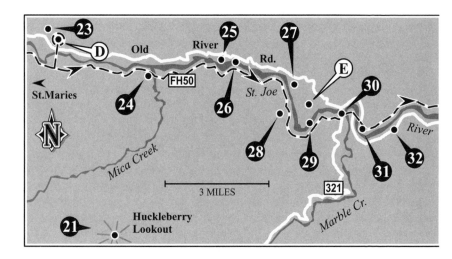

the 1940s. He donated part of the right-of-way for this bridge and access road. The old Calder Bridge stood from 1934 to 1990.

Calder General Store
Turn left on Railroad Ave.
Mr. Neely and his French partner built the store in 1916. In the early days there was a shooting in town, and the trial was held on the porch of the store. The man was found not guilty because it was determined the victim died of the infection, not the gunshot wound. Because of a fire in 1953, the store was torn down and rebuilt with cinder blocks salvaged from Farragut Naval Training Station. It is the oldest business on the St. Joe River.

Buell Sawmill Site
Across from the store on the left
The Buell's operated a sawmill here for many years. Frank Buell's son Glen referred to the mill as the Slab and Knot Hole Lumber Company or the Limber Limb Lumber Company. It finally became profitable during WWII by supplying lumber to Farragut Naval Training Station.

Go back to the St. Joe River Rd. and turn left

24 Mica Creek
Mile 27
A homestead in Mica Meadows in the upper Mica Creek drainage served as a halfway house between St. Joe City and the Marble Creek homesteads.

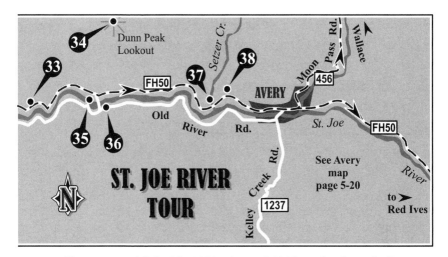

ST. JOE RIVER TOUR

A post office was established in 1902. Around 1908 a school was built.

Extensive logging occurred in this area. In 1916 a log flume was built from near the headwaters to the river, along with a railroad to take logs to the flume. A locomotive was barged up the river and cabled to the isolated railroad. Later when the Blackwell Lumber Company built a logging railroad up Crystal Creek from the St. Maries River, it reached into Mica Creek close enough to cable another locomotive down to the isolated Mica Creek tracks. The flume was used into the 1930s.

25 Herrick townsite and Railroad Logging
Mile 28.3

Fred Herrick owned mills throughout the area and had several lumber camps in the St. Joe. He established a camp at the mouth of Big Creek for the construction of a logging railroad into the Big Creek drainage in 1910. The 1910 Fire destroyed Herrick's logging railroad and the timber in the Big Creek drainage. Herrick rebuilt and extended the Big Creek railroad and salvage logged for two years. Herrick had a Milwaukee Road depot, two hotels, a general store and a saloon. The Herrick school operated until 1937. There was also a CCC camp here and another up Big Creek.

Logging and Forest Service crews were in Big Creek in 1910 fighting the Trout Creek Fire. The fire trapped three crews when it blew up on August 20. From a Forest Service crew of 19, eighteen died at the Dittman homestead in a tributary of the West Fork of Big Creek. Beauchamp, two homesteaders and 13 others died at the Beauchamp homestead. The other crew took shelter in the creek, and all survived. Most of the firefighters who died are buried in St. Maries. Other Big Creek firefighters escaped the 1910

Fire across the Coeur d'Alene-St. Joe Divide, though some of those died too, when the group sought shelter in a mine near Wallace. The Dittmans were not at their homestead because Mrs. Dittman was giving birth to twins.

26 Bellows Dairy
Mile 28.5

While James Montgomery was milking a cow on this ranch, he was shot and killed by a transient he had hired to help him pull stumps. In 1927 Harris and Annetta Bellows moved to the Montgomery place. In 1928 Harris built a cable footbridge over the river here. The 1933 flood destroyed the bridge, but the CCC rebuilt it. The first floor of their frame house was flooded and they also lost six milk cows and three steers. In 1934 Harris built a log house and two barns higher up on the hill. The 1938 flood was 18 inches higher than the 1933 flood. In 1938 the Bellows began a milk run and delivered milk to Avery for the next 19 years. They also sent cream via the train to a creamery in Spokane. They sold hens, eggs and extra garden produce, as well as hay to the logging companies to feed the workhorses.

27 Erling Moe Mill Site
Mile 31.4

This flat was a homestead and in the 1930s became a CCC camp. Erling Moe built the largest mill on the Swiftwater on this flat in about 1951. A spur track from the Milwaukee Road came off the main rail line west of the Pocono siding to access the mill. Some mill workers boated across the river to the mill before a bridge was built. The mill burned in the 1970s and only a round concrete footing remains.

28 Spring Creek Cabins
Mile 31.9

These cabins were originally built as a hunting and fishing camp. Later they were used for a logging camp and now serve as recreational rentals.

29 St. Joe Lodge
Mile 33.5

In the late 1960s this was the Ragan's Musical Museum. It became a restaurant and, for a while, they kept a cougar outside in a cage.

E Marble Creek Side Trip
Mile 34 turn left

Truss Bridge

The old suspension bridge was replaced with this bridge brought from Alaska in the late 1960s. A stronger bridge was needed to carry steel for power line construction between Dworshak Dam and Thompson Falls.

Less than a quarter-mile up the Northside Rd. turn left onto the Potlatch Rd.

Marble Creek Store
On the left

The community got its start supplying the railroad crews but it was the lumberjacks who kept it going. At one time two stores supplied lumberjacks in this area of rich timber. From about 1920 to about 1970 the McQuade family operated this store. It had a restaurant, rooms upstairs and, for a while, a post office.

Sheep Corral Site

Heading west on the old Milwaukee Road grade a few hundred feet and on the right is the spot where a sheep corral was located. After the 1910 Fire, grass was plentiful and sheep were hauled in by rail for summer pasture. Ninety-pound males were shipped on the Milwaukee Road to Chicago to market in the late summer. Other sheep corrals were located near Big Creek and at Adair on the railroad above Avery. The last sheep were shipped out in 1955. In the 1970s, the Forest Service's yellow metal signs could still be found on the slopes above the river. The signs read: "NO SHEEP GRAZING BEYOND THIS POINT."

West of the sheep corral a few hundred feet and on the same side of the tracks was the Marble Creek Depot. It was a "class D" depot found commonly at the railroad's smaller stations. The freight room was taken off the depot after 1950, and the remainder of the building was removed when passenger service was discontinued in 1961.

Turn around and go back to the St. Joe River Rd., turn left

 Marble Creek Interpretive Center
Mile 34.2

 Marble Creek Bridge
Mile 34.25

This bridge replaced a truss bridge built by the CCC immediately upstream in the mid-1970s. It was constructed as part of the four miles of road realignment and reconstruction west of here.

32▸ Old River Road
Mile 34.7
This road was built in the mid-1930s and replaced the wagon road above the tracks on the opposite side of the river.

33▸ Milwaukee Road Grade
Mile 34.9
From here to Avery the highway is built on the railbed of the Milwaukee Road, which abandoned its track in Washington, Idaho and much of Montana in 1980. By 1991 this paved road was open. The old road is visible across the river.

34▸ Dunn Peak Lookout
Mile 35.6, look straight ahead
The 20-foot tower was built in 1958, replacing the original lookout built in 1932. The lookout has a good view up and down the river valley and across the river as well. It's at the end of the ridge that spurs off Cedar Mountain at Storm Mountain. Between Storm Mountain and Dunn Peak is Flash Peak. To add to the tumult, Dunn Peak was earlier called Thunder Peak. In 1969 it was "manned" by a woman. A road was built to the lookout in about 1958. Since the 1970s the lookout has not been manned except during lightning bursts.

35▸ Hoyt's Flat, Stanley Ranch and Avery Ranger Station
Mile 40.6, turn right
In the 1890s Charlie Hoyt built a saloon, restaurant and seven cabins establishing one of the first resorts along the St. Joe River. By 1910, up to 10,000 people lived at Hoyt's Flat logging or working on road or railroad construction. Al Stanley homesteaded in 1921 and in 2007 the family still owned the land. A veteran's CCC camp was located here but only the office building remains, serving as a home. Stanley built log cabins in the late 1930s and rented them to tourists. In 1962 the Forest Service bought land from Stanley to build the ranger station. The FS paid the highest price it had ever paid for a piece of land up to that date.

Turn around and go back to the St. Joe River Rd., turn right

36▸ Hoyt Creek Steel Truss Bridge on the right
The Sailor Boy, Franklin and the Mastodon Mines took out low-grade copper

in the Slate Creek area. A wagon road extended to the St. Joe River as early as 1914. When the road was built between Marble Creek and Avery, the CCC built this bridge in 1934 to access the Slate Creek Road and Hoyt Flat.

37 Site of 1910 Fire Deaths
Mile 43

One crew fighting the Setzer Creek Fire had a camp near the head of the Storm Creek drainage in 1910. When the winds came up on August 20, a new fire reached the camp from the west. Though warned of the danger, the crew had not foreseen the arrival of a new fire. All 27 in the crew perished. Twenty-six of the firefighters were moved from temporary graves in Storm Creek to the 1910 Firefighters Circle in the Woodlawn Cemetery in St. Maries.

38 Pinchot Ranger Station site
Mile 43.8

A Forest Service ranger station was built here in 1905. Ralph Debitt, his wife, Jessie, and their children lived here. Ralph was the ranger and Jessie served as postmaster. The ranger station was in the railroad right-of-way and was moved to the Avery site. A typhoid epidemic that killed many railroad construction workers also claimed the life of Debitt's eldest daughter, Marie. Two more children were born to the Debitts here.

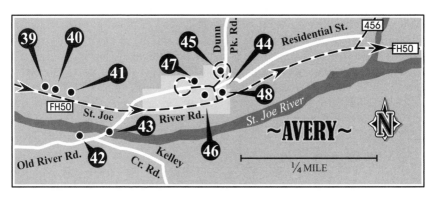

39 Avery Rail Yard Site
Mile 45.5

As the valley bottom widens here, the road enters the site of the rail yard at Avery. From here, and for almost the next 2 miles, three sets of tracks existed: the main line and two siding tracks. At the roundhouse there was a third siding, various spurs and the turntable. At the depot the main line was accompanied by seven siding tracks. This point also is the beginning of what was the railroad's electrified division. From here, and for 438 miles into Montana, an overhead wire brought electricity to the electric locomotives that pulled the trains over the mountains. The Milwaukee Railroad ended operations in the St. Joe Valley in 1980, although the Potlatch Corporation hauled logs from Avery to St. Maries on the line for three more years. In the early 1990s the railroad grade was widened and raised for the construction of the highway. Rock and earthen material was blasted from the foot of the mountains along the grade below Avery. The highway runs through the rail yard site.

40► Potlatch Log Landing
Mile 45.75, on the right
Many trains made up solely of log cars left Avery from this landing. The logs went to the Potlatch Mill in St. Maries. The logs arrived here by truck, mainly from the south. The 1910 Fire and 1934 Fire denuded the mountains to the north. This was also the site of a Japanese community (on the left side of the sewer drain field, north of the highway at the Potlatch Landing, west of the railroad yard site). The Milwaukee Road agreed to hire Japanese labor as part of the lucrative silk trade it had with the Japanese. The Mountain Park Hotel hired Japanese women as cooks. The Japanese continued to settle in Avery until after WWII, but by the 1950s few remained.

41► Roundhouse Complex, nothing remains
Mile 46.1
The roundhouse was located between the road and the river. It was actually only about a quarter-round with a turntable that turned the locomotives toward the 12 stalls where repair and maintenance work was done. A water tank, sand tower, fuel tanks, a restaurant, a bunkhouse, a blacksmith shop and a car shop were also located here.

42► Avery School
Across the river
This brick building was built in 1923. Because of a large number of logging and family camps in the area, seven teachers were needed to teach the 87 pupils attending the school in the late 1950s. When logging Camp 44 and the railroad workers left the area, the school population decreased. To finish high school, students went to St. Maries or other communities.

43► CCC Bridge
Mile 46.6
Built in 1935 by the CCC, this bridge replaced a wagon-width swinging bridge. Before 1931 there was not a road between St. Joe City and Avery and

the only way in was on foot, by rail or poling canoe. The CCC was under the jurisdiction of the Army out of Ft. George Wright in Spokane. The Forest Service and private contractors supervised the work projects.

46.8 miles junction of Old River Road, turn left

Avery and the Milwaukee Railroad depot in the center and the sub station on the right, 1969.

~Avery~

This junction of the St. Joe River and the North Fork of the St. Joe is where Sam "49" Williams homesteaded in 1886 and the spot was known as North. When the railroad was completed in 1908, the station was named Avery after William Rockefeller's grandson.

By 1915 Avery had two hotels, a billiard hall, a drug store, a school, icehouses, bunkhouses, a doctor's office and a jail. The waterworks was in the draw above the ranger station on Avery Creek. Avery's depot and most of its houses and apartments remain from the railroad era.

44 Ruth Lindow Park

On the right
This park was created to honor Ruth Lindow, a long time Avery citizen, after the substation was torn down. Railroad Substation 14 housed transformers that received power from the dam at Thompson Falls, Montana, and sent that power out along the rail line.

45 Avery Historic Ranger Station

Up the hill toward the Avery Work Center

Since 1907 this site has been in continuous use as a Forest Service administrative site. Avery's first ranger, Ralph Debitt, and wife Jessie worked out of this station. The cabin was built in 1908 and served as the ranger station until 1967 when headquarters were moved to Hoyt Flat.

The two smaller log cabins were built in 1922 and 1923, and the large bunkhouse in 1928. Other buildings, such as a barn and cookhouse, have come and gone. The log foundation of the bunkhouse was restored in the late 1970s. Among the most recent additions are the apartments at the rear of the site, built in 1981.

Turn around

46 Railroad Depot and Fishpond

The Milwaukee Road depot, sitting at the original track grade, included the yard office for railroad officials as well as for those who coordinated the arrival and departure of the many freight and passenger trains that went through Avery each day. The telegrapher and dispatcher communicated with the trains, with the awaiting train crews, and with the yardmaster. Next to the yard office was the waiting room and next to that was a 24-hour restaurant. The Interstate Company, a concession company for the Milwaukee Road, ran this "beanery" for most of its existence. A spur track came up alongside the back side of the depot, the north side, and brought such things as ice and coal and other supplies to be unloaded here for delivery to other railroad buildings or to other town businesses.

Next to the depot was a small park featuring a fishpond stocked with trout. The fishpond remains one of Avery's biggest attractions. After the jail was destroyed, the jail cell was moved west a few hundred feet near the fishpond.

47 The Avery Trading Post

Apparently built in 1942 by Bud Pears, the Avery Trading Post was one of three taverns near the depot, the hub of activity for the community. The other two taverns were the Antlers in Kelley Creek and Mahoneys up the river road toward the CCC bridge. In later years the Trading Post acquired the nickname "The Pub." Many a full keg has been rolled into The Pub and many an empty keg rolled out. The tavern hosted poker games in the back room. Farther back the Pears had their living quarters.

Beer is served on a long, polished bar of "Tennessee cedar" overlooking it are the remains of Stanley "Hook" McGuire. It is said the remains were brought down from the Yukon, including a hook on one arm that had been amputated, and the leg bone and boot still stuck in a huge bear trap.

Return to the St. Joe River Rd. and turn left

48 Scheffy's General Store and Motel On the left

The store was originally a railroad employee residence, as were the two houses between it and the substation. Over the years a hotel and a jail were also located in this area. The year after the railroad began operation, five "flats" were built to house railroad families. Each had four spacious apartments, or flats. Around 1920 the fifth flat burned. They were heated by coal, as were most homes in Avery. Local lore indicates that the third flat was used as a morgue during the 1910 Fire. The river road went right by the front steps, and the main line and east yard of the railroad were just beyond that.

In Avery you need to decide which route you want to take home. At the intersection of the St. Joe River Rd. and Moon Pass Rd. is the 29 mile Moon Pass route to Wallace, which is gravel, and takes about an hour and a half. Another route is the St. Joe River Rd. to St. Regis, Montana. From Avery to St. Regis is about 58 miles and then on I-90 about 100 miles back to Coeur d'Alene. Fourteen miles on the Montana side are not paved but it is a good gravel road. The other alternative is to return on Hwy 3 and go back the way you came, or when you get to St. Maries take Hwy 5 to Plummer and Hwy 95 to Coeur d'Alene

Go to page 5-29 to continue on to St. Regis

Moon Pass Rd. to Wallace (For the more adventurous)

Numbering of mileposts along this route begins in Wallace and ends at milepost 29 where the road reaches Avery and the St. Joe River

The old Moon Pass Road is visible in most places from the current county-maintained road that uses the old railbed. The old road began as a wagon road in about 1907 when the railroad was under construction. Wagon loads of supplies were hauled from Taft, Montana, to Avery over the road. There was also a stage, which was merely a Studebaker wagon rather than a coach, that operated while the railroad was under construction.

The Forest Service extended the road to Wallace up the "Little" North Fork over Moon Pass by the 1930s. Shoshone County took over maintenance of the road in 1951. The Milwaukee Road's right-of-way for the first nine miles out of Avery became the Shoshone County Road in 1989.

Graves
Mile 28.5
Between the road and the river near the riverbank are the graves of three individuals. One small girl of about 3 or 4 years old became ill on the passenger train passing through Avery. Shortly after she and her mother disembarked to see a doctor, the child died. Resident Doris Pears gave up her cedar chest to be used as a coffin, and the small body was buried at Forty-Nine Gulch. Also buried there were an unknown man, who was cut in two at the railroad yards, and a man named Spores from Tekoa, Washington, who was killed in a snow slide at Adair and likely buried here only temporarily.

The Milwaukee Road Olympian *derailed one mile above Avery on the North Fork of the St. Joe River, during the 1933 Flood.*

Site of December 1933 Train Wreck
Mile 27.85
In December 1933 heavy rains combined with melting snow swelled the rivers of the region. On December 21, 1933, the westbound *Olympian*, Train 15, wrecked at this spot when a bridge, weakened by the flooding North Fork, collapsed. The bridge cut across the outside of a curve in the river; earthen fill now covers the area where the bridge used to be. The railroad's Deer Lodge superintendent of electrification suffered back injuries, and

locomotive engineer Gouyd received some broken ribs when electric locomotive 10309 (a Westinghouse Quill) plunged nose-first into the swollen river. Passengers on the train were evacuated to Avery on speeders. The flood caused so much damage to the rail bed between Avery and St. Regis, Montana, that the Milwaukee's trains were rerouted on Northern Pacific tracks east of Spokane for nearly three weeks.

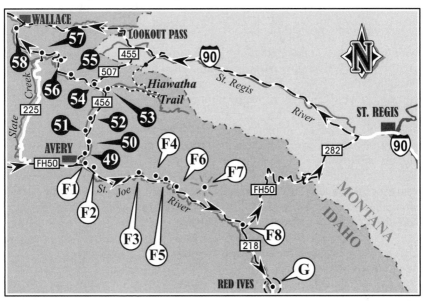

51 ▶ 1934 Fire
Mile 26
The area north of here to the far edge of the Hammond Creek drainage and everything south to Avery, from ridge to ridge east and west, and extending westward into Storm Creek and Slate Creek, was burned in the fire started at the roundhouse in Avery in 1934. In all, over 20,000 acres were burned. CCC boys were among the firefighters.

52 ▶ Stetson Trestle
Mile 24.2
The Stetson Trestle is one of nine high steel bridges between Avery and the Montana border that were used by the Milwaukee Road. This crossing of the North Fork was originally accomplished with a wooden pole trestle. Only two of the original bridges were steel. The ballast baskets on this bridge and on the high bridge over Big Dick Creek were removed in 1988 and concrete slabs were installed to provide a one-lane driving surface for automobiles and trucks.

53 Pearson Trailhead Access to the *Hiawatha Trail*
Mile 20.1

The *Hiawatha Trail* was opened in 1998 and provides mountain biking and hiking opportunities on the old Milwaukee Road railbed from here to East Portal, Montana. The *Hiawatha Trail* is named after the *Olympian Hiawatha* passenger train. One eastbound and one westbound, *Hiawatha* went through here each day from late 1947 to early 1961. Until 1947 the Milwaukee's fast passenger train was called the *Olympian*. That service began in 1911 along with the slower *Columbian* that also came through daily each way. Around the time of WWII another passenger train called the "Butte local" ran through daily each way. The *Olympian* and *Columbian* (and the *Olympian Hiawatha*) were Chicago-to-Seattle trains.

To provide a relatively straight track through the mountains, the railbed had to cut across the many spur ridges and creek canyons. This was done with tunnels and trestles. The most impressive is the St. Paul Pass Tunnel (Taft Tunnel), 1.6 miles (8771 feet) long, with an elevation of 4170 feet in the center of the tunnel. This and other civil engineering feats can be witnessed along the *Hiawatha Trail*, as well as the beautiful mountain scenery. From here the road no longer follows the railbed.

Cross Lucky Swede Creek which flows past the Lucky Swede Mine upstream from here

54 Lucky Swede Mine
Mile 18.6

The Pearson brothers of Minneapolis operated the Lucky Swede Mine. A shaft, nearly a mile in length, produced only two carloads of ore. The mine had its own generating plant. After 10 years of labor and a sizable investment by Minneapolis stockholders, the only salvageable commodity were the mine tailings, used as fill for the Avery-to-Wallace road.

55 Bullion Mine
Mile 17, junction with Bullion Creek Road 507 to Montana and access to Bullion Mine

Most of the nearly 100 people who died in the 1910 Fire died in the St. Joe River Country. The Bullion Fire was part of the 1910 disaster. Two crews were fighting the fire from different sides. When the Big Blowup occurred, S.M. Taylor's crew sought refuge in the Bullion Mine. However, eight of the crew in the mine suffocated. Access to the mine was by way of a wagon road off the Mullan Road that intersected with the Northern Pacific Railroad near the Borax Mine in Montana. The bodies were taken back to the railroad and by rail car into Wallace. They were buried in the Nine Mile Cemetery.

56➤ 1928 Fire

Mile 12.65

In 1928 a forest fire burned from here to the Coeur d'Alene-St. Joe Divide and all the land that can be seen to the west of here. The fire extended west beyond Mastodon Mountain. In all, it burned over 15,000 acres.

57➤ Coeur d'Alene St. Joe Divide Trail 16

Mile 8.7

Trail 16, two miles east of Moon Pass, connected with an Indian trail that connected Coeur d'Alene Indian villages along Lake Coeur d'Alene and the Coeur d'Alene River with Pend d'Oreille Indian villages along the St. Regis River and the Clark Fork farther east. The trail left the South Fork of the Coeur d'Alene River at Wallace and left the ridge of the Bitterroot Divide to drop into the St. Regis River several miles east of Stevens Peak. The peak was named for Isaac Stevens, the first territorial governor and the leader of the 1853 railroad survey party.

58➤ Slate Creek Road 225

Mile 3.7

The Slate Creek Road was built from Wallace to mines in Slate Creek. By 1914 it reached all the way to the St. Joe River.

59➤ The 1910 Fire and Pulaski Interpretive Sign NR

(on the right) Less than a mile from Wallace

The tunnel forest ranger Edward C. Pulaski and his men took refuge in during the 1910 Fire is about two miles upstream on the West Fork of Placer Creek. The fire trapped him and his crew of 45 men. He led his crew into an abandoned mine tunnel and held them there until the fire passed. Six men died, but Pulaski's prompt action saved the other members of the crew.

Enter Wallace, Idaho

Go on to Tour 7 page 7-51 or take I-90 and return to Coeur d'Alene

 **St. Regis Side Trip** (For the more adventurous)
From Avery on the St. Joe River Rd. continuing to St. Regis, Montana

(F1) Trail 186
Mile 47.7
*This trail and the divide trail were Indian trails, used largely by Coeur
d'Alenes and Pend d'Oreilles. When Ward Peak Ranger Station, at Quarles
Peak, was built in 1919-20, the trail on the Bitterroot Divide (state line)
connected this point to the Avery Ranger Station.*

(F2) Upper Log Landing
Mile 47.8 (Picnic Area)
*This area was developed after the highway was built from Marble Creek to
Avery in the early 1990s. Fill material was brought in from that construction
so that now the road sits several feet higher than the level where the log
landing and tracks were situated. The tracks joined Track 6 in the middle of
the East Avery Yard. Though the Forest Service owned the tracks, the
Milwaukee Road locomotives were used to bring in the empty flat cars and
take out those cars loaded with logs.*

(F3) Packsaddle Campground Entrance
Mile 51.2
*Prospectors Jimmy O'Brien and Charles Ferguson were working near the
head of the St. Joe River when, on Sept. 8, 1888, heavy snows began to
fall, making it impossible for them to cross the Bitterroots. They started
down river with two horses and a dog. Out of food and nearly exhausted,
they finally reached the flat now known as Packsaddle. They killed their
horses for food, left their outfits in the trees, and built a raft. Rafting down
river, they made it to another prospector's camp near Calder, then on to Fort
Sherman in Coeur d'Alene for the winter. Neither one would ever tell what
happened to the dog, but one of the packsaddles remained in the tree for so
many years that the tree grew around it, hence the name. In 1918, a camper
sawed the tree down.*

*Also at this site is a tiny bench above the road chosen as a burial site for a
Forest Service packer, Arch Smith, and for newborn infant, Sophie Margaret
Schmalhorst, who died in 1929.*

(F4) Turner Campground
Mile 56.1

When Mary Elizabeth Turner was in her 60s, she came to Turner's Flat to cook for her two sons, Eugene and Jessie. She often wrote in her diary about the solitude of the homestead: "Am so tired and lonesome, could cry my eyes out." Men from the Turner Flat CCC spike camp built a suspension bridge and trails in this area in the 1930s.

F5> Allen Ridge Trail 17
Mile 56.5
The lower part of the Allen Ridge Trail 17 was constructed to provide access to the river face for the Wyssen Skycrane logging system, which was introduced to the St. Joe in the 1950s. Invented in Switzerland by Jakob Wyssen, it was designed to work on steep terrain with cables running high over the trees, eliminating the need for many roads and skid trails. The Wyssen Skycrane lowered logs on a long cable to log decks at the river bottom where they were loaded onto trucks. The operators of this equipment came from Switzerland. Several married local women and made their homes here. The operations ended in about 1967.

F6> Tin Can Flat CCC Camp
Mile 58.3
The CCC built many roads, lookouts and trails as well as fought fire and planted trees from 1933 to 1942 in the St. Joe Country. They wore surplus olive fatigues from WWI. Tin Can Flat was one of the many CCC campsites in the area.

CCC boys grubbing out ribes as blister rust control during the fall of 1933.

 Halfway Hill
Mile 60.6

*Roughly speaking, Halfway Hill was halfway between Sam "49" Williams'
claim at the mouth of the North Fork of the St. Joe River and the St. Joe
Quartz Mine. The St. Joe Quartz Mine was in a draw north of the river
downstream from Bluff Creek. The mining company had four cabins along
their access trail. They built the trail in 1903 from North Fork (Avery) to the
mine. Heavy equipment, needed to operate the mine, was shuttled
laboriously up the river by barge. But before any more than a sample of ore
was taken out, the head of the company absconded with the funds and went to
Europe. The Theriault family purchased the equipment, floated it back down
the river to Avery in 1912, and later moved it to the family claim at Harvey
Creek. Bobby Stauffer, local trapper and prospector, worked the St. Joe
Quartz Mine and did assessment work. During prohibition he produced a
little bootleg whiskey which made it more productive than most mines in the
area.*

F8 Old Montana Trail Turnout and Interpretive Sign
Mile 75.1

*The trail between De Borgia, Montana, and Tensed, Idaho, followed an old
Indian trail. Prospectors and miners used this trail in the late 1800s. Pack
strings brought goods back and forth between Montana, Idaho and
Washington through the early 1900s.*

**At the junction with Road 218 and St. Joe River Road you can take a 12-
mile side trip to Red Ives or continue on the St. Joe Road up Gold Creek
to cross the Bitterroot Divide into Montana. The two-lane paved road
leaves the St. Joe River to head over the summit (5,813 feet). The road at
the summit turns into two-lane gravel until two miles from St. Regis,
Montana, where the pavement resumes. Near the summit there are
views of Ward Peak (elevation 7,312 feet), over which the Montana Trail
passed**

G Red Ives Ranger Station Side Trip

*Road 218 is the number of the St. Joe River Road from Avery to Spruce Tree
Campground. The road below Avery is numbered Forest Highway 50.
Elevation at the junction with the St. Joe River Road is 3343 feet.*

Set odometer to 0
**Road 218 is paved but narrow to Red Ives and gravel to Spruce Tree
Campground. There are few turnouts for the entire 12 miles**

The CCC completed the road from Avery to Red Ives in 1938, except the four miles closest to Avery. The route ends at the Spruce Tree Campground a short distance from Red Ives. Before 1938 road access to Red Ives was over the 57-mile Kelley Creek-Bathtub-Beaver Creek route.

Mile 0.1, Informational sign for St. Joe Wild and Scenic River, including map and Whitewater classifications of the river's reaches

In 1978 Congress included the upper St. Joe River in the National Wild and Scenic River system under the Wild and Scenic Rivers Act of 1968. The St. Joe is classified as a recreational river from Avery to Spruce Tree Campground, and as a wild river from Spruce Tree to St. Joe Lake.

Red Ives Ranger Station ⬚NR
elevation 3,711, Mile 9.7

Red Ives was the name for a redheaded placer miner who had a shelter at this site. The Red Ives Ranger Station was established in 1932, when the Ward Peak and Pole Mountain Ranger Districts were combined. The CCC built the structures at the ranger station beginning with the administrative building and the garage in 1935. In 1937 a barn and waterpower house were constructed. The ranger station staff wintered in Avery until 1969. It has not been an active ranger station since 1984. The ranger's residence is now a recreational rental.

Red Ives Ranger Station from the pasture, 1946.

Generator Plant at Red Ives

Mile 9.8

The generator plant provided hydroelectric power to the Red Ives Ranger Station from 1937 to 1960. Water arrived at the plant through a wooden pipe from a dam a half-mile up Red Ives Creek and had sufficient head to provide five kilowatts of power.

Forest Fire of 1889

A large forest fire burned nearly 50,000 acres in the upper St. Joe Country in 1889. It burned almost the entire headwaters above Timber Creek and undoubtedly burned many more thousands of acres in the adjacent Clearwater Country and Clark Fork Country. Much of this area was re-burned in 1910. The 1910 Fire burned tens of thousands of acres immediately downriver as well.

Turn around and go back to Forest Hwy 50. Turn left to go back to Avery or right to go onto St. Regis and I-90

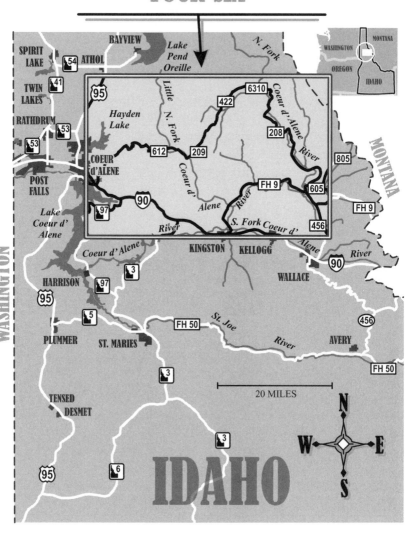

This tour, for the more adventurous, starts at the Fernan Ranger Station in Coeur d'Alene and follows Forest Road 268 along the north shore of Fernan Lake, over the Fernan Saddle and down the Little North Fork of the Coeur d'Alene River, up Leiberg Creek over a divide to the main North Fork of the Coeur d'Alene River drainage, and to I-90. The tour covers 125 miles and takes most of a day especially if you make many stops. Camping, hiking, and fishing opportunities abound.

The road around Fernan Lake is narrow, winding and traveled by logging trucks. From the Fernan Saddle it is impassable by auto when covered by snow (November to May). Some of the roadway is gravel but along the North Fork of the Coeur d'Alene River the road is a two-lane paved route. Check with the Fernan Ranger Station office (208-769-3000) for road conditions and maps before traveling.

Fernan Lake in the foreground and Lake Coeur d'Alene and the Potlatch Lumber Company in the distance, about 1925.

❶ Fernan Ranger Station

2502 E. Sherman Ave. Set odometer at 0

The Forest Service purchased the land for this ranger station in 1937. The Civilian Conservation Corp (CCC) crew from Beauty Bay constructed the original buildings in 1938. The shop and warehouse are the only CCC buildings remaining. In 1961 the station was named after an early homesteader in the area, John Fernan. Originally the district and station were called Coeur d'Alene Ranger Station and District but the District is now referred to as the Coeur d'Alene River District. Buildings constructed by the CCC were destroyed in 1959 and in 1990 to make room for Interstate-90.

❷ Fernan Village

John Fernan, a Civil War veteran, arrived in 1878 as a soldier at Fort Sherman. His wife, Mary Jane, joined him a year later to become the first white woman to raise a family here. They raised six children at their Fernan homestead on the west side of the lake near the ranger station. Fernan had a very modest little house, rented boats for day use on the lake and raised alfalfa hay in the area north of the lake where Fernan Village is today. Renowned local saddle maker Sam Theis bought the property and continued to rent boats and raise hay. He provided his field for rodeo grounds during the 1930s and 40s. He remodeled a large barn into a home for his family on the lakeshore. Until its incorporation in 1957 Fernan Village included only two homes, a ranger station and the Sourdough Club. The Sourdough Club was located east of the I-90 westbound entrance ramp. It was a popular and unique nightclub featuring a tunnel entrance, a bar ceiling lined with old dollar bills and a dance floor ceiling decorated with brightly colored neckties. It operated from the 1940s to 1979.

❸ Cattle Crossing

0.7 miles turnout on the left with the cattle crossing on the right side bank next to the shore

When the CCC built the road in the 1930s they constructed three cattle crossings (tunnels) under the road to let cattle reach the water. This is the first of the cattle crossings along this road. This crossing served the Monard's ranch which was on Fernan Hill. The second cattle crossing is on the west side of the Moate house and the last is in front of the K- Bar Ranch.

❹ Moate Lake House

1.5 miles, 5132 Fernan Lake Rd.

Tom Moate homesteaded this area and built a house up the hill. His son Robert built this vertical log cabin on Fernan Lake in 1954. It was one of the first houses built on the lake.

❺ Fernan Lake Road

There was only a pack trail along the lakeshore before the Forest Service built this road. The main road into the valley and to the east end of the lake was by way of French Gulch and over the ridge to a point near Lilypad Bay. The Fernan Lake Road is the primary access road from Coeur d'Alene to the Little North Fork of the Coeur d'Alene River and the Coeur d'Alene National Forest. It took nearly 20 years to build a one-lane road over the saddle. In 1922 when the surveys for the road were completed the availability of heavy equipment was limited. Beginning in 1934 the CCCs did much of the difficult rock removal and fill by hand. Bulldozers helped to finish the one lane road with turnouts by 1941. Several large hand-laid rock culverts and traces of rock walls built by the CCC are visible along the road. The completion of this road stimulated the regional economy by providing access to timber for the nationwide housing boom after WWII and access to agricultural lands, mining claims and recreational opportunities. The road provided access to Fernan Lake, Huckleberry Mountain and its fire lookout, Deception Creek and the Experimental Forest. In the 1950s improvements were made to the road to accommodate the heavy logging truck use. In 1968 only the first 4 miles of the one-and-half-lane road were paved but by 1979 it was paved to the saddle.

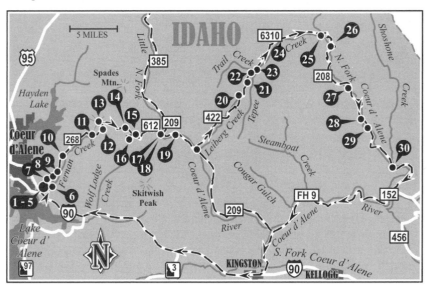

❻ Fernan Lake

Fernan Lake is a half-mile wide at its widest point and 2.3 miles long. The lake is relatively shallow with depths up to 20 feet. The lake freezes most winters and is popular for ice-skating and ice fishing. Early residents, like the Kelly's, cut 50-pound blocks of ice from Lilypad Bay, hauled them to their farm by sleigh and stored them in an icehouse.

❼ CCC Rock Work

2 miles

Here is a good example of CCC rock work remaining along the north side of the road built above a rock culvert. Four much larger hand laid rock culverts are located near the top of the Fernan Hill Road on curves near State Creek. The culverts are only visible if you hike down into the drainage along the north side of the road. The fact that these rock structures are still there and still in use after all these years is a testament to the workmanship of the Civilian Conservation Corp.

Bridge at the head of Fernan Lake. The bridge was torn down and the end of the bay was filled c. 1950.

❽ Bridge Site, Lilypad Bay and Wetlands

2.3 miles

This turnout was the site of a bridge that crossed Lilypad Bay. Cattails, camas and wapato (also known as Indian potato) are found in the wetlands. When I-90 was built, a culvert was placed at the west end of the lake causing water to back up and flood much of the meadow land on the east end of the lake and into Fernan Valley. An old trapper's cabin and barn were also flooded on the east end of the lake. At one time the meadows extended all the way up past Rondeau Gulch to the private shooting range.

❾ Kelly Homestead

3.7 miles, 8449 E. Fernan Lake Road (K-Bar Ranch)

William Kelly came to Fernan in 1886 and lived on the homestead with his wife and nine children. The homestead included a house, barns, cellar, well, 150-tree orchard, 160 feet of ditching, 25 acres under cultivation and another 25 fenced acres. The original house burned in 1897. A two-story log house was built just below the horse barn and it burned, too. The family lived in the chicken house until a third house, built with cedar siding on the outside and knotty pine on the inside, was built in the same spot. This house was burned down in the spring of 2005. Two large log barns, over 100 years old, are all that remain of the original homestead. One of the barns and an attached dairy barn are visible from the road. The barn used for the Kelly Dude Ranch is set back in a narrow draw.

The Kelly's operated a Dude Ranch as early as the late 1890s. They offered horseback riding, hayrides and rustic log cabins with outhouses. June Kelly Lunceford remembers the Coeur d'Alene Indians camped in the meadow along Fernan Creek near the Ranch in the 1920s and 1930s to dig camas in the spring. Later in the summer the Indians would go to the top of Huckleberry Mountain to pick berries.

A dance hall and bar were built in 1937. The dance hall burned in 1947 and Jennifer Gookstetter (a Kelly descendant) built her home on the spot. The last guest log cabin from the Kelly Dude Ranch was moved to the pond, visible along the left side of the road. Members of the Kelly family no longer own the K-Bar Ranch but family members still own portions of the original acreage in Fernan Valley.

⑩ Rondeau Farmstead

9742 E. Fernan Lake Road at the confluence of Rondo Creek and Fernan Creek on the right (east) side of the road
This land was originally part of the Kelly Homestead of 1200 acres and is the only piece of land in the valley where Fernan Creek has water in it year round. In the early 1900s William Kelly sold the land to Charlie Rondeau, a saddle maker. The log cabin, outhouse, barn and chicken house are part of that original farmstead. The small log cabin and rock cellar were built into the slope and are the oldest buildings. The barn and chicken coop are said to have been built during the 1940s. Charlie Rondeau married Alice Bruher, the daughter of Louis Bruher, who owned the property upstream.

Rock wall remnants along the road edge near the beginning of the driveway to this farmstead are from the original road built by the CCC in the 1930s. When the Forest Service built the road right up against Charlie Rondeau's log cabin he was so angry and distraught that he was never the same. John Kelly hauled the lumber, with a team of horses, needed to build a second house. It has been added onto and remodeled.

⑪ Fernan Saddle, elevation 4,061

At 10.7 miles take FS Road 612

The large parking area here serves snowmobile riders. In the winter, Road 612 is groomed for snowmobiles.

⑫ Windy Ridge

13 miles

Off to the right is Skitwish Peak. In the distance is the St. Joe/Coeur d'Alene River Divide. The forest in this area is second growth Douglas fir forest intermixed with western white pine, western larch, ponderosa pine, grand fir, western red cedar and mountain maple.

At mile 14 continue on FS Road 612. This is the end of the paved road and the junction of FS Road 434 that goes to Wolf Lodge Saddle

⑬ Huckleberry Mountain

As you continue up Fernan Road there is a ridge on the left that ascends from Fernan Lake to Huckleberry Mountain. In the early 1920s Huckleberry Mountain was used as a Forest Service lookout consisting of a crow's nest in a snag and a log cabin with a cupola on the ground. Between 1928 and 1931 a standard 7' x 7' cabin was built on the site for a cost of just over $1,000.00. It was destroyed in 1950. Forest Service Trail 28 follows the ridge above the path of an earlier trail that was in use before 1906 by homesteaders and trappers. Today the area is a popular mountain bike and ATV recreation site.

⑭ Spades Mountain Lookout

14.2 miles, pull out in the turnout on the left and look back across Burnt Cabin Creek drainage

Spades Mountain Lookout began in 1917 as an observation point from a tree perch with a platform. The lookout was reached on foot by way of a trail up the East Fork of Hayden Creek and Deerfoot Ridge. In 1926 a wood tower was constructed at a cost of $998.00. Lookouts lived in tents until a 12' x 14' cabin was built on the mountain at a cost of $524.00. Between 1940 and 1941 a 50' L-6 steel tower was built to replace the wooden tower. In 1952 the cabin was replaced by a 14' x 14' cabin moved to Spades Mountain from Hudlow Peak. In 1963 this tower was replaced with a 67' L-4 treated-timber tower and the steel tower was given to the state of Idaho. With binoculars you can see that this current tower has a cabin on top with a flat roof. At one time there were 989 fire lookouts in Idaho and by the late 1990s only 196 remained.

17 miles is the Five Finger Saddle, continue downhill on FS Road 612

Cottage one at Deception Creek. Experimental Forest, Oct. 1962.

⑮ Deception Creek Experimental Forest

19.6 miles (the actual entrance to the Experiment Station is west of the Honeysuckle Campground)

Deception Creek was on the route of an old Indian trail between Coeur d'Alene and the Little North Fork of the Coeur d'Alene River. This was also the first route used by early homesteaders who came by way of what eventually became the Huckleberry Mountain Trail 28.

Isaac Sand homesteaded in 1904 and logged the white pine here. After the Coeur d'Alene National Forest was established in 1906 the land was withdrawn from homestead entry and the Forest Service began acquiring the homesteads on Forest Service lands. In 1913 Isaac Sand died and his wife Mary refused to sell to McGoldrick Lumber Company. Eventually the Forest Service acquired the land and finally in 1931 Ranger Haynes of the Honeysuckle Ranger Station burned all of the homestead buildings. A log chute on Sand Creek and a sluice dam on Deception Creek are the only remnants of Isaac Sand's operations.

The Experimental Forest was dedicated in 1934 to find better methods of growing trees. The entire Deception Creek drainage is part of the Intermountain Forest and Range Experiment Station. It included small and large residences, a garage/warehouse, outhouses, an administrative building, bridges and an office on Sand Creek just west of the Isaac Sand homestead. The barracks were built in Spokane and trucked into the forest in 1936. When superintendent Elton Bentley, his wife Doris and three children arrived, they were impressed with the hardwood floors, plaster walls and furnace in the house. Problems with vandalism forced the Forest Service to dismantle the station in 1982.

⑯ Bill Moore Gravesite
FS Road 612
In September 1906, Bill Moore and two companions were on their way to
Coeur d'Alene and spent the night in a cabin near here. The next morning,
Bill fell off his horse, dead from a heart attack. His partners buried him,
went on to Coeur d'Alene and reported his death. A storekeeper to whom
Bill owed money came out and dug him up to see if he had any cash on him.
He didn't. The cabin was destroyed when the road down Deception Creek
was built in 1934 and Bill Moore's grave is under the road near the mouth of
a small creek named for him.

⑰ Burnt Cabin Creek Railroad
21.4 miles
About four miles north of the Honeysuckle Campground the railroad
extended between Garwood and the Little North Fork area. There were
many logging railroads in the Coeur d'Alene National Forest but the most
ambitious was the Burnt Cabin Creek Railroad. The Ohio Match Company
began construction of the 25 mile-long railroad in July 1923. The railroad
extended from Garwood over the mountains and down Burnt Cabin Creek
into the 70 million board feet of timber the Company purchased in the Burnt
Cabin drainage. The railroad was later extended down river to Cascade
Creek and upriver to Iron Creek. In twenty years of operation more than a
quarter-billion feet of logs were hauled on the railroad. The railroad was
abandoned in 1944 when the company started trucking logs directly to Coeur
d'Alene Lake. Portions of the railbed were made into the Ohio Match Road,
which goes east from Garwood.

⑱ Honeysuckle Ranger Station site
21.5 miles (at the bridge crossing the Little North Fork)
The Honeysuckle Ranger Station was located near the mouth of Skookum
Creek, which is located downstream (to the right) on the right side of the
river. The original structures built after 1911 included a two-room log cabin
and a small tool shed. From 1923 to 1932 other structures were added using
lumber salvaged from logging structures such as flumes and cabins that were
abandoned in the area. During the Depression a CCC Camp was built as a
summer work site in the area. After the work program ended many of the
permanent structures were leased from the Forest Service as summer homes.
When the structures became unsuitable for use, the buildings were destroyed.
The District became part of the Kingston Ranger District.

The Winton Lumber Company built a logging camp, flume, log rollaway, and splash dam at the mouth of Skookum Creek in 1918. Before roads and logging trucks reached this area, a series of splash dams was built along the Little North Fork to facilitate floating logs to downstream mills. Chutes and flumes are trough-like structures used to transport logs. Chutes were often greased to allow the logs to slide either downhill or to be pulled by horses. Flumes were filled with water to float the logs to streams or rivers. Telephone wires were strung between logging camps, dams and other logging structures to coordinate the release of water needed to transport logs to the river. The flumes, splash dams and other logging structures have rotted or been washed away by frequent floods but, with a sharp eye, some remnants are visible.

Winton Lumber Company operations on the Skookum Creek sale. On the left is a chute and on the right is a flume. This flume cost $9,000 per mile to build. Notice the large rollaway on the right where logs are waiting to go into the flume. Some of the camp buildings are visible in the background, 1924.

After you cross the bridge over the Little North Fork of the Coeur d'Alene River turn right on Road 209 to Magee

⑲ Delaney Splash Dam (Interpretive Sign)

24.2 miles. Get out of the car to see the remnants of the dam and to read the sign: Transporting Logs by Water

In the 1920s and early 1930s log drives were the main method of transporting logs out of the lower portion of the Little North Fork of the Coeur d'Alene River.

This log dam at Delaney Creek was one of seven splash dams on the Little North Fork. Logs were cut, skidded by horses and delivered to the river by a system of chutes and flumes. The logs were piled in decks at the water's edge or stored in the ponds above the dam. When the spring thaws swelled the river, water and logs were released through the gates and splashed from dam to dam. The logs rolled and pounded, riding the crest of the flood to the main Coeur d'Alene River. In slack water the logs were gathered into rafts. Steam-powered tugboats towed the rafts to lumber mills along the river and Lake Coeur d'Alene.

Leiberg Creek and Road 422 junction, turn left toward Magee
26.6 miles (Mileposts begin here at 0, set odometer to 0)

John B. Leiberg was commissioned in 1860 to survey the forest resources in what is now northern Idaho and the adjoining Bitterroot Mountains in western Montana. It would be 38 years before he finished surveying and reporting on the 10 million acres of forest. During the time of his survey there were many destructive fires but Leiberg estimated there were 31 billion board feet of timber still standing in the Coeur d'Alene area in 1898. From Leiberg's final report eastern lumbermen started projecting their plans westward.

On the left is an area that was not burned in the 1910 or 1919 fires. The Ohio Match Company owned this block of timber containing mature white pine but when the area was surveyed, it appeared there was no way to get the timber out. The area was referred to as the Lost Block. In 1940 Ohio Match built Road 612 to truck the timber to Coeur d'Alene.

The Winton Lumber Company established the majority of the timber claims south of Burnt Cabin Creek and logged into the early 1930s. They constructed an elaborate system of log chutes, flumes and sluice dams on Copper, Skookum, Leiberg, Laverne, Picnic, Mineral, John, Canyon and Deception creeks that were tied into a larger system of seven splash dams. The dams were located at Breakwater (furthest downstream), Leiberg,

Bootjack, Honeysuckle, Tom Wright, Cathcart and No-Name Dam (furthest upstream). The entire system was connected by a telephone communication system that timed the holding and release of water at each dam all along the Little North Fork of the Coeur d'Alene River during spring log drives. The logging operations required numerous logging camps along the river. Many of these logging camps eventually became ranger stations, CCC or Blister Rust Control (BRC) Forest Service work camps.

In 1918 the Wintons built logging Camp 22 on Leiberg Creek. A log flume along Leiberg Creek transported logs into the holding pond formed by the Leiberg Dam on the Little North Fork of the Coeur d'Alene River. The splash dam, built in 1919, had two 14-foot sluice gates and one 16-footer.

⑳ Leiberg Saddle
Mile 6.1, Continue on Road 422
This travel route began as a pack trail and wagon road during the late 1890s and early 1900s following Leiberg Creek to Tepee Summit by way of Hump Creek, then down Tepee Creek to Magee's homestead. Early trappers, miners and homesteaders used the road hoping to find their fortune. The Forest Service ran telephone line along the trail between ranger, guard and lookout stations in the early 1920s and then built a road in 1930. In 1949 the Forest Service built a road over Leiberg Saddle along the same route in use today.

In the summer this is a good area to spot wildflowers including: Indian paintbrush, fireweed, daisy, white yarrow, Japanese sweet clover, St. John's wort, wild rose and golden pea. Huckleberries and serviceberries ripen in late July and August.

Continue on to Magee

㉑ Halsey Homestead and the Barker Sawmill
Mile 11.6
Homer Halsey's mother homesteaded 85.82 acres at the mouth of Halsey Creek along Tepee Creek in the early 1900s. In the winter of 1912 the Halsey's daughter died and was buried here on the east side of Tepee Creek. The Halsey log cabin was home to Charlie Magee during the winter months beginning in the 1920s until his death in 1934. In 1946 R. C. "Bob" Barker built a sawmill here on this land then owned by the Erickson's who were ranchers on Trail Creek. The mill did not have a planer and produced only rough cut lumber. By 1950 the Forest Service built this improved road

allowing Barker to truck two loads per day over Leiberg Saddle to Coeur d'Alene. The sawmill operated until the early 1960s and included a large teepee burner (a teepee-shaped structure used to burn sawdust and waste wood), five cabins, four bunkhouses, storehouse, cookhouse and the original Halsey log cabin. The foundation of the teepee burner can still be seen. The Forest Service eventually acquired the homestead as well as other private properties in the nearby drainages.

Barker sawmill, 1949.

㉒ Trail Creek Work Camp Site
Mile 12.8
This house, built in 1925, was the residence of the assistant ranger for Magee Ranger District and was being used in 2007 by Idaho Department of Fish and Game. In addition there were thirteen bunkhouses, two bathhouses, several employee buildings, powerhouse, mess hall, meat house, wood shed, and recreation hall. The site was used as a CCC camp in the early 1930s and from the 1940s to the 1960s as a BRC camp. At times the CCC camp housed as many as 400 men who furnished manpower for trail and road building, timber harvest, tree planting and blister rust control. From the 1970s to early 1980s the camp was used as a Youth Conservation Corps Camp and from the 1970s to the 1990s as the school district's Outdoor Education Camp. In 1999 the camp was dismantled.

Cross the bridge and turn right on FS Road 6310

23 Magee Ranger Station
Mile 13

Charles Magee came to Lakeview on Lake Pend Oreille in 1890. After a couple of years he sold his property there and homesteaded here on the Coeur d'Alene River. During the winter, Magee trapped beaver, marten, mink and other fur-bearing animals. He had a good string of pack and riding horses and during the summer he packed parties of fisherman a distance of 22 miles from Lakeview to his homestead where they would stay in tents for a week or more. Magee died in November 1934 and is buried in Athol.

The Magee Ranger District was active from 1908 to 1973. The Forest Service constructed the house, office, warehouse, bunkhouse, barn and other structures between 1922 and 1935. During WWII, the Army Corps of Engineers built a 900-meter long emergency airstrip. A radio building was added in 1954 and a powerhouse was built in 1976. In 1980 a man traveling from Murray took a wrong turn at Prichard and drove upriver instead of down river. He became stuck in the snow at the Magee Ranger Station. To set a signal fire he burned down an Army Air Corps cabin, a warehouse (where the concrete slab is still visible) and began to burn down the barn. Snowmobilers rescued him 2-3 weeks later. The ranger's house is available for rent.

24 Independence Creek
Mile 17

Independence Creek flows into the North Fork of the Coeur d'Alene River here. From the Lakeview Mining District on Lake Pend Oreille a wagon supply route came over the Pend Oreille Divide down Independence Creek to the Tepee Creek area in the 1890s. Tepee Creek was named by Charlie Magee for a teepee that his sister's husband Jack Needham had used as an overnight stop on this trap line in the 1880s. Magee thought he was on the same creek as the teepee but he later found the remains of the teepee at the Junction of Callis and Trail Creek but the name stuck. This area was burned in the 1910 fire. Logs from here were driven down the North Fork and then the Coeur d'Alene River to the Winton Mill at Rose Lake.

25 McPherson Meadows
Mile 20.5

Frank McPherson lived here from 1920 until his death in 1980. He did seasonal work for the Forest Service and in the winter he ran a 70-mile trap line for mink, otter, marten, coyote and other fur-bearing animals. It was estimated he traveled 2,000 miles in a winter. He purchased the private land in the meadow area from Eric Pete Pearson in 1920 with his partner Herb Stone. Stone sold out his share a couple years later. McPherson also homesteaded the abandoned homestead originally filed by Ferguson and the late George Hamilton. McPherson died at the age of 80. It is still privately owned but a log tool shed, in the meadow on the right just before the pavement begins, is the only original building remaining. In 2004 McPherson's cabin was moved to the Shoshone Work Center.

26 Rock City CCC Camp Site
Mile 27.4 (Big Hank Campground)
This area, known as Big Hank Meadows as early as 1905, was used for the Rock City Guard Station, a McGoldrick logging camp, Rock City CCC spike camp, and now is a Forest Service campground. Today the Big Hank Cabin (Rock City Guard Station) is on the North Idaho College campus at the Museum of North Idaho's Fort Sherman Museum.

27 Yellow Dog Ranger Station Cabin
Mile 32.3 look across the river through the trees
One story has it that Yellow Dog was named for Yellow Dog Smith who was on the wrong end of a lawsuit with the Bunker Hill Mine. Remains of a log cabin are visible behind the trees, on the east side of the North Fork of the Coeur d'Alene River near the mouth of Yellow Dog Creek. The Forest Service built a cabin as a small guard station in 1929.

28 Devil's Elbow Campground
Mile 34.6
Devil's Elbow was named for large rocks that stuck out from the bedrock in the river that could cause a boat to flip. A pack trail went around the rock point here and forded the river nearby. When the Forest Service built the road up river in 1934 the rock was blasted and the obstacle was removed. The 1933 flood forced the men at the CCC camp to leave.

29 Kit Price Campground
Mile 36.5
Kit Price Campground is a misspelling of the original homesteader's name of Kid Price. Kid Price signed the original homestead deed in 1914. Local lore places Kid Price near Murray during the gold rush period from the 1880s through the 1890s when he ran a group of hooligans and toughs from his cabin on Prichard Creek. After consuming their fair share of spirits while languishing around the cabin, the gang entertained themselves with numerous volleys of gunfire at whatever target pleased them. It was known in Murray

that when the shooting could be heard in the direction of Kid Price's cabin it was not the most opportune time for travel down Prichard Creek. When the gold dredge worked through that section of Prichard Creek where the cabin once stood, the dredge master reported that several pounds of spent lead bullets were recovered from the dredge's gold tables.

30 ▶ Shoshone Work Center
Mile 39.5, rest stop
The Shoshone Work Center was the Big Creek Ranger Station site from 1907 to 1920. Shoshone Creek was originally known as Big Creek until the 1960s. The name was changed to avoid confusion with the Big Creek in the St. Joe National Forest. From 1912 to 1914 the Forest Service shared the site with the Stack Gibbs (Winton) Lumber Company as a logging camp.

From 1933 until 1941 this was CCC Camp F-132. The men were involved in road construction along the North Fork of the Coeur d'Alene River and Shoshone Creek, building lookout towers, fire access trails, a grounded telephone system between the lookouts and guard stations and they also built the dike on the east side of the camp along Shoshone Creek to keep the area from flooding.

As the economy boomed after WWII a large block of mature white pine became accessible in the Yellow Dog drainage and a woods camp was again established at the site. With extra timber dollars the Forest Service began to develop the site as a work center in 1955 with the construction of a mess hall, two barracks and a small fire cache. Additional buildings were constructed in the 1960s through early 1980s to accommodate an ever-increasing Forest Service woods crew.

The Young Adult Conservation Corp used the camp from 1977 to 1981. The Forest Service continued using the camp on an intermittent basis through the early 1990s. Several attempts were made by the Forest Service to have the camp converted into a minimum-security prison to be run by the State Corrections Department but the local outcry ended this endeavor. The Work Center served as an administrative site from 1921 to 1999. In 1999 the Forest Service issued a special use permit to the Inland Northwest Lutheran Outdoor Ministries to use the Work Center as an outdoor education facility, known as Shoshone Base Camp.

Junction to Murray Forest Hwy 9
Mile 45.9 Turn right to return to I-90 and Coeur d'Alene

See Tour Eight page 8-14 for sites from Prichard to I-90

Coeur d'Alene Mining District
~TOUR SEVEN~

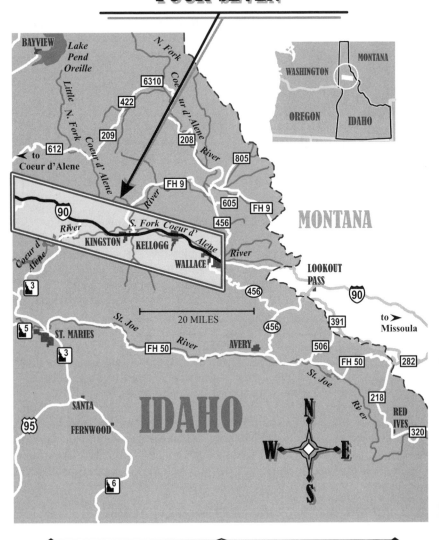

Starting from Coeur d'Alene and ending at Wallace this tour is about 120 miles round trip and can take all day if you visit the museums and other attractions. The route follows much of old Hwy 10. However, if you do not have the time and want to stay on I-90 we have included the mileage/mileposts from the Idaho/Washington state line so you can see the sites that are visible from I-90.

The Coeur d'Alene Mining District is filled with interesting sites and things to do. Once in Wallace, we encourage you to pick up the free *Historic Wallace Idaho* booklet which includes a walking tour of the buildings in Wallace, Wallace-Burke Historic Canyon Creek Milepost Tour and information on Mullan and other sites in the area that are not included in this tour book. Opportunities for biking and walking abound on *The Trail of the Coeur d'Alenes*. For information, call the Historic Wallace Chamber of Commerce at 208-753-7151.

❶ Yellowstone Trail

Traveling east on I-90 from Coeur d'Alene look to the left up the hillside as you approach Exit 22

Cut into the hillside above the Interstate is the Yellowstone Trail. This was the first highway through North Idaho and was built between 1914 and 1916. The Yellowstone Trail, Hwy 10 and now Interstate-90 followed much of the same route as the Mullan Road, the first engineered road connecting the Great Plains with the Northwest. Captain John Mullan and his crew built the 624-mile road linking Fort Benton, Montana with Fort Walla Walla, Washington between 1859 and 1862. The first automobile trip from Wallace to Coeur d'Alene, on the Mullan Road over Fourth of July Pass, was in July of 1911 and took five hours. From 1914 to 1916, much of the Mullan Road was improved or bypassed and became known as the Yellowstone Trail. In 1926 the Yellowstone Trail was renamed U.S. Hwy 10 and then in the 1960s and 1970s was re-designated in various sections as Interstate-90.

❷ Fourth of July Pass, elevation 3,069 feet

Prior to 1932 the road went over the top of this pass. Motorists usually had to stop for a break at Lee's Lodge which was located near the summit. The lodge featured a zoo which included two bear cubs named Pete and Repeat. They entertained customers by taking a soda pop bottle (one the customer bought for the bear) into their claws and drinking it. In 1932 a tunnel bypassed this road, which in turn was bypassed in 1957 by I-90. The old tunnel was buried and the current road base is about at the level of this tunnel.

A soda pop drinking bear at Lee's Lodge on the Fourth of July Pass, circa 1935.

Ⓐ Mullan Tree Historic Site Side Trip
Take Exit 28, then turn left and proceed to the Mullan Tree Historic Site, interpretive sign and half-mile trail
This is believed to be the site of the first 4th of July celebration in the state of Idaho. John Mullan's crew completed the work on this segment of the military road during the week of July 4, 1861 and carved "MR July 4, 1861" on a tree here. The tree was blown down and the section of the tree with the blaze is on exhibit at the Museum of North Idaho in Coeur d'Alene.

From Mullan's journal:
July 4, Thursday, gave the expedition a holiday, to commemorate the day. Issued to working parties extra issues of molasses, ham, whiskey, flour, and pickles, for a 4th of July dinner. . . Day spent pleasantly and harmoniously in camp, which was six and a half miles east of Wolf's Lodge prairie and

branded one hundred ninety-six miles from Walla Walla. *In the 1860s travelers and pack strings, including one camel caravan, going to and from the Montana gold fields used the road, but sometime after 1865 maintenance ceased and use declined. After an inspection tour of the West in 1877 General William T. Sherman ordered the construction of Fort Missoula and Fort Coeur d'Alene (later named Fort Sherman) and the repair of the Mullan Road, which was accomplished in 1879. Travel on the road increased immediately. General Frank Wheaton reported in a letter accompanying Sherman's inspection reports that after the army had repaired the road:* "The amount of travel over it during the past thirty days in both directions has surprised us here [Fort Coeur d'Alene]. Every few days, wagon trains are passing, and several intelligent parties just off the road, with whom I have conversed, predict a very heavy traffic over the route next spring. One drove of twelve thousand sheep passed east over the road three weeks ago, and bands of horses are continually moved on it."

Mullan Statue

William A. Clark, Jr. of Missoula, Montana, donated six 14-foot high marble monuments to mark the route of the Mullan Road through Idaho. Designed by Edgar Paxson they were installed in Post Falls, Coeur d'Alene, Kellogg, Wallace, Mullan, and St. Maries. This statue was moved from Coeur d' Alene, where it had been erected in 1918, to Fourth of July Pass where it was dedicated with the Mullan Park in 1921.

Return to I-90 and continue east toward Kellogg

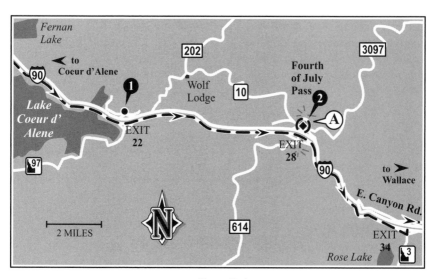

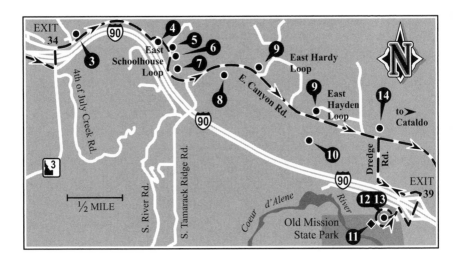

Take Exit 34, Rose Lake/St. Maries then turn left (north). At the yield
sign set the odometer to 0 and turn right (east) onto Canyon Rd. Most of
Canyon Rd. is the original Yellowstone Trail (Hwy 10), although some of
the road was re-aligned when I-90 was built.

❸ Canyon Garage

0.2 miles near the corner of Fern Cr. Rd. and Canyon Rd.
Frank Durning had a garage at Rose Lake but when the mill closed in 1920s
he moved the business here to take advantage of the highway traffic. The
original Canyon Garage was destroyed by fire in 1924 and was rebuilt. After
the highway was re-aligned, he built the house in 1936 and the accompanying
garage on top of the road. If you go northwest on Fern Cr. Rd., near the
garage, you can see a small bridge on the left, probably built in 1921 that
carried the Yellowstone Trail across the creek. Northwest of this bridge is the
site of the original Canyon School which was commonly known as the Green
Schoolhouse. The yellow sheet metal building on Canyon Rd. was the
Canyon Garage.

1.2 mile,s turn left on School House Loop Rd.
Canyon School Loop Rd. was the original Yellowstone Trail until a highway
revision (the present Canyon Road) bypassed it in 1936. Early travel
required frequent stops. Remnants of motels, gas stations and stores are found
along this route.

❹ Canyon Store

**27659 Canyon Rd. on the east corner of Canyon Rd. and School House
Loop Rd.**

This was Darrell Wall's second store. The first was the log cabin further down the road. When a new alignment of U.S. Hwy 10 was constructed in 1935-36 he moved his business here in 1937. Judy McKivers bought and expanded the building adding a bar, service station and grocery. In 1960 during the construction of I-90 the building was placed on skids and moved north to make way for the new highway. Carl Nordstorm lived on School House Loop Rd. and ran Nordstrom's logging company for many years. One day, in the 1960s, he came home and said to his wife Evelyn, "Guess what, I just bought Judy's store." Evelyn replied, "I'm not running that beer parlor." However, their daughter Donna and her husband Ronnie Rex were interested so they bought the property and ran it for a short while and then it became a residence for Ron.

❺ Wall's Service Station

1.5 miles on the left. (If on I-90 just after the Rose Lake Exit look left (north))

This log building was Darrell Wall's first service station, country store and home along the Yellowstone Trail. When he moved down the street, Sam and Lenore Adams bought it in the late 1930s and it became a residence.

❻ Canyon School

1.5 miles

Originally a grange building it was remodeled several times and since the 1950s it has served as the second Canyon School.

❼ Almond Farm

27769 E. School House Loop Rd.

In 1904 Herman Almond built this home for his bride-to-be who was coming from New York. The wedding never took place because his bride married his brother. Herman remained a bachelor the rest of his life. In 1937 Delmar Kerns purchased the property, added onto the house and started a dairy farm. Terry Sverdsten purchased the home in 1980.

When you see the "Do Not Enter" sign turn to the right and then left (east) on Canyon Rd.

❽ Arnhold Farm

29266 Canyon Rd.

Tony and Hannah Arnhold settled here about 1910. Their sons Frank and John continued to live and work on the farm until the mid 1990s. John never married and Frank married Frances Miller of Cataldo in 1954. The family sold farm produce and milk to the creamery. While running the farm the brothers worked on the Coeur d'Alene Mine dredge that operated on the Mission Flats until it closed down in 1968. John then took a job at the Morning Mine Shop where mining equipment was repaired. Frank stayed home and ran the farm. In the late 1980s the farm was sold to Dennis Wright, with the agreement that Frank, Frances and John could stay there until they died. When Frank died in 1994 Frances moved to Coeur d'Alene and John stayed on the farm for a few more years before also moving to Coeur d'Alene. Latour Baldy and Frost Peak can be seen in the distance behind the house.

❾ Hardy and Hayden Loops

These loop roads are remnants of the Yellowstone Trail. Hayden Loop and Hayden Gulch are named for Mathew Hayden who homesteaded land east of here near the intersection of Canyon Rd. and Dredge Rd.

❿ Mission Flats

2.9 miles (If on I-90 mile 37)
Before the Post Falls Dam was constructed in 1906 hay fields covered this area. Coeur d'Alene Mine owners operated a dredge on this flat from 1932 to 1968 pumping millions of tons of mine tailings from the river onto the flat. Tailings are the sand-like wastes that are left after ore is crushed and the metals removed. The portion of I-90 across this flat was built using these tailings. Heron, ducks and other waterfowl can be seen here.

To go to the Cataldo Mission turn right at Dredge Rd. This road is also part of the original Yellowstone Trail, which used to go to the Mission. In 1923 the present Canyon Road bypassed Dredge Rd.

From I-90 take Exit 39

⓫ Old Mission State Park

This 18-acre park, established in 1975, contains an interpretive center and a half-mile historic trail with exhibits and audio stations. Another trail starts at the west cemetery and leads across Mission Flats to where the Coeur d'Alene Indians camped. For information call 208-682-3814.

⓬ Cataldo Mission ⓝ🅡

Coeur d'Alene tribal leader Circling Raven had a vision that one-day men wearing black robes would bring spiritual power and teaching to his people. So, when word of a missionary named Father DeSmet came to the Coeur d'Alenes they eagerly sought him out.

This was the third site for a Catholic mission with the Coeur d'Alenes. Father Anthony Ravalli and the Coeur d'Alenes constructed the Mission between 1850 and 1853. Designed in Greek revival style by Father Ravalli, SJ the Old Mission is the oldest standing building in Idaho. Made of earth and timber, it measures 90 feet high and 40 feet wide. All the upright timbers, more than 25 feet long, were hewn and planed by hand with a broad axe. Wooden pegs were used throughout the church to secure all structural members together. The four-foot thick foundation is made of native stone and held together with mud.

Because of the increased mining and settlement, the Coeur d'Alene Indians moved to DeSmet in 1877. The Mission site was essentially abandoned in 1909. In the late 1920s, the community supported preservation efforts to save the dilapidated church building. In the 1970s, a fundraiser headed by Henry L. Day and aided by a State Legislative grant, provided funds for the complete restoration of the church as a national bicentennial project.

⑬ Parish House NR

Brother Achilles Carfagno, SJ, supervised the construction of the Parish House in 1887-1888. It was restored in 1987.

Go back on Dredge Rd. to Canyon Rd. and turn right (if traveling I-90 continue east toward Wallace)

⑭ Whiteman Lumber Company

32887 Canyon Rd. Intersection of Canyon Rd. and Dredge Rd. on the left (north).

The Whiteman Lumber Company is the oldest continuous operating mill in Idaho. Harry Whiteman built the first sawmill in Fourth of July Canyon in 1929. In 1933 the mill was moved to Cataldo where it was nearly destroyed by the 1933 Flood and then by two arson-suspected fires. After the second fire swept through in 1935 the Sunshine Mining Company helped finance the construction of a new sawmill at this location. Whiteman supplied the Sunshine Mining Company with mine timbers during WWII so the mine could produce strategic metals for the war effort. Harry Whiteman's sons Wesley, Laddie and Keith ran the mill and were principal suppliers for the Sunshine Mining Company until the 1970s. The mill was sold to Brad Corkill in 1988. When the mines shut down, Whiteman Lumber continued to operate because of the mill's circle mill used to cut the large logs. Most of the mills today are specialized for small logs. At one time Whiteman Lumber Company cut as many as 100 different types of underground timbers of various sizes and shapes for the mines.

⑮ Kootenai Cabins

34009 Canyon Rd.

Father Joseph P. Cataldo patented 640 acres of land in this quarter section in 1889. In the early 1900s Glen and Marian Downey settled here. Marian Downey recalled seeing Coeur d'Alene Indians camped in the draw behind their home near the spring. Glen Downey, a well-known local rock mason in the area, built seven roadside tourist cabins along with a bathhouse. The log cabins included hand-laid rock floors and outside they were decorated with brick and rockwork. The location along the highway made it a popular stop for travelers and tourists beginning in the late 1920s until the mid-1960s. Work crews that rented cabins included the State Highway Department which leased the cabins for their engineers and crew while re-aligning the new road between Cataldo and Fourth of July Canyon in 1935. The Downeys lived in the main cabin that also served as an office. The Monteiths purchased the property in 1973 and also lived in this cabin until their new home was built. The cabins have been inundated by floodwaters several times since the 1933 flood. In 2006 only four cabins remain, one is used as a guesthouse by the Monteiths.

⑯ Road Curve

According to local lore the road curve that begins at the Kootenai Cabins and ends at Cataldo is the longest road curve ever constructed on a road in the United States.

⑰ U.S. Hwy 10 Bridge

At the bridge over the Coeur d'Alene River (From I-90 just before Exit 40)

If you look to the left (upriver) at the west bank past the rock outcropping you can see the abutments of the old bridge. During the August 1919 dedication the bridge nearly collapsed when too many people crowded onto it. Many accidents occurred because of an abrupt turn before the bridge so the Yellowstone Trail/U.S. Hwy 10 was re-aligned and the bridge you are traveling on was opened January 1, 1935.

~ Cataldo ~

From I-90 Exit 40

The Coeur d'Alene Indians had a village here known as *Sq'wt'u̱*. Patrick J. Whalen, the first homesteader in this area, platted the town of Cataldo. The town is named for Father Joseph Cataldo, SJ, who served at the Old Mission from 1865 to 1870. Patrick J. Whalen built a log cabin and operated a ferry across the Coeur d'Alene River connecting to the Mullan Road.

When the Oregon Railway and Navigation Company came through in 1889 Whalen discontinued his ferry. The first post office opened in 1893. Mathew Hayden, Whalen's brother-in-law, owned a boarding house and saloon about the same time as Whalen built his two-story Whalen Hotel in 1894. The Whalen Hotel with its large porch and balcony was a favorite stopping-off place for everyone, including Indians. Although Whalen's name is not prominent in local history his brother-in-law's is. Whalen encouraged Mathew Hayden to settle in the area homesteading near Cataldo in Hayden Gulch and at Hayden Lake.

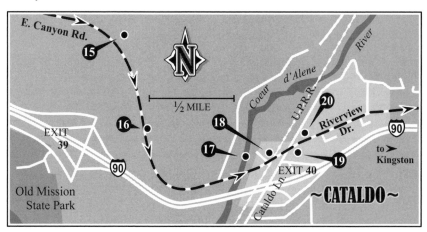

By the early 1900s Cataldo thrived as a supply point with a sawmill, two stores, logging company, hotel, bars and a restaurant. Cataldo was the crossroads for the Yellowstone Trail (Hwy 10), Latour Creek Road and the Oregon Washington Railway and Navigation Company (Union Pacific). A trailhead for the *Trail of the Coeur d'Alenes* is located here.

⓲ Mission Inn
36179 E. Canyon Rd.
John Burns and Art Norris operated the Owl Tavern in this 1934 building. In the mid-1930s George Snyder bought the tavern and by 1938 it was called the Cataldo Beer Parlor. In 1944 he sold it to his brother Tom who ran it until 1976. This was a popular restaurant and bar for loggers and miners. Tom kept a lot of cash on hand and cashed checks for local miners who played poker in the back room. In 1983 it was called Bodine's.

After the intersection the road becomes Riverview Dr.

⓳ Ewing's Inn
36312 E. Canyon Rd., on the right (Cataldo Inn)

The original Ewing's General Store burned so Mr. Ewing rebuilt a little store in front of what was left of the Old Pioneer Hotel in 1947. Ted Snyder bought and ran the business for many years.

㉒ Snyder's Grocery and Cataldo Post Office
On the left after the intersection
Ted and Cleo Snyder built this clapboard frame structure in 1926 and opened the Cataldo Post Office and Snyder's Grocery. In 1947 Joseph and Harriet Miller purchased the grocery and post office and operated it as Miller's Grocery and Post Office. Their son Jim married Dorothy McGillivray and the second generation of Millers purchased the store from his parents in 1956. The year after the 1974 Flood the Cataldo Post Office was moved across the street from the Mission Inn into a new building. The store closed in 1977. Jim and Dorothy Miller and their son Virgil started a restaurant in1983 naming it the 3rd Generation Restaurant because three generations of Millers operated businesses here. They closed after the 1996 Flood.

～ Kingston ～

(If on I-90, Exit 43)
William R. Wallace (no connection to Idaho's first Territorial Governor, also named William Wallace) was a land speculator. On a cold Christmas Day in 1883 he and a partner surveyed this area expecting it to become a major supply center for the Prichard Creek gold diggings. But, with the discovery of silver-lead claims above Canyon Creek (east of here), and the Hunter claim at Mullan, along the main stream of the south fork, he redirected his attention to what would become his namesake, the town of Wallace. Steamboats provided transportation up the Coeur d'Alene River to a landing in Kingston during the late 1800s. Kingston flourished briefly and then declined. A Forest Service ranger station was built at Kingston along French Gulch Road (located on the south side of I-90) in 1934. The ranger station operated until 1973 as the administrative site for the Kingston Ranger District in the Coeur d'Alene National Forest. The building became a private residence in 1979.

Continue on Riverview Dr. across the Coeur d'Alene River Rd. (If on I-90 look to the left or north after Exit 43 for the next three sites)

㉑ Kings Inn
43073 Riverview Dr. on the left
Opening in the late 1800s the Kings Inn has served as a hotel and tavern. Owner Oscar Williams purchased a beautiful oak back-bar, and matching front-bar in 1927. At one time the ceiling was higher creating a gap between

the bar and ceiling. Patrons, primarily loggers and miners, would throw silver coins trying to land them on top of the bar. If they made it they got a free drink. We wonder who came out ahead. Evidence of the many floods along the Coeur d'Alene River is visible on the walls and floor of the inn.

The building was very narrow and partitioned off from a barbershop. Boarders roomed upstairs and took meals downstairs. Originally there was a balcony facing the street on the second floor and a big front porch. During the late 1920s Billie Shewmaker remembers her grandmother Kate Brown ran the Kings Inn and during the winters kids jumped off the balcony into the snow bank below.

22 Kingston Grade School
43143 Riverview Drive on the left
The Kingston Grade School was built in the 1920s to replace the original one-room schoolhouse that was situated next to the river and north of the grade school building. The new school was used for grades 1 through 10. After 10th grade students would transfer to Kellogg High School for grades 11 and 12 until the new Kingston High School was built in 1930 across the road. Grade school children were transferred to the new school in Pinehurst in 1957. The building has been remodeled into apartments with small balconies and a stairway added onto the front of the building.

Behind the Kingston Grade School, east of Riverview Drive on the hillside, a rock retaining wall can be seen. This is a remnant of the original Coeur d'Alene River Road. The hillside road was abandoned when the Forest

Kingston gym on the left, grade school center and high school on the right. Notice the old Coeur d'Alene River Road on the center hillside; circa 1940.

Service constructed the new river road from Kingston to Enaville in the 1940s.

23 Kingston High School
43164 Riverview Dr.

Built in 1930 this building served as a high school until 1955 when students were transferred to Kellogg. The 5,000 square-foot main floor has six classrooms, principal's office, library room, and a 1,200 square-foot auditorium with stage. The 5,000 square-foot basement contained a woodshop, coal furnace, coal storage bin, bathrooms, and classrooms. It changed hands many times before Dr. Stan Shapiro purchased the property in 1991. He found campfire burns on the stage floor and graffiti on the walls. He replaced 150 panes of glass in his extensive restoration work.

Another large building, now gone, was located near here and used for the gymnasium and cafeteria. It was later used by the VFW and was easily spotted from the highway by the large VFW letters painted on the roof.

24 Smith House
Silver Valley Rd. on the right at the first pullout by the speed limit sign

Frank and Elizabeth Smith had 160 acres here in 1883. Mr. Smith and his boys cut virgin timber for the house and floated the logs downriver to the sawmill at Cataldo where they were made into lumber. With horse and wagon they brought the lumber back and built this 2-story, 12-room home between 1890 and 1895. They raised nine children (eight boys and one girl) here. Elizabeth died in the mid-1920s and Mr. Smith lived here and rented part of it until he died in the early 1940s. It remained in the Smith family into the 1950s.

Turn right on Shiplett Overpass, go over I-90, and turn left on Silver Valley Rd. (If on I-90 near the sign for Exit 45)
Jack Shiplett homesteaded up Pine Creek and operated a Standard Oil service station located about 200 yards east of the overpass along old Hwy 10. He was also a Shoshone County Commissioner. When I-90 was built the location of the station was moved to Division Street in Pinehurst. In 2006 it was still operated by Shiplett descendants.

Shiplett & Son Gas Station, circa 1946.

~ Coeur d'Alene Mining District (Silver Valley) ~

Historically the South Fork of the Coeur d'Alene River and the Coeur d'Alene Mountains have been known as the Coeur d'Alene Mining District. The term Silver Valley began to appear in the late 1970s when the mines in the area exceeded the total silver production of the famed Potosi District of Bolivia where silver had been mined since the 1500s. In 1985 the silver production of the district passed the one billion-ounce level and by the end of 1999 the total output had climbed to 1,150,000,000 ounces.

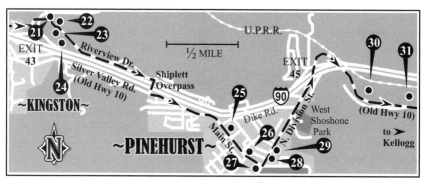

~ Pinehurst ~

(If on I-90 Exit 45)

When Captain John Mullan came through this area it had a large stand of yellow pine and he named the area Pine Prairie. The town, founded in the 1880s, was first called Pine Creek then named Pinehurst by Dr. Thomas Mason. In the western end of the Coeur d'Alene Mining District several mines operated, primarily during WWII, along the East Fork of Pine Creek including the Sidney, Constitution and Highland Surprise Mines. The Sydney Mine included a mill and a tram that extended over the mountain to connect to the Bunker Hill Zinc Plant. The Constitution Mine (later known as Spokane Idaho Mine) also had a mill. The West Fork of Pine Creek produced only small prospects. The Pine Creek Lumber Company mill yard was located where the school and library are today. Hoyt McClain as kid in the 1920s, remembers seeing acres of drying lumber stacked here and that it was a great place for hide-and-seek. The population was 2,500 in the late 1960s.

25 Aro Cabin

708 Main St.

This cabin was originally built on the John and Ailie Aro homestead located on the North Fork of the Coeur d'Alene River a quarter-mile upstream from Enaville and the "Silver Bridge," along the east side of the railroad tracks.

John Aro worked on the railroad and he and his family ran a boarding house with this cabin serving as a sauna for railroad workers. The cabin survived the 1933 Flood but the boarding house did not. After the Flood, the Aros moved down river and decided to turn the sauna into a two-room cabin. After renting the cabin out for many years they planned to burn it down. Instead Vernon Vork bought the cabin and in the late-1970s it was dismantled, numbered, moved and reassembled by Vernon and his son Calvin. When they were taking the cabin apart they found a 6-inch thick layer of dirt and old wool clothing in the ceiling used for insulation. It became Vernon Vork's taxidermy shop until he died in 1989. Later Calvin Vork used it as a saddle shop and then as his workshop. The logs are carved with the names of Aro and Kuisti family members and others who used the cabin.

26 Pine Creek Community Baptist Church NR
210 Main St. (Community Bible Church)
Architects Tourtellotte and Hummel were known for the nostalgic revival of the log cabin. Many Idaho buildings of this design were built by these architects, including a church in Pierce built the same year. The original part of the church was finished with full dovetailed joints in the logs by Finnish miners who were members of the congregation. This log church is one of the finest examples of this type of architecture in the State of Idaho. Howard Simpson was instrumental in organizing the Church and dedicated the building in 1933. Parishioners recall 17-year old June Yearout preaching in this as well as in other churches in the area. It was said that the young woman's quiet manner and angelic appearance contributed to the conversion of many loggers and miners. In about 1940 contractor Dan Etherton jacked up the building, which had no foundation, and used a 'fresno' (a scoop device pulled by horses) to dig out the rocky soil for a foundation and basement. The building also housed the school before the construction of the Pinehurst Grade School.

27 Morbeck Grocery
2 S. Division on the right (Crown Electric)
The Morbeck brothers operated several stores throughout the region. Walter Morbeck built this grocery store in 1937 and operated it until he died in 1967. His wife Vivian kept it open until 1970. Brothers Rusty and James Wilbur purchased the store and renamed it Wilbur's in 1971.

At the 4-way stop turn left onto Division

28 Lee's Grocery and Post Office
3 N. Division (Watts Electric)
Lee McClain opened a grocery store in a 15-foot by 30-foot space with $500

in groceries about 1937. Pinehurst's first post office operated out of Lee's Grocery in 1937 with Lee's wife Nettie McClain serving as the first Postmaster. She held the position for 34 years. In the early 1940s Everett Arvidson opened an appliance store here. During WWII he sold refrigerators without compressors because they were unavailable due to the war. People needed ice for the refrigerators so Everett opened an icehouse, which was also used as a locker plant before home freezers. When the compressors became available he installed them in the refrigerators people had already purchased. In 1966 Sherman and Lawanna Watts bought the appliance business but Arvidson continued to sell televisions from the store.

㉙ Tall Pine Drive-In
203 N. Division
Everett and Lois Arvidson owned the property and the Town brothers built the restaurant in 1957. It was named for the tall pine located in front of the building. The Town brothers thought their wives would run the drive-in but after a year they sold it. The Tall Pine is locally known for their milkshakes.

Go under I-90. You are again traveling on the Yellowstone Trail/U.S. Hwy 10 (Silver Valley Rd.) I-90 bypassed the area from Pinehurst to Smelterville in 1954. (If on I-90 look right for Hwy 10)

㉚ Old Cedar Stumps
(If on I-90 at about mile 45.7 look right (south))
In the late 1890s and early 1900s ranchers logged their property in the valley to provide wood to the mines that were dependent on steam power. Huge quantities of wood were needed to generate steam and the valleys and surrounding hillsides were cleared of all useable timber. These tree stumps are remnants of the cedar groves that were cut down during that time. Washington Water Power Company constructed the world's longest high voltage transmission line to the Coeur d'Alene Mining District in 1903 making it the first mining district in the world to utilize electric power and eliminating the need for steam power generated by wood.

㉛ Page Tailings Pond
If traveling on I-90 mile 46.2 look to the right (south) side (South Fork sewage treatment area)
The Page Mine, located south of the tailing ponds near the head of Silver Creek at the top of Upper Page Road, is associated with mining claims staked in 1886 known as the Corrigan Group. The Federal Mining Company (forerunner of ASARCO) purchased the claims between 1904 and 1908. The ore-body contained lead, silver and zinc. The zinc made separation of the metals difficult and operations were sporadic until a new mill was built in

1926 and the mine placed on a profitable base. The Page Mine operated from 1926 to 1969 and was a leading producer of lead and zinc producing 14.6 million ounces of silver and 270,000 tons of lead. The Page Pond was created during the 1940s to contain mine tailings.

㉜ Three Toots
At the corner where Lower Page Road meets old Hwy 10
This is where the first railroad, the Oregon-Washington Railroad and Navigation Company (Union Pacific), went through this area. When the train rounded the curve west of here the engineer would sound three toots on the whistle so that everyone would clear the tracks.

㉝ The Boat Restaurant
47240 Silver Valley Rd.
The Boat was the first drive-in eating establishment in west Shoshone County. Ike and Vance Corbeill constructed the original Boat for John Penney. L.B. Page and Penney filled in the mouth of the draw, partly with tailings from an old mine dump, taking some two years to complete the fill by hand-sluicing methods. Captain John Penney "launched" (opened) the Boat Saturday, June 21, 1932 with the building portraying the top of a Mississippi riverboat. They sold confections, ice cream, soft drinks and tobacco. In 1933, they were offering chop suey. Mrs. L.B. (Etta) Page managed the Boat for many years. Mr. and Mrs. George Sala bought the Boat in 1948 and in 1952 they sold it to Linville who operated it until the 1960s when he sold it to Tex Galbreath. In 1966 Galbreath tore down and replaced the original Boat with this building.

~ Smelterville ~

(If on I-90 Exit 48)
This area was originally part of Kellogg until the Bunker Hill smelter began operations in 1917. The Bunker Hill Company sold lots and the town began but it was not until 1930 that the name Smelterville was officially selected and the post office was established in Harry Brown's grocery. The highway came through town and Smelterville had a thriving downtown with half a dozen bars, several restaurants and two theatres. In 1956 Smelterville was bypassed by I-90.

㉞ Concrete Roadway
The old concrete you are driving on is a remnant of the original highway paved in 1930. The Yellowstone Trail had been officially renamed U.S. Highway 10 in 1926 (even though people still refer to it as the Yellowstone Trail) and the paving was part of a massive highway program in the late

1920s and 1930s to upgrade the road from Coeur d'Alene to Mullan.

㉟ Smelterville Feed Store
619 Main St.
Built in 1943.

㊱ Johnson's Café
316 Main St. (Sterling Silver Café)
Hazel and Oscar Johnson operated a cafe in the 1940s and 1950s.

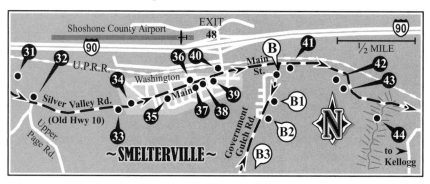

㊲ Harry's Grocery
301 Main St. (Happy Landing Bar)
In 1929 Harry and Vi Brown leased the building from Walt Reynolds and opened a store. It was not yet an official town and Harry Brown was known to stand up on the grocery store counter to give speeches promoting the new town of Smelterville. Vi wrote to Washington, D.C. for information on getting a post office for the town. It was suggested they change the name to Van Rena but Smelterville won the vote and the first post office was established in Harry's Grocery. Brown hired his sister Allene Waggoner as the first postmaster for a short time then Vi became postmaster. In 1932 the Browns moved out and "Peg Leg" Pete (because he had a peg leg), opened a bar called the Black Cat in this building.

㊳ Wayside Market and Smelterville Post Office
215, 217 and 223 Main St.
Postmaster Vi Brown was watching out the window for the train carrying the mail when one day she saw her husband Harry digging a hole. She asked him what he was doing and he said, "Why, I am building my store." Harry Brown built this complex, which included a store, a post office with living quarters and a drug store in 1931. Harry Brown lost the store during the Depression but three generations of women related to Harry worked in the

Smelterville Post Office: Harry's sister and her daughter, Harry's wife and her sister, Harry's daughter and granddaughter. In 1946 Bill and Hazel Noyen bought the building and expanded the store several times during the 58 years they owned it. In the late 1960s the post office was expanded into the drug store. Their son Gary took over the store and in 2004 sold it to Doug Burmeister.

215 Main St. was used as the Pix Theater and later became a bar called the Cinnabar, then it was used as the Eagles Lodge and finally it became the local roller-skating rink. Phyllis Allingson remembers going to work at the theater so she could earn a bag of popcorn and a free movie for sweeping the floors after the afternoon matinees. The front top of the building has been removed.

㊴ Rostead Dance Hall and Apartments
125 Main St.
Before the 1930s this building was a dance hall where families came and children often slept outside on benches piled with coats while the parents danced inside. In the late 1930s it was converted to apartments. During WWII many war brides lived here while they waited for their husbands to return. Billie Shewmaker recalled that after the war, when she and her husband lived here, refrigerators were scarce so they used an orange crate mounted to the back wall outside with a wet gunnysack over the crate to keep food cool.

㊵ Log House
106 Main St.
Built in 1928 this log cabin was occupied by Mrs. Connolly and her two daughters Molly and Jean Murray.

Continue on Hwy 10

━━━━━━━━━━━━━━━━━━━━━━━━━━━━━━━━━━━━━━

Ⓑ Government Gulch Side Trip
0.4 miles, turn right on Government Gulch Rd.
Government Gulch may have been so named because during the mining wars in the 1890s some of the soldiers camped up this draw.

Ⓑ1 Bunker Hill Assay Office
606 Government Gulch Rd. (Silver Valley Lab)
Chemist and research engineers' offices, which had previously been located at the Bunker Hill Mine, the Lead Smelter and Zinc Plant, were consolidated into this assay office in the 1960s.

Government Gulch is on the right where the Zinc Plant was located. Later the Fertilizer plant was also located up this gulch. The first section of Silver King School is visible up Government Gulch on the left side of the road. On the left is Sweeney Heights, Bunker Hill slag pile in the foreground and the Smelter. Highway 10 and the Union Pacific Railroad are in the foreground; circa 1945.

ⓑ₂ Silver King School
797 Government Gulch Rd.
Ore laden trains heading to the Zinc Plant passed the back of this 1920 school providing a distraction for the students, especially the boys. In 1929 there were 125 pupils. An addition was added in 1949 and a year later four classrooms, bus garage and gym were built. In 1952 Silver King became part of Smelterville. The building was closed in 1982. School District 391 uses the property for a bus garage and maintenance area.

ⓑ₃ Bunker Hill Zinc Plant
Continue 0.5 miles and turn around at the gate
The Bunker Hill Electrolytic Zinc Plant operated here from 1928 to 1981 refining zinc ore by an electrolytic process. Bunker Hill produced 17% of U.S. primary lead, 15% of refined slab zinc and 15% of refined silver. The buildings still standing were used as a warehouse and an ore processing building (the long structure). All the other zinc plant facilities were torn down, including six 2 and 3-story Colonial style homes across the road from the Zinc Plant which housed top plant staff.

Go back to Hwy 10 and turn right.

At the intersection of Government Gulch Rd. and Hwy 10 set odometer to 0

㊶ Sweeney Mill and Concrete Flume

0.1 mile on the right at the intersection of Government Gulch and Hwy 10 (If on I-90 Milepost 48)

Only remnants of foundations and a concrete flume from the Sweeney Mill are visible. The town site and mill were named for their founder Charles Sweeney. He consolidated most of the major mines of the Coeur d'Alenes into the Federal Mining and Smelting Company. In 1901 the $55,274 mill at Sweeney opened partially equipped and handled 400 tons of ore a day. In 1903 Washington Water Power contracted the building of six brick power stations, each eighteen feet square and thirty feet in height with step-down transformers providing power for the mines between Sweeney and Burke.

Billie Shewmaker recalled that in 1939, just before graduating high school, she and friends went to the closed down Sweeney Mill during the night. Each kid took turns standing on the conveyor belt that ran up several stories to the top of the mill while another kid ran the crank. The trick was to jump off of the belt before the conveyor belt looped around.

㊷ Smelter Plant and Bunker Hill Slag Pile

0.3-0.4 miles, Hwy 10 (If on I-90 mile 48.5 to 49.5 look to the right (south))

Just before the incline on Highway 10 there is a road inside the fence on the right that leads to the former smelter site. This was initially a railroad line into the Smelter and up to the Zinc Plant in Government Gulch. The large mound to the north is what is left of the Bunker Hill Smelter slag pile. Silica, iron, cadmium, lead, arsenic and small amounts of lime made up the black slag pile which is now covered with dirt and has grass growing on it. East of, and adjacent to the slag pile is the Bunker Hill tailings pond containing waste product from the milling operation and some mine wastes. The slag pile and the tailings pond are the Superfund Site's central impound area. Before the Bunker Hill complex closed in 1982, the Company produced between 15 and 20 percent of the U.S. requirements for refined lead and zinc, each metal with hundreds of uses. Nothing remains of the Lead Smelter.

The Lead Smelter operated from 1917 to 1981 smelting ores and concentrates from local mines and mines located in Canada, Alaska, South America, Australia and Greenland. The smelter processed the ore and concentrates by blending, roasting and blast furnacing. The molten blast furnace metal was further processed (skimmed) to remove various metals, mainly antimony, copper, silver and gold. In 64 years the Smelter produced over five million tons of refined lead and 486 million troy ounces of refined silver. The Electrolytic Zinc Plant turned out 2,982,000 tons of refined zinc in its 53-year life.

Two concrete smoke stacks, one 610-feet tall at the Zinc Plant and another 715-feet tall at the Smelter Plant were constructed in 1977 at a cost of $11.5 million to meet clean air standards for sulfur dioxide. In May 1996 the smoke stacks were toppled because the cost of maintaining the aircraft warning strobe lights every 200 feet was too great.

43 ▶ The site of Bunker Hill management housing
On the right as the road curves the houses were up on the hillside
The Bunker Hill Company built and owned about 10 large homes on this hillside for their middle management personnel so they could be close to the job.

44 ▶ Deadwood Gulch
1.1 miles, Hwy 10
The second gulch to the right is Deadwood Gulch where many working class people settled. The smoke from the smelter was so bad that gardens could not grow. At the mouth of the gulch Keesey had a general grocery and gas station and Ross Oil had a bulk storage plant for Shell Oil products. For about a quarter of a mile on both sides of the road, ore concentrates were stored in the open.

If on I-90 take Exit 51, tour sites 1 through 6, turn right on Division St. and start with the Chamber of Commerce/Kellogg-Wardner Depot at 10 Station Ave. on page (7-25)

~ Kellogg ~
First named Milo, the town site of Kellogg was established in 1885. A year later its name was changed to honor Noah Kellogg, discoverer of the Bunker Hill Mine. In 1887, the Coeur d'Alene Railway and Navigation Company built the first railroad into Kellogg. The Bunker Hill Company was the main employer and provided electric power and water for Wardner and Kellogg for many years. The Company also built the first school, the Wardner hospital and the Kellogg Y.M.C.A. Kellogg became the center of the Coeur d'Alene Mining District. In 1912 the population was 1,650 and by 1917 grew to 3,500 with 1,000 students and 36 teachers in the school system.

Page 7-22

❶ Bunker Hill Crusher Plant and Mine Dump Station

1.9 miles, Hwy 10, south of McKinley Ave.

This area is the old Bunker Hill Mine yard. Look to the right (south) on the hillside, the tall concrete structure with the partially burned roof was the dump station/Crusher Plant for mine ore from the Bunker Hill Mine. This is where the ore was first dumped, crushed to gravel size and then went into a concrete bin from which it was pulled into the mill (concentrator). There was a conveyor over McKinley Ave. to the concentrating plant located on the north side of the road. To the east was the compressor to make compressed air for drills used underground. The Nordburgh compressor was relocated behind the Staff House Museum.

❷ Bunker Hill Warehouse and Engineering Building

1021 McKinley Ave.

On the hillside behind this 1956 building is the main portal of the Bunker Hill Mine. The Kellogg Tunnel extends a little over two miles from this site to the ore-bodies beneath Wardner. The tunnel was completed after five years of work in 1902 and eliminated the need for the tram from Wardner. The mine employed 400 of the 2,100 Bunker Hill employees. At various times underground workers numbered as high as 800. The Bunker Hill was twice as large as any two of the other 100 mines that operated in the Silver Valley. In 1982 Bunker Hill ceased operations after 94 years. Bob Hopper bought the mine and operates it on a much smaller scale.

❸ Bunker Hill Assay Office

1020 McKinley Ave.

Built in 1962-63 it was used by Bunker Hill for only a short time until they consolidated assay offices up Government Gulch.

❹ Bunker Hill Company Main Office

834 McKinley Ave.

From the 1890s until the 1990s Bunker Hill's main office was located here. During the labor troubles in 1899 the miners blew up the office along with the mill. Bunker Hill lost all its records. The office was rebuilt and has been added onto many times. Although Bunker Hill closed in 1982 about 75 people worked here into the 1990s.

❺ Staff House Museum

820 W. McKinley Ave.

This Colonial Revival house was built for Stanly and Estelle Easton in 1906. Easton began his career with Bunker Hill as a laborer in the mine in 1897. He served in an engineering capacity, and later became manager of operations in 1903, first vice president and general manager in 1927, moved up to the presidency in 1933 and then served as chairman of the board from 1954 until 1958. In 1923 Stanly, Estelle and their three daughters moved to Coeur d'Alene and the house was converted to a residence for single staff of the Bunker Hill Company. In 1940 it was moved to this location from just down the street. After the closure of Bunker Hill the building remained empty until it was given to the Shoshone County Mining and Smelting Museum in 1986. The Museum features mining and smelter equipment and historical and cultural exhibits. For information call 208-786-4141.

 Lincoln School
514 McKinley Ave.
The Lincoln School was dedicated on Lincoln's birthday in 1906. A pair of carved griffins above the doorway appear to guard the school entrance.

Turn left (north) at Hill St.

Notice the metal sculptures
Local sculptor David Dose created eleven sculptures throughout the town.

After crossing the South Fork of the Coeur d'Alene River turn right on the Frontage Rd. and then right on Division

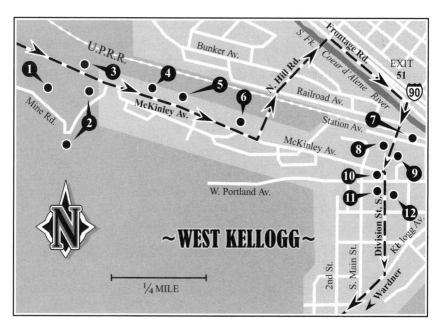

❼ Kellogg-Wardner Depot

10 Station Ave. (Chamber of Commerce)

The Oregon Railway & Navigation Company constructed this brick passenger depot between 1909 and 1914. It was built to replace the Wardner passenger depot but its name changed to the Kellogg-Wardner Depot in 1914 to reflect the growing importance of Kellogg. Union Pacific Railroad owned the building until 1993 when the Wallace Branch of the Union Pacific ceased operation. When the railroad was going to tear down the building, community members requested that it be saved and in the 1990s the City of Kellogg assumed ownership of the depot. In 2002 the depot underwent historic renovation to become the Historic Silver Valley Chamber of Commerce and a railroad museum. For information call 208-784-0821 or www.historicsilvervalleychamberofcommerce.com

❽ Owens & Atkins

2 S. Division St. (In Cahoots)

This one-time confectionery and 5 and 10-cent store with a soda fountain downstairs was a popular hangout for young people in the early part of the twentieth-century. But by the 1980s it was the Kopper Keg. In 1991 it was one of the 58 establishments shut down by an FBI crack down on gambling and prostitution. About 150 FBI agents from throughout the West descended on the Silver Valley in more than 70 vehicles, making this the biggest police raid in the state's history. The strike teams hit mostly bars in Shoshone County as well as Elks Clubs in Wallace and Kellogg. The agents seized $544,000 worth of gambling machines and other devices. What appeared to be a crackdown on illegal gambling in the Silver Valley was actually an evidence-gathering operation and the culmination of a two-year investigation into the Shoshone County Sheriff's Department.

A grand jury in Boise indicted the sheriff in 1992 on federal charges that he not only ignored prostitution and gambling operations but that he accepted bribes and prevented state and local law enforcement from intervening. As the first trial got underway in Moscow, the defense argued that the sheriff was being used as a scapegoat for more than 100 years of blatant, illegal activity in the Silver Valley. His attorney noted that Shoshone County sheriffs have always faced the serious dilemma of upholding the law and being booted out of office in the next election or ignoring the law to keep constituents happy with the possibility of facing criminal charges. The first trial ended in a hung jury. The second trial, held again in Moscow in 1993, resulted in the sheriff's acquittal.

❾ Noah Kellogg's Homestead

105 S. Division St. (Mansion On The Hill Bed and Breakfast) on the left
Noah Kellogg and his wife Dora homesteaded here in 1893. After 1897 it
served as a boarding house under several owners. In 1944 John George
purchased some of Noah's property and rebuilt the home for his family. Dana
Musick purchased the property and in 1998 began restoring the home using
old photos and information gathered from the John George family.

❿ John Mullan Statue 🆖

Division St. and McKinley Ave. on the right

⓫ Post Office

302 S. Division St. on the right
Built in 1937 by the Depression era Works Progress Administration this post
office was chosen as the one post office in the whole state of Idaho to receive
a mural. Above the postmaster's door is a mural of Noah Kellogg with his
burro painted in 1941 by Fletcher Martin. This is Martin's second design, the
first depicted two miners carrying a third out on a stretcher. Several
community groups rejected this "Mine Rescue" design because of its
suggestion of disaster.

⓬ Pleasant Homes

305 S. Division St. across from the Post Office
This 3-story house was a boarding house for single miners and newcomers,
especially Italian and Norwegian immigrants.

Continue up Division St. for about 2 miles

~ Wardner ~

The Coeur d'Alene tribe had a village in the area of Wardner. In 1885 the
town was named Kentuck. That same year Noah Kellogg, or as legend has it
his jackass, discovered the outcropping of lead-silver ore here that became the
Bunker Hill and Sullivan Mine. Founded in the fall of 1887 the town was
named after James Wardner who became one of Kellogg's partners. In 1890 a
10,000-foot long aerial tramway was built to transport mine ore from the
mountainside above Wardner to the mill in the Kellogg area.

In 1891 Mrs. Hood was in her Wardner home, located under the tram, when a
bucket of ore slid down the cable, hit another bucket and dropped it 70 feet
onto Mrs. Hood, killing her. Two other women in the house survived. In
1902 Bunker Hill completed the two-mile Kellogg Tunnel and hauled ore
from it to the mill, doing away with the tramway. Mining crews were

gradually shifted to the lower tunnel. Many businesses in Wardner opened stores in Kellogg to accommodate the increased population of Kellogg. The term Twin City was used by several businesses including Twin City Furniture, Twin City Hardware, and Twin City Fuel. A slaughterhouse, which produced most of Wardner's meat products, was located up this gulch. On the left you'll see a street sign saying Slaughterhouse Gulch. In 1912 the population was 1,650, the same as Kellogg, but by 1916 it had declined to 1,350.

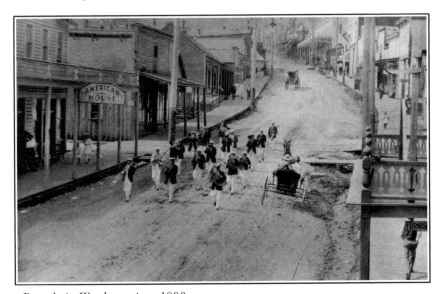

Parade in Wardner, circa 1890.

⓭ Red Men's Hall

Between 314 and 330 Main St.
Built as a men's club, the building was temporarily used in the 1930s as a school while a modern brick grade school was under construction.

⓮ Wardner Gift Shop and Museum

650 Main St.
The museum building was built about 1888 and served as a second-hand furniture store and boarding house. Chuck Peterson purchased the building and two lots for $100 from Dan Chisholm and in 1982 opened the Gift Shop and Museum. In 1995, Wardner became the first Silver Valley town to be on the Internet. A couple of local entrepreneurs set up a webpage, putting the camera in a birdhouse on the upper right hand corner of the City Hall providing a live telecast of the Wardner Gift Shop and Museum. The webcam attracted stories on NPR, the front page of the Spokesman Review and Grit

magazine. For several years, tour buses filled with Japanese tourists would stop at the gift shop to meet the long-time mayor of Wardner, Chuck Peterson, and wave at their friends back in Japan. Unfortunately vandals destroyed the camera.

⑮ Bunker Hill Mine

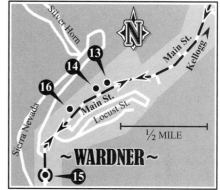

Up this road a few thousand yards
This is the site of the original Bunker Hill and Sullivan Mine workings beyond the gate. Public access is restricted. This road was the access road to Jackass Ski Bowl, which later became a part of Silver Mountain Ski Resort. Public access today is via the gondola.

Turn around and go back down Main St.

⑯ Colonial Tavern

Main St. on the left (Shady Lady Saloon)
This is one of the oldest buildings in Wardner. It was built in the early 1900s replacing a burned out frame building built in about 1889. The rock wall is a common feature of many of the buildings in this community.

Continue down Division St. and turn left on Kellogg's Main St.

This is the older part of Kellogg. We suggest parking near Market and Main and walking the area.

The Alpine Village theme was developed when the community was facing an economic downturn after Bunker Hill closed in 1982. As residents looked at ways to draw tourists into Kellogg they talked to other communities that used themes to enhance their image. After much debate it was decided that Kellogg would take on the appearance of an Alpine Village. As time goes on businesses are restoring their original facades.

⑰ 401 Main St. (Shoshone News Press)

The Wardner News was established in 1886 in Wardner and the Kellogg News was established in 1911 operating out of the McConnell Hotel in Kellogg. By 1914 the weekly papers combined and were listed in the City Directory all at this address under three names: Kellogg-Wardner News, Wardner-Kellogg News and Wardner News Kellogg. In the mid 1980s it became the Shoshone News Press.

⓲ 402 Main St. (Silver Needle)
In 1918 a blacksmith shop was in the back portion of this building. In 1928 the whole building housed a car repair shop and dealership.

⓳ 322 Main St. (Silver Needle)
Built in 1926 this building was also an automobile dealership and garage.

⓴ Federated Church
314 Main St.
Although this building wasn't built until 1923 the Congregational and Methodist churches were established in Wardner in the early 1890s. In 1902 the Plymouth Congregational Church moved to Kellogg followed by the Methodist Church in 1915. In 1932 the two became the Federated Church. In the 1990s the Federated Church building became the Masonic Temple. In 2004 the building sold to the Sterling Mining Company.

㉑ Sears Store
313 Main St. (Silver Valley Appliance and Mercantile)
Built in 1948 this building served as a Sears store until the late 1990s.

㉒ 311 Main St. (Shoshone County Food Bank)
In 1916 William McKinney ran a hardware business here. It also served as a second-hand store in 1928.

㉓ Blackwell Reminder Printing Co.
309 Main St. (Progressive Printing, Inc.)
Built about 1920 the northern part of the building housed Blackwell's Daily Reminder Printing and from the 1930s to 1950s they published a mimeographed paper containing mostly advertising. In the 1930s and 1940s the southern part of the building was the John H. Gaby Men's Store featuring clothing, dry cleaning, and later a Laundromat.

㉔ 307 Main St.
In 1918 the Kellogg-Wardner Business College was located on the second floor. They advertised that they had two faculty members and a "Night School for Foreigners" along with Rational Typewriting, the Palmer Method of Business Writing, shorthand and bookkeeping. From the 1930s into the 1960s it housed the Liberty Theater. A small part was, for many years, the office of Mike Waggoner, a fuel (coal & slab wood) provider. This is part of the I.O.O.F. building. By 1928 the Liberty Theatre took over most of the building.

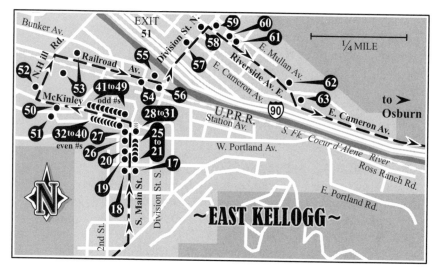

25▸ Odd Fellows Hall
301-305 Main St.

This brick complex was built about 1890. 305 Main St. was the entrance to the Odd Fellows Hall (I.O.O.F.). In the early 1900s it became Liberty Billiards and the Odd Fellows Hall moved into the upper floor where they had lodge rooms, a kitchen and some apartments. About 1915, 303 Main became Joe & Henry's Liberty Billiards and in the 1960s it became Dick & Floyd's Liberty Billiards and then Liberty Billiards. The building had a game room and bar in the back portion and a soda fountain with food in the front. In 2006 the soda fountain was still in use. In the 1940s, Bud Moe printed a small mimeographed paper called "The Eye Opener" in a space on the second floor. The shop at 301 Main on the corner was Mann's Variety Store and later became a stationery store. The basement of the I.O.O.F. was a skating rink in the 1930s but is best remembered when it was the K Klub, a popular dance club for teenagers in the late 1940s and 1950s. It continued to be used as a dance hall for many years.

26▸ Stone's Grocery
302 Main St. (Sass Jewelry)

This building housed many businesses over the years including Samuel McGregor Billiards and a saloon. Sass Jewelry came to Kellogg in 1944 and operated in several locations before moving here in 1987.

27▶ McConnell Hotel

212 Main St.
Built about 1912 this block was referred to as the McConnell block. The Hotel had all the modern amenities for that time. The Seely family owned the building for 52 years until 1967. This four-story building housed the J. E. Jones Brokerage Corp., local and New York Stocks and later became Pennaluna & Company Brokerage. For many years the V.F.W. held their meetings here.

28▶ 211 Main St. (Main Exchange)

The Princess Theatre was located upstairs. In the 1930s and 1940s Oscar Reiman's pharmacy held contests for high school kids to win $5.00.

29▶ 209 Main St.

The 1916 city directory listed a drug store owned by Emil Bonham at this location.

30▶ 207 Main St.

A cigar and confectionery store operated here from 1918 into the 1930s.

31▶ Seelig Block

205 to 201 Main St.
This block was built about 1912 with Seelig Grocery on the corner at 201 Main St. Beginning in the 1910s, 205 Main St. housed several clothing stores including Baker Clothing Co., Morrows Department Store and in the 1960s Patano's Men's Wear. A barbershop was located at 203 Main in 1918. As early as the 1930s and into the 1950s the Korner Klub, a nightclub with live music and dancing, operated in the basement. Buster Brown and the Curly Heads performed here. A fire in 1951 destroyed part of the building.

Turn left on McKinley Ave.
McKinley Ave. was part of Hwy 10 until 1933.

32▶ 103 to 117 McKinley

If you look at the roofline of this 1903 brick building you can see architectural features that tie these storefronts together. Drugstores, billiards, restaurants, soft drink and grocery stores operated here. The 1916 Directory lists the Wardner Hospital on this block.

33▶ Brayer Bakery

106 McKinley Ave. (Uptown Hair Studio)

John Brayer built this building in 1909 and it was called the City Bakery and Confectionery. The building then became Pat's Grocery. During the 1970s and 1980s it was Ed's Rexall Drug.

34▶ 108 McKinley

In 1912 the Elgin Creamery Company Ice Cream operated here and then in 1915 it was a five-and-dime store. Between 1918 and 1928 a saloon was in the storefront with a stage business in the back.

35▶ Worstell-Thornhill Company

110 McKinley (Twin City Furniture)

The Thornhill Company was established in 1885 in Kellogg and sold furniture, carpets, crockery and household goods and furnishings. This building was built about 1910 as the Worstell-Thornhill Furniture & Hardware. The proprietor, Mr. Thornhill, was also a local mortician. In 1960 Jon Pierce and Ewing Little purchased the business and renamed it Twin City Furniture and Hardware, later dropping hardware from the name.

Parade in front of 103-117 McKinley Ave., about 1915.

36▶ 114 McKinley (Silver Valley Alternative School)

In 1916 Kellogg Hardware Company occupied the building. In the 1960s Sass Jewelry was located here.

37▶ Stein's Grocery

115 McKinley Ave.

Papesh Meat Company was an early occupant of this 1910 building. Ed

Stein purchased the business in 1929. During the Depression he kept at least two men working by rotating them in the meat market and on the delivery truck. Stein operated a grocery until 1950 when he sold to his four sons. In 1955 they moved to a new store on Cameron Ave.

㊳ White's Shoes
116 McKinley (Meister Burger)
White's Shoe Shop moved from across the street to this location in the mid-1910s. In 1918 White's moved to Spokane and a telegraph office occupied this space.

㊴ Vang's Shoe Shop
117 1/2 McKinley Ave. (Bitterroot Mercantile)
Ole Martin Vang moved from St. Maries to Kellogg in 1914 and rejoined White's Shoe Shop in Kellogg. When White moved to Spokane, Ole opened his shop in 1918 here. Ole retired and his son Lloyd took over the business. Retirement didn't agree with Ole and he opened the Central Shoe Shop in 1937 in competition with his son and remained open only a few years. In 1987 before Lloyd retired at age 84 he was the oldest active businessman in Kellogg.

㊵ 118 to 122 McKinley
Between 1914 and 1916 Yost Garage Co. was located in 120-122 McKinley. They advertised as an auto garage, general blacksmithing and woodworking along with tires and tire repairing. Between 1918 and 1928 the Kellogg Auto Center occupied these storefronts including a garage and auto showroom. During WWII the auto showroom at 118 McKinley became the Office of Price Administration (OPA) where residents picked up their ration cards. Within a week after the end of the war, the owner of the auto center forced the OPA to move so he could reopen his show room.

㊶ 123 to 125 McKinley Ave.
Cement block was used to build these two buildings. The First National Bank at 125 McKinley was built in 1909 with an large arched front window. Later it was J.N. Mattmiller Agency advertised as "Kellogg's Department Store of Quality Insurance and Real Estate". A jewelry store and mining office were located at 123 McKinley between 1915 and 1918.

㊷ Twin City Hardware
124 McKinley Ave.
Built after 1915.

Looking east on McKinley Ave., circa 1950.

43 Y.M.C.A.
200 McKinley Ave.
The Bunker Hill & Sullivan Mining Company built the Y.M.C.A in 1910. The 1917 city directory listed it as a $40,000 fully equipped facility. It operated for 70 years with the company providing much of its operating expenses. Almost everyone who worked for the Bunker Hill had a membership in the Y. It included a bowling alley, gymnasium, swimming pool, reading room, boxing ring and Bunker Hill's hiring office. Until the 1990s, a spacious room on the second floor housed the Masonic Hall.

44 Rio Club
201 McKinley Ave.
Built around 1900 this building housed the Rio Club Bar and dance hall downstairs with hotel rooms upstairs. It changed owners throughout the century and went from hotel to boarding house to brothel. It re-opened in 2004 as the Kellogg Rio Hotel.

45 McKinley Inn Hotel
206 McKinley on the right past the Elks
Built about 1918.

46 211 McKinley (Senior Center)
J.C. Penney operated here.

47 213 McKinley (Inland Lounge)

This building was built in 1910 as a billiards parlor.

48 215 McKinley (Wah Hing Chinese Restaurant)

Built in 1911 it served as a millinery and florist. In 1928 a restaurant and variety store operated here.

49 Melody Lane

217-219 McKinley
Built about 1911 it was a saloon and dance hall. During the 1940s it became Melody Lane and continued as a dance hall and saloon.

50 Robinson Motors

323 McKinley Ave.
Built in 1947 this block-long building was originally Robinson Motors, which sold Studebaker cars.

51 Union Legion Building

On the hillside (Kellogg Bowling Alley)
Built prior to 1915 for the Wardner Industrial Union and the American Legion it included a 12-lane bowling alley, bar and two large meeting halls upstairs, one for each organization. The Wardner Industrial Union owned 60% and the American Legion owned 40%. Bunker Hill advanced the money to build it and kept an employee on the board to break any ties concerning the building. Bunker Hill was soon paid back with the profits from slot machines. Farragut sailors during WWII frequented this hall for dances. The building was sold in the late 1980s.

Turn right on Hill St. (To view sites 1-6 on page 7-23 continue straight)

To your right is Teeters Field, named for one of the early superintendents of the school district.

52 Scout House

4 S. Hill St. on the left
Built in 1944 by the Bunker Hill Company and the American Legion this building is constructed of logs donated from Bunker Hill's waste log pile. A large number of logs were used in the mines and when they were replaced they were put into a pile. Good ones were selected for this building. The American Legion Kellogg Post 36 has sponsored Kellogg's Scout troop since 1919. In 1953 Bunker Hill deeded the property to the City of Kellogg

for the children of Kellogg. The Boy Scouts and the community continue to use the building.

Turn right on Railroad Ave.

Bull Pen Site
Along Railroad Ave.
During the mining war of 1899 Martial Law was declared and Federal troops rounded up and guarded 528 miners in a makeshift prison called a bull pen. The Union miners were accused of highjacking a Northern Pacific train loaded with 90 cases of stolen dynamite and blowing up the Bunker Hill concentrator plant and office in Kellogg.

Union Pacific Freight Depot
21 Railroad Ave. (Excelsior Cycle & Sport Shop)
This wooden freight depot was built between 1909 and 1914 for the Oregon Railway & Navigation Company (OR&N) or its successor the Oregon Washington Railroad Company, which were affiliated with the Union Pacific Railroad. It was built on the west end of the first Wardner OR&N Depot and the two buildings stood side by side for many years as the freight warehouses for the thriving "Twin City" mining towns of Wardner and Kellogg. Bob Douglas recalls delivering mail from the depot up to the post office on S. Division St. two times daily and operating a Railway Express out of the depot in the 1950s when the Union Pacific owned it. The building was sold to R.D. Lane and then to Bob Douglas who donated the depot to the City of Kellogg. It was used as a recycling center and later as a city storage area. In November 1999 the depot was leased to Excelsior Cycle. Although extensive remodeling was done to make the depot suitable for a bicycle shop, care was taken to retain the character of the building using existing features such as freight doors, arches, original window frames and windows.

55 16 to 1 Saloon
14 Railroad Ave. (Longshot Saloon)
Built in 1892 this building served as the 16 to 1 Saloon until 1914. It is rumored that the saloon was a house of ill repute. It was the Depot Grocery from 1916 to 1943 and from 1944 to 1989 it was the Tip Top Bar.

Trail of the Coeur d'Alenes
The Oregon Railway & Navigation Company raced against its rival, the Coeur d'Alene Railway & Navigation Company, to build a railroad into the Coeur d'Alene mining region from Spokane, Washington. In November 1889 the track reached Kellogg-Wardner where a wooden passenger/freight depot

was built. The OR&N Company merged into the Oregon Washington Railroad Company by February 1911 and later became the Union Pacific Railroad. The Wallace branch extended to Wallace and operated until 1993. In the 1990s work began on converting the Union Pacific Railroad grade into a rail-to-trail. The trail is open to non-motorized users year-around. In the winter when snow is sufficient the section of trail from Wallace to Mullan is open to snowmobiles. The entire *Trail of the Coeur d'Alenes* is handicapped accessible.

Turn left on Division St., continue under the freeway

This part of Kellogg is known as Sunnyside or Downtown. The area around McKinley Ave., where you just came from, is called Uptown. When I-90 came through in the 1960s it split the town.

57▸ Yellowstone Trail Garage
1 W. Cameron (Dave Smith Motors)
The Yellowstone Trail Garage was located here beginning in the late 1920s. It was owned and operated by Albert Wellman, Sr. and later by his sons, Albert Jr. and Charlie Wellman. The garage sold Dodge and Plymouth products. The gas pumps faced Cameron Ave. which was the highway. In the 1970s Dave Smith moved his automobile dealership from Wallace to Kellogg. He died in a scuba diving accident in 1994 and his children continued the business.

Yellowstone Trail Garage during the late 1930s.

58> Rena Theatre

310 N. Division
Built in the 1930s the Rena Theatre was part of the Simon's Amusement Company, which started in 1915-1918. They had theatres in Wallace, Kellogg and Mullan.

Turn right (east) on Riverside Ave. Until 1933, the route you just traveled through Kellogg was part of Hwy 10 and followed Riverside to Division to McKinley. In 1933, Cameron Ave. became the highway route (called the Kellogg By-Pass) and remained so until bypassed in the 1960s by I-90.

59> Lang's Grocery Store

401 N. Division Northeast corner of Riverside & Division Streets
This brick building started as Lang's Grocery store. It served several businesses over the years including Brack Motor Supply, Propane By Lane, O.K. Rubber Welders tire store and tire repair shop and TeleSystems, Inc. TeleSystems was one of two competing cable TV companies serving the Silver Valley. In 1998 the two companies were racing to bring in high speed Internet service to the Silver Valley in order to convince customers to switch providers. Because of the competition, Kellogg and Wardner got high speed Internet long before Coeur d'Alene. Cable TV cost $17.95 a month from either provider. A few years later, when USAMedia purchased TeleSystems cable TV rates doubled in a single month.

60> American Lutheran Church

Elm & Riverside Ave.
The office area and the back section were constructed in 1939 with living quarters for the pastor and his family upstairs. In 1948 the sanctuary on the east side was added. Volunteers from this church also built the Our Savior Lutheran Church in Pinehurst. In 1964 the Fellowship Hall and Sunday school rooms were added on the west side. Until the mid 1970s area mining companies provided free bus service for children attending Sunday school swelling the attendance to 225.

61> Pik Kwik Grocery

104 E. Riverside Ave. (St. Vincent de Paul)
The Chaffee family operated the Pik Kwik Grocery for many years.

62> Gas Station

218 E. Riverside Ave.
Known as Guy Belle's place, it was owned and maintained as a service

station until the day he died. Belle's widow, Velma, continued to live in an apartment on the second floor of the building.

Hwy 10 passed behind the Miner's Hat but the road now dead ends. Turn right in front of the Miner's Hat then left on Cameron Ave.

⑥ Miner's Hat

300 E. Cameron (If on I-90 mile 51.9 on the left or north side (Miner's Hat Realty)

Built in 1937 to replicate a miner's hat, this was Kellogg's first drive-in restaurant. Mrs. Etta Page, proprietor and cook, was known throughout Shoshone and Kootenai Counties for her famous Coney Islands, caramel milkshakes and banana cream pies. In 1967 Ted Reynolds and Don Rumpel opened a new real estate office and called it Miner's Hat Realty.

The Miner's Hat, circa 1955.

⑥ Crystal Gold Mine

51931 Silver Valley Rd. (Cameron Ave. changes to Silver Valley Rd.) (If on I-90 mile 51.9 on the left or north side)

In 1879 Tom Irwin, a gold prospector, discovered a gold-bearing vein near Montgomery Gulch. He became the first miner to work a quartz vein in Shoshone County. In 1881 he blasted the hillside down to hide the mine, leaving his track, ore car and tools inside with the intention of coming back. No one knows where he came from, where he went or what happened to him and his crew to keep them from returning. The land around the mine was eventually homesteaded. In the 1960s an I-90 road construction crew discovered the mine and moved the freeway away from the site. In 1991, the owner of the property noticing water seeping from the bank hoped to find a spring and dug in with a backhoe and partially discovered the mine portal. In 1996, Bill Land, a retired miner, and his wife Judy bought the mine, cleaned up the property and began operating a mine tour for tourists. Evidence of blasting done over 100 years ago is still visible. The mine is open year-round for tours. Call 208-783-4653 for information and hours.

ⓒ Elk Creek School Side Trip

(If you are on I-90, milepost 53.5 to your left or north side). For a closer look at the school turn left on Butts Rd. (the road before the school), go one block to Elk Creek Rd. (the original Hwy 10 alignment) and turn right.

Built in 1938 with an addition in 1944 this was the third Elk Creek School. In 1942 windows shattered in this building when 25 tons of dynamite exploded in the powder magazine at the mouth of Big Creek, about a mile away.

At the stop sign turn right
Just beyond the stop sign is an old Yellowstone Trail bridge, built in 1924, crossing Moon Creek.

Turn left on Silver Valley Rd.

65 Elk Creek Swimming Hole

The filled-in area on the north side of Silver Valley and Moon Gulch Rd. (If you are on I-90, milepost 53.5 to your left or north side)

Many residents remember this as a favorite place to swim and ice skate. The water was clear, but unfortunately it contained mining residues. They did not pose a hazard to human health, however the EPA ordered the pond filled in. Locals referred to it as Polio Pond, although no cases of Polio were ever attributed to it.

Elk Creek Swimming Hole, 1965.

66 Moon Gulch

In 1938 the Idaho Fish and Game trucked elk into the Coeur d'Alenes from Yellowstone National Park. The first truckload arrived at Moon Gulch near Kellogg and contained as many as 22 elk. The second truckload brought the total number to 74. Mr. Wilson of Coeur d'Alene Hardware sponsored the two truckloads of elk.

If you are on I-90 take the Big Creek exit, (Exit 54) and turn right for the side trip or left for the Miners' Memorial Statue. There is a trailhead for the *Trail of the Coeur d'Alenes* here.

D Big Creek Side Trip

Turn right on Big Creek Rd. and at the I-90 interchange set your odometer to 0.

D1 The Sunshine Mine Silver refinery

About one mile

In the early 1980s the Sunshine Mine was able to use a process they developed that refines copper silver ore to a purity of 99.5%. This involves a modified nitric-sulfuric-acid pressure leach followed by electrolytic deposition. Sterling silver "925" contains 7% copper. In the mid-1990s they moved to another location within the mine that was producing a lead silver ore and had to discontinue using this process. The process required a copper silver ore. Once they discontinued using the refinery the concentrates were shipped to East Helena, Montana.

D2 Sunshine Mine's General Manager's House

1227 Big Creek Rd.

Built in 1935 this house served as the home for the General Manager of the Sunshine Mine. Harry Cougher, former Sunshine Vice President, purchased the home. In October 1980 Sunshine Executive Vice President E. Viet Howard was living here when Shoshone County sheriffs investigated an explosion on the lawn near the street. No one was hurt and damage was minimal. The bombing was linked to the Sunshine miners' strike. One month earlier a miner who had crossed the picket line found a bag of 11 sticks of smoking dynamite under his truck.

D3 Crescent Ore Chute

1.8 miles, on the right

The surface workings are just barely visible. This mine operated sporadically from 1917 to 1981 producing over one million tons of ore and over 26,000,000 ounces of silver. First incorporated in 1902 as the Big Creek

Mining Company, it was acquired by the Bunker Hill and Sullivan Mining and Concentrating Company in 1922.

D4▷ Sunshine Mine Surface Plant
About two miles
The Yankee Lode, discovered in 1884 by True and Dennis Blake, was a mediocre producer for 30 years. The Blake's homesteaded in a meadow at the mouth of Big Creek and sold vegetables to get by. The mine changed hands several times before it paid off in 1927. By 1937 the mine set a single year production record of 12 million ounces and through 1980 produced more than 300 million ounces of silver. The mine still holds a number of production records. The 1937 single year total of over 12 million troy ounces is still the highest underground silver mine production ever. It also has produced more silver in a sixty-year period than any other single silver mine in the world. This total of over 380 million ounces is over twice the combined total of all of the mines that made up Nevada's famous Comstock Lode. Although there are still some reserves left in the mine it would take significant investment capital to bring it back into full production.

Turn around in the parking lot, back go under the freeway and turn right on the frontage road and continue east.

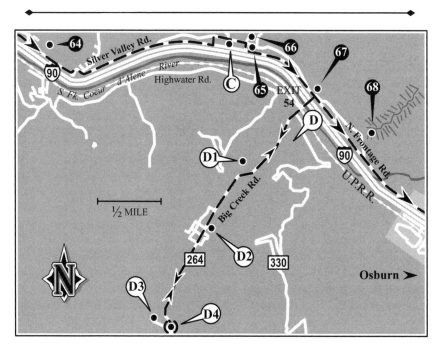

 Miners' Memorial Statue

The Sunshine Mine fire was one of the worst hard rock mining disasters in U.S. history. On May 2, 1972 there were 173 men underground on the day shift when a fire broke out in the wood timbering of the Sunshine Mine. Eighty men escaped and 91 died of suffocation from carbon monoxide.

Continue east on the frontage road.

68 Prospect Gulch

About a half-mile from the interchange, look for the highway department compound on your left (north).

It is believed that the first "official" placer gold in this region was taken from Prospect Gulch on the other side of these buildings. The term "official" is used because there were several reliable and rumored gold nuggets found in the Coeur d'Alene river system, but until this find in the late 1870s, no claims had been filed and no commercial workings had been developed. Reports of gold being found by Native Americans date back to the mid-1850s. A.J. Prichard staked the Evolution claim just east of here near the Frontage Road bridge. He also blazed the Evolution Trail up Prospect Gulch and on to his gold discovery in the Eagle/Murray area. Wyatt Earp was known to use this trail to transport supplies to his bar in Eagle City.

Keep right and go under the interstate and then left at the junction of S. Johnson St. and W. Yellowstone Ave. into Osburn. If you would like to visit the Gene Day County Park turn right and go about 1/4 mile. This site is the old Steven's ranch. Local kids would hike along the railroad tracks to reach a favorite fishing pond located here. In 1975 the park was dedicated as the Gene Day County Park. Brothers Eugene, Harry and Jerome Day were among the partners of the Hercules Mine.

Yellowstone/Mullan Ave. through Osburn is the original Hwy 10 alignment.

1 The Polaris Mill

Behind 1223 Yellowstone Ave. on the hill. (If on I-90, it is mile 55.95 off to the right or south side

The series of connected buildings against the hillside that resemble a stair step arrangement is typical of many of the concentrating mills in this area. This layout allowed gravity to do much of the work. Weldon Heyburn, who later became a U.S. Senator from Idaho, discovered the Polaris mine in 1884, the same year as the earliest discoveries elsewhere in the Silver Valley. This claim, like many others in the mining district, would go through a number of mergers and/or working agreements with larger operators. Eventually, it emerged as part of the Consolidated Silver Corporation. The combined total production of the combined claims reached 27 million ounces of silver. The mill was built in 1937 and operated until about 1981. There are some known reserves remaining.

~ Osburn ~

(If on I-90 mile 57)
When Captain John Mullan built the road through this area in 1861 he had a construction camp here. The town was originally named Georgetown for Lee George, one of the owners of the town site. When the Union Pacific Railroad came through, S.V. William Osburn built a trading post and platted the town. The name Georgetown was submitted as the name of the post office but was not accepted because there was already a Georgetown in Idaho. The name was changed to Osburn for the storekeeper and first postmaster in 1887. In 1890 Osburn competed to replace Murray as the county seat but lost out to Wallace in 1898. The Two Mile Wagon Road up Two Mile Creek north of the I-90 interchange was the first wagon road to connect the south fork and north fork of the Coeur d'Alene River. The population in 2000 was 1,545.

❷ Burns-Yaak River Lumber Company Site
Just past Fillmore St.
All that remains of the sawmill that operated here from 1966 until 1975 are two teepee burners and a foundation. The mill had a dry kiln and planer mill producing timbers for the mines and dimensional lumber. Jim Burns operated the mill and then sold it to the Pack River Company.

As the road curves take a right on Yellowstone Ave.

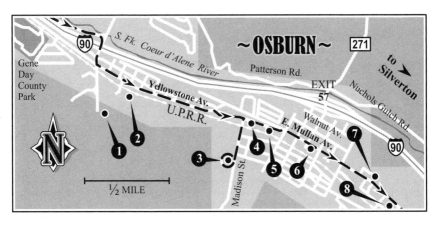

❸ Day's Cemetery turn right on Madison St. and then turn around after the cemetery.

Plots in this cemetery were free to valley residents as a gift from Harry L. Day who deeded the land to Osburn in 1896. In 1982 the City of Osburn leased additional land from the Bureau of Land Management for cemetery use and fees are charged to maintain the grounds.

❹ Cameron Apartments

185 W. Yellowstone Ave. (Yellowstone Apartments)
The concrete foundation for the Cameron Apartments was originally part of an outbuilding for the Day's ranch. The apartments were built originally with garages underneath in 1937-1938. During WWII it was the bomb shelter for the town of Osburn.

❺ Osburn Lumber Company

115 W. Yellowstone Ave.
Building contractor Ben E. Johnston purchased the Osburn Lumber Company from C.H. Perkins in 1965. In 1967 Altas Tie Company of Coeur d'Alene acquired the company and changed the name to Atlas Building Center, Osburn Branch. They noted that the increased activity in the silver market, development of a ski bowl and a general upturn in building starts in the area were positive factors of economic growth.

~ Yellowstone Trail ~

As you turn onto Mullan Ave.
Mullan Ave is the original alignment of the Yellowstone Trail/Hwy 10. The highway passed through the center of Osburn but the section where you turn (while heading east) to go to the Barrel was bypassed in 1949. East of the Barrel, the Yellowstone Trail ran alongside the UPRR to east of the County Shops where it crossed the river and stayed on the north side (now Silverton) until re-crossing to the south side near the mouth of Lake Gulch.

Go right where the road comes back to Mullan Ave.

❻ Zanetti Brothers

301 E. 3rd St.
In 1935 the Zanetti Brothers took over Mohr's Service Station for their concrete business. The sign on the building is the oldest continuous working neon sign in the entire Northwest, possibly the west coast.

❼ Rock Waste Pile

The industrial area across the street from City Hall at 921 Mullan Ave.

(If on I-90 mile 57.5)
This was the site of a mill constructed by Hecla Mining Company during WWII. They reclaimed the flood plain from Silverton to Big Creek, screened out the sand and gravel and re-milled it to reclaim 27,000 tons of lead and 50,000 tons of zinc lost in earlier processing. Zinc combined with copper produces brass used for artillery and small arm shells. The large pile of rock adjacent to the freeway is the rock waste from this process.

⑧ Osburn Locker Plant

1043 Mullan Ave.
The Martins first owned the Osburn Locker Plant. In the early 1940s not many people owned freezers, or ones big enough for all of their food, so they would rent lockers at a locker plant. Patrons were given a key and the front door was always open so they could go in anytime to retrieve their frozen foods out of the rented locker. Blocks of ice could be purchased for 30 cents. Henry Sciuchetti ran the locker for many years.

Keep right on Mullan Ave.

⑨ Coeur Mine Surface Plant on the right

Right before 1341 Mullan Ave. (the Barrel House) look behind the house and up the hill (Mile 58.05 if on I-90)
As you get to the east end of town just past the Silver Hills School, look up the canyon on the right. The buildings, midway up the hill, are part of the Coeur Mine complex. Production at the Coeur Mine began in 1974 and by the end of that decade the company had recovered its investment capital and was operating in the black. Almost from the beginning, it ranked among the nation's top five silver producers. The mine produced 24,388,563 ounces of silver.

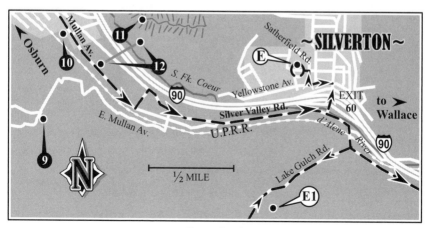

⑩ The Barrel

1341 Mullan Ave.

The road in front of the Barrel was the original Yellowstone Trail. A prominent Kellogg businessman, Pete Albinola, started the Barrel Restaurant as one of his last business ventures. Henry Johnson was contracted to build the barrel-shaped restaurant sometime in the late 1920s or early 1930s. The barrel portion of the building was originally painted orange although there is no relationship to A&W. The George family purchased it in the 1940s and built a living quarters addition to the restaurant. June and Robert Hamer bought the Barrel in 1947 and offered curb service and car hops. A projector pointed out of the small upstairs window to a large screen along the west side of the lot. People would watch the movies from their cars while local kids sat on the logs in the parking lot. Car hops filled burger orders as the movie played. The Hamer's daughter, Karen, recalls her mom running upstairs to splice the film together to keep the movies going while she was filling burger orders to a full lot below. Local teenagers listened to and respected Mrs. Hamer. In her starched white, buttoned-up "cooks uniform" she waded through crowds of drunken kids with motorcycles and cars to break up fights between the rival kids from Wallace and Osburn. June contracted MS but was able to continue to work with the help of family, friends, neighbors and customers. Merrill Fields hooked up an automatic lift to get her wheel chair up to the second floor living quarters. She sold the Barrel in 1970.

The Barrel Café, Osburn, 1963.

⑪ Osburn Fault

From the Barrel look left (north). (If on I-90 mile 58.1 on the left (north) side in the barrow pit along the ridge)

The gray material on the north side, in the barrow pit along the ridge, is ground up material in the Osburn Fault. The Osburn Fault is a major right-lateral slip fault and has been traced from the vicinity of Coeur d'Alene to east of Superior, Montana passing under the city of Osburn. The lateral movement in the Silver Valley has been estimated from 12 to 16 miles with a vertical displacement in the thousands of feet.

⑫ Coeur Mine Tailings Pipeline

Over the road (If on I-90 mile 58.3)

In the 1960s a pipe from the Coeur Mine was built across the old highway to reach the tailings dump just east of the Barrel Restaurant and north of the river.

The road loops back to Silver Valley Ave. Then turn right on W. Yellowstone Ave. and continue east towards Silverton and Wallace on old Hwy 10.

 **~ Silverton ~**

(If on I-90 Exit 60)

This area was first known as "West Wallace". It was the site of Markwell's Dairy. He was a partner in the Hercules Mine. It became known as Silverton in 1941 when the post office was established.

Ⓔ Shoshone County Infirmary Side Trip

Turn left on Markwell Ave. at the Silverton sign and go under I-90 and left on Yellowstone Ave. then right at Sather Field

(The field was named for Norman Sather, a Hecla, and later a Bunker Hill Mill superintendent, who worked hard to develop a football field.)

Shoshone County Infirmary

This three-story brick building was built by Shoshone County in 1916-17 and served as a nursing home to care for the infirm. In the 1918 flu epidemic the county added the building behind this one. In 1928 when the second floor above the kitchen was added an architectural error resulted in the need for an 18-inch ramp in the hallway to make the addition meet in the hallway. The county owned 160-acres and the grounds had gardens, orchards and livestock. The basement has two solitary confinement cells that were used for housing the insane. Jail cells in the back were used for women and juveniles.

The Forest Service moved its administrative headquarters for the Wallace Ranger District into this building in 1974 after the new Good Samaritan Nursing Center was opened. In 2005 the Forest Service moved to a new building in Smelterville.

◆――――――――――――――――――――――――――――――――◆

Continue east for less than a quarter mile and turn right up Lake Gulch and go about one mile to the Galena Mine parking lot.
(If on I-90 at mile 59.4 look to the right)

Galena Mine, 1961

(E1)▷ **Galena Mine**

Some of the early claims that make up the Galena were located in the late 1800s although it was not until the 1950s that development work and investment capital were successful in developing a working mine. Since then, the Galena has been the nation's leading silver producer seven times. In 2002 it became the third mine in the region to produce over five million ounces in a single year. Traditionally the Galena is the lowest cost producer in the region, and has around seven years of known reserves, plus opportunities to develop more. In 2004 the lowest level of mining was at 5,500 feet.

Turn around and return to W. Yellowstone Ave. and turn right.

⑬ Wine's Auto Court

60330 Silver Valley Rd. (If on I-90 mile 60.4) (Molly B'Damm Motel)
Wine's Auto Court was built in 1939 and is typical of early motor courts along the old highways. This design was also used on the Wine's Auto Court in Spokane, Washington. The oldest section extends north and south and the office is the second oldest section. The Pabst Brothers added the last section of three to four units in the 1940s. It was called Myles' Motel in 1957. When Jack Hull bought it in 1979 it still had the small garages attached next to each unit. He remodeled the garages into additional units.

⑭ Log Cabin

60448 Silver Valley Rd. log cabin on the right (If on I-90 mile 60.5)
Brothers Enar and Gunnar Mattson built this cabin for Wilson Miller in 1939. Art and Margaret Linn bought the cabin and lived there for many years. The brothers were noted craftsmen and built log homes throughout the area. Art worked as a hoist man at the Galena Mine and other area mines and lived here until he died in 1983.

⑮ Stairs to Nowhere and Rock Wall

A little past the cabin on the right (If on I-90 look to the right or south at the Exit 61 sign)
Gene Fellin, Frank Brawl, Faust Voltolini, Angelo Frank, and Mr. Argala built this rock wall and steps in 1934-35. They were among a team of craftsmen, whose names and faces changed over the years, who completed many projects in the area including the rock work on the Idaho side of Lookout Pass, Dobson Pass, Kings Pass, and up Placer Creek.

These rock steps next to Daly Gulch lead to the top of a bench where a large three-bedroom house was built about 1915. Harry Voltolini remembers the Hendrickson family as the first occupants. Mr. Hendrickson was the Shoshone County Sheriff and he had three boys, Blackie, Sam and Ray. Blackie and Sam were killed in World War I and Ray, at the age of 18 or 19, ran a newsboy peddlers and collection business. In the 1950s another Shoshone County Sheriff, Morris Ogilvie, lived here. It was torn down in late 1980s because of contaminates from the Caladay Mine located on the hillside above. Common minerals located at the Caladay included lead, silver, zinc and copper.

(If on I-90 Exit 61) NR

Wallace's downtown is a fine example of turn-of-the-century architecture. For information about Wallace's historic buildings pick up the "Historic Wallace, Idaho" pamphlet at one of the museums or visitor's center. This tour does not repeat what is in that excellent publication.

For the Coeur d'Alene Indians the area near Wallace is called "Wide Forehead" or "Wide Surface Under the Hair" *Ni' aq'qn*, which probably refers to a wide ridge or mountain.

With the discovery of a silver-lead claim above Canyon Creek, and the Hunter Claim along the main stream of the South Fork, William R. Wallace built a cabin at the large cedar swamp near the confluence of several canyons in May 1884. The next year his wife Lucy joined him and then became postmaster. The post office department would not consider the application under the name Placer Center, so she filed under the name of Wallace over her husband's objection. William Wallace subdivided the area into building lots and soon the town became a supply point for the mining district. By the late 1800s railroads provided transportation in and out of Wallace. In 1890 the business district burned, but was quickly rebuilt and grew to be the third largest town in Idaho with a population of 2,000 including twenty-eight saloon keepers, ten lawyers, five doctors, one teacher and one preacher. Shoshone County had the largest population in the state in 1890. In 1898, the county seat was moved from Murray to Wallace. From 1884 into the 1980s, mines around Wallace were responsible for about half of the nation's newly mined silver each year. Over 1.2 billion ounces of silver have been produced in Shoshone County making it the Silver Capital of the World.

16 Visitor's Center and Mining Heritage Exhibition

View the outside exhibits of large mining machinery and pick up a walking tour here (the "Historic Wallace, Idaho" tour is available here). 208-753-7151

17 Hercules Mill Foundations

From the Visitor's Center look across I-90

The Hercules Mill was completed in 1911. At one time the mill operated twenty-four hours a day regularly producing double its rated capacity. In 1942 the mill stopped production. After the equipment was salvaged in 1958 a controlled burn destroyed the concentration plant and the rest of the buildings burned accidentally in 1976.

Continue into downtown Wallace

18 John Mullan Statue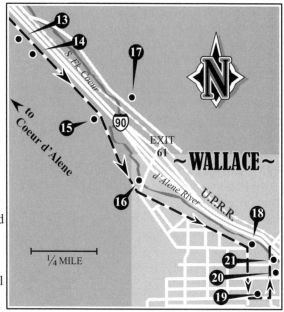

On the left as you go around the corner.

Follow Fifth St. and turn left at Bank St. The Mullan Road came through this swamp in 1859. The route became the Yellowstone Trail, then Hwy 10. When planning to replace Hwy 10 with I-90, citizens and historic preservation advocates worked to place the town's old buildings on the National Register of Historic Places.

A north hillside elevated bypass was chosen to pass through the downtown and the freeway was completed in September of 1991. By this time, all the traffic lights on the interstate system had been retired except one, the one at the corner of 7th and Bank streets here in Wallace. It was given a funeral worthy of its fame, and retired to the Wallace District Mining Museum.

19 Wallace District Mining Museum
509 Bank St.
The museum first started in a small building next door at 507 Bank St. in 1956. By 1972 the Rice's Bakery building (built in 1945) was available for museum use. With some remodeling, the museum reopened as the Coeur d'Alene District Mining Museum. The name was later changed to Wallace District Mining Museum to avoid confusion with the city of Coeur d'Alene. The Museum focuses on life on the western frontier, local history, and the region's mining accomplishments. Call 208-556-1592 for information.

Turn left (north) on Sixth St. then right on Cedar.

20 Bi-Metallic Building
605 Cedar (Oasis Rooms a brothel Museum)
Built in 1895 as a hotel and saloon the original wooden structure survived the 1910 fire but was rebuilt in brick the following year. It is uncertain when the

Bi-Metallic Saloon/Hotel became the Oasis Rooms, a brothel. There were five brothels operating in Wallace in 1973 when a Boise Statesman article charged a politician with agreeing to go easy on law enforcement in North Idaho in exchange for a $25,000 campaign contribution. By the time the article was in print, Wallace's brothels were closed. However they did not stay closed. Locals recall the front doors were locked but the back doors were open and it wasn't long before front door business resumed. The last recorded date in the registry was in January 1988. The occupants then left in a hurry, leaving their personal belongs which are on exhibit. 208-753-0801

㉑ Northern Pacific Railroad Depot NR
219 Sixth St. (Northern Pacific Railroad Depot Museum)

Built in 1903, the Northern Pacific Depot is a two-story chateau style brick and stucco structure. The bricks were originally imported from China and concrete panels are made from mine tailings. The Depot was closed in 1980. In 1986 it was moved 200 feet to this location to make way for the completion of I-90. The Northern Pacific Railroad Depot Museum recreates a 1910-period railroad station and traces railroad history in the Silver Valley. 208-752-0111

Moving the Northern Pacific Railroad Depot, 1986.

Continue to explore Wallace, return to Coeur d'Alene via I-90 or take Tour 8 to Murray and down the Coeur d'Alene River back to I-90 at Kingston.

Although this tour ends at Wallace, you are a short distance from the starting point for the *Route of Hiawatha Rail Trail*, which is located just over the Montana border. Take Taft Exit 5 just east of Lookout Pass. The parking area is 2 miles from the exit. The 15-mile downhill biking/hiking trail begins with the 1.7-mile Taft Tunnel. If on bicycles, helmets and flashlights are required. Call 208-744-1301 or visit www.silvercountry.com for trail fee, hours of operation, bike rentals, and bus ride schedule back to the top and other information.

Dobson Pass to the Coeur d'Alene River
~TOUR EIGHT~

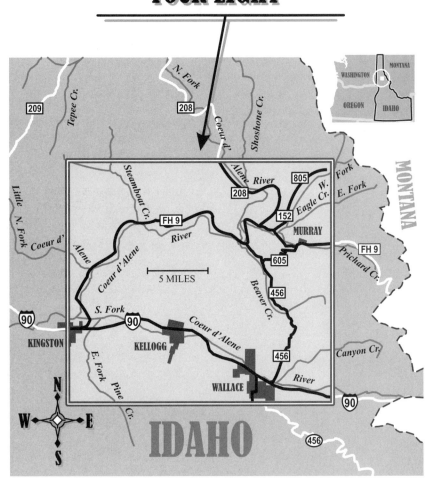

This tour begins in Wallace and goes over Dobson and Kings passes to Murray and down the Coeur d'Alene River to I-90 at Kingston. The route covers about 50 miles plus your mileage to and from home. It takes 3 to 4 hours depending on stops. Although the route is maintained by Shoshone County for bus travel, it is for the more adventurous so please check road conditions at 208-753-5475 Mon.-Fri. 8-5. This is the region where gold was first discovered in the Coeur d'Alene Mining District.

In Wallace go to the Northern Pacific Depot Railroad Museum at 619 Sixth St. and set the odometer to 0 and proceed north on Sixth St., under the freeway and up Nine Mile Canyon (Forest Service Road 456) towards Dobson Pass.

The McKinnon House and its eccentric murals and sculptures, circa 1980.

❶▶ Mural

0.1 miles behind the Down by the Depot RV Park building which was the Pacific Fruit Warehouse

Jerry McKinnon, a local artist and some would say eccentric, created these murals and sculptures. He lived on the hillside in a house which has since burned. For over 23 years McKinnon painted murals and collected junk to create three spaceships. The place is in bad condition and only one spaceship remains. One of the spaceships was a room and another had hundreds of mirrors which reflected the sun. He collected materials for his house and locals recall seeing McKinnon with his bicycle loaded with lumber. McKinnon's other claim to fame was his ability to rope a post from 30 feet away with his back turned.

❷ Sierra Silver Mine Tour
0.7 miles

The Cathella Mine prospect was pursued commercially in 1900 and it has changed hands many times over the years. In the 1960s an aggressive exploration program producing assays of about 1/2 ounce of silver per ton of ore determined there was not enough silver to warrant putting the mine into production. From 1977 to 1982 the mine was used as a lab site for the Wallace High School vocational education program. It was the only program of its kind in the United States on a high school level.

In 1982 a non-profit organization formed to develop the mine into a touring mine with the mission of educating current and future generations about the history and current practices of hard rock mining in the Coeur d'Alene Mining District. This underground tour uses historically correct narratives, exhibits and live demonstrations of mining machinery. Tours operate May through September with tours leaving every half-hour beginning at 9:00 a.m. Tickets for the mine tour must be purchased at 420 5th St. in Wallace. The ticket also includes a brief tour and historical overview of Wallace aboard a vintage open-air trolley on the way to and from the mine.

❸ Nine Mile Cemetery
1.0 miles

Just as you enter the cemetery, park and walk to the left to see the graves of men who fought in the 1910 Fire and died in the Pulaski Tunnel. Another 1910 Fire gravesite is located up the hill about 150 yards. To the right of the main cemetery road is the grave of Wallace Mayor Herman Rossi who was acquitted after shooting his wife's lover in 1916. There are many prominent miners buried here. Continue through the cemetery passing the urn wall and keep right to return to Nine Mile Canyon Rd.

❹ Slaughter House and Wallace Meat Company

1.3 miles on the left
There were two slaughterhouses here; the City Meat Company on the east side of the creek and the Wallace Meat Company on the west side near the cemetery. The small brick structure on the left hillside is the last remaining building of the Wallace Meat Company. The City Meat Company also operated the Meat Market in downtown Wallace.

❺ Sunset Branch of the Northern Pacific Railroad

The Northern Pacific Railroad had a branch line from Wallace to the mining hamlet of Sunset about one-half mile up the East Fork of Nine Mile Creek. The railroad grade can be observed on the east side of the road from Wallace to the fork of Nine Mile Creek.

❻ Black Cloud

2.4 miles
The mill for the Black Cloud mine operated here in the early 1900s. The Black Cloud, one of the claims making up the Dayrock group, was discovered in 1884 by Oscar Wallace, son of the founder of the town of Wallace and nephew of Lew Wallace, the author of *Ben Hur*. These mining claims were primarily silver and lead producers. Period mining machinery can be observed behind a chain link fence fronting what was the Caron Machine Shop. Boxing was a favorite pastime in the district and many matches were held here.

❼ Zanettiville

2.6 miles on the right
Shortly after homesteading here in 1886 Petro Zanetti returned to Italy to marry Irena. Together they returned to settle in Wallace. With their twelve children (eight boys and four girls) they tended livestock, raised crops and worked their mining claims. In the early thirties, two of the sons and Lew Hanley started Triangle Trucking, a small trucking company located above Zanettiville across from the Dayrock Mine. They bought out Hanley and moved to Osburn under the name Zanetti Brothers. The siblings worked together to become a prominent business family in the Coeur d'Alenes.

Where others came to discover a gold bonanza, the Zanetti's discovered good solid business in the rock, sand and gravel industry; general contracting; tourist establishments and rental properties.

⑧ Dayrock Mine
2.9 miles

Incorporated on Nov. 30, 1923 the Stratton Mines had five patented and seven unpatented claims. It was a very promising property when the Day family acquired control of it in 1924. In 1928, president F.M. Rothrock and manager Henry Day changed the name of the company to Dayrock. The company bought the adjoining claims and eventually had 47 patented and 22 unpatented claims. The mine had 22 adits (nearly horizontal passages leading into a mine) driven for a total of 21,508 feet, (4 miles) underground.

Dayrock Mining Company eventually became part of Day Mines Inc. which was formed in 1947. In 1948 this was the first mine in the district to use sand to fill in the mined-out areas. By the mid 1950s other mines in the district used sand-fill. Hecla Mining Company acquired the company from Day Mines in a hostile takeover in 1981. Virtually all of the mining accomplished in the region owes part of its history to the Day family.

Interstate Mine, 1923.

⑨ The Road to the Tamarack and Interstate-Callahan Mines
3.5 miles

The Tamarack and Interstate-Callahan mines, both notable producers in their day, are located on this road.

⑩ Dobson Pass, elevation 4,179 feet
5.8 miles is the top of the pass
Dobson Pass may be named after William Dobson who came to the area in
1879 with his partner Tom Irwin (the prospector with the first gold claim east
of Kellogg). William Dobson was the first elected surveyor of Kootenai
County. The current road follows much of the original 1887 Wallace to
Murray stage route. In 1891 the stage fare between Wallace and Murray was
reduced from $3.50 to $2.50. The Sunset Stage route was added several
years later to reach the small communities of Sunset, Interstate and, possibly
Tamarack. The last Wallace to Murray stage was August 5, 1911 after 26
years in service. Clay Speck and John Morrison (State Senator) were two of
the stage drivers and owners of the stage line. The road on the far right goes
to Sunset Peak; the road on the left, Forest Service Road 424, follows the
divide between the South and North Forks of the Coeur d'Alene River. This
area is a favorite spot to gather huckleberries.

⑪ Beaver Station
8.6 to 10 miles at the confluence of Dudley Creek and Beaver Creek
This is about half way between Wallace and Murray and was an important
stopping point and transportation hub. Where the road drops down into
Beaver Creek there were several homesteads and mining claims. This point
at the bottom of the Dobson Pass road was known as Beaver Station and
served as a stage stop and social center for area residents. The first building
built in 1888 was known as Red's Place and it burned. Then a two-story
building about 25 feet by 60 feet opened in 1889. Beaver Station later was
known as Delta. Nothing remains today.

⑫ Camp Ferguson
9.6 miles, look to the meadow on the left
John "Lon" and Zoe Ferguson bought the Benjamin Hemminger homestead
at the confluence of Dudley Creek and Beaver Creek. The spot became
known as Ferguson Lodge (Station). In the meadow along the west side of
the road there was a very large barn and one and a half story log house that
served as a stage stop along the Two-Mile Stage Route to Murray. The barn
was used to hold extra teams of horses for the stage line. Ferguson operated
an underground still nearby in the abandoned Rex Mine. He was known as
the "King of the Bootleggers" and provided whiskey for the whole county.
John Ferguson was killed on a curve along the Dobson Pass Road and Mrs.
Ferguson built a memorial monument for her husband. The monument was
later moved to the Wallace Cemetery. Bunker Hill bought the property and

donated it to the YMCA for use as a summer camp. In 1940-41 the YMCA began using the property and later the Boy Scouts camped here. Bunker Hill built a swimming pool in the 1950s but it is now filled in.

⑬ Lorenzi Homestead (Chapen Home)
4190 Beaver Creek Rd., 11.7 miles on the left
Pete Lorenzi emigrated from Italy in 1900 and a few years later his brother Mike followed. The brothers were hard rock miners who were expert "hand steelers". Mike married Laura and the family homesteaded here on Beaver Creek. Their daughter Nelda married John Chapen who then moved to the family farm, where they farmed hay and raised beef cattle. Some of the first trails into the Eagle and Murray gold camps were the Evolution and Jackass trails from the South Fork of the Coeur d'Alene River, which descended into Beaver Creek along the ridge between Alder and White creeks directly behind their home.

The town of Delta, 1883.

⑭ Delta
12.8 miles (nothing remains)
The gold camp town of Delta was located at the confluence of Trail Creek and Beaver Creek. At its peak, the population reached 1,500 with one-fourth of its buildings being saloons, dance halls and gambling houses. The Mascot Gold Mining Company purchased the land in 1902 and the town of Delta was dissembled and salvaged. The company assumed gold had washed

downstream and ended up near Delta so they dredged the area for the gold but returns were minimal. However the gulch produced some of the biggest gold nuggets ever found in the region. In 1995 a 3-ounce gold nugget was discovered.

⑮ Trail Creek

About 13 miles turn right on County Road 605 towards King Pass and Murray

Along this route for about a mile and a half, wooden flumes and ditches were built to transport water to support extensive hydraulic mining activities. Hydraulic mining involved the use of huge nozzles called *Giants* which washed away entire hillsides leaving piles of gravel. This type of mining was outlawed in California in the 1880s and discontinued in this region before 1900. Nearly 2 million dollars of gold at $16 an ounce was extracted from the area. Stories of the size of the nuggets found vary. One of the largest gold nuggets, weighing 13 pounds, and worth between $3,000 to $4,000 was found in Trail Creek. It was cleaved with an axe to be shared by two of the

Hydraulic operations on Dream Gulch near Murray, 1884.

partners. The discovery was kept from the third partner. Evidence of modern-day prospecting is visible on both sides of the road.

16▸ Kings Pass, elevation 3,319 feet

16 miles
Coming down from Kings Pass you can see large dredge piles that were left by the Yukon Dredge. Watch out for four wheelers (ATV riders).

17▸ Dredge piles on Prichard Creek

16.6 miles look for a clearing in the trees and look down
The Yukon Gold Company, dominated by the Guggenheims, disassembled a dredge in Alaska and barged it to Seattle and then by rail to Murray. The dredge was used between 1917 and 1926 and took out over a million dollars in gold. Approximately 7 miles of Prichard Creek were dredged ending upstream at the mouth of Granite Creek. The total recovery was $1,500,000 with a profit of $500,000. Gold was selling for $20.07 per ounce.

18▸ Murray GAR (Grand Army of the Republic) Cemetery

18.4 miles on the right
Established in Jan. 1884, gold rush pioneers and colorful characters are buried here including Molly b'Damn and Andrew Prichard. For many years, it was believed that Addison O. Toncray was the individual that Mark Twain had used as inspiration for his book *Huckleberry Finn*. It has since been determined that Twain used an individual named Tom Blankenship as Huck's "role model". Since it was believed at the time of Toncray's death in 1906 that the story was real, the Washington Post ran a story on it to inform those in the nation's capital about his passing. News stories, however, are not particularly accurate or reliable. In this case, the grave is mistakenly marked 1900 but should be 1906.

Proceed into Murray across Thompson Pass Rd. onto Walt Almquist Ave. and turn right on Prichard Creek Rd.

~ Murray ~

Many early gold seekers arrived in winter by trails over Thompson Falls Pass, just to the east of Murray. In January 1884 the town was founded and named in honor of George Murray, a part owner of one of the claims. Murray was the Shoshone County seat from 1884 until it was moved to Wallace in 1898. At its peak the population was over 3,000 and the town had many businesses including a hardware store, four drug stores, four hotels, a shoe store, five restaurants, two newspapers, three general stores, a bakery, two banks, a feed store, post office, theater, houses of ill repute and 38 saloons. More than 400,000 ounces of gold have been mined in the Murray area.

The Idaho Northern Railroad surveyed for a track from the mouth of the Coeur d'Alene River up the North Fork and Prichard Creek and past the town of Murray in 1899. On Dec. 13, 1908 the town celebrated the arrival of the first train. In 1911 the line was taken over by the Oregon Washington Railway & Navigation Company (OWR&N). When a track washed out close to Murray in Dec. 1917 the line between Prichard and Paragon (6 miles above Murray) was abandoned.

The stage at Murray. Looking northeast toward Montana from the left is the Warren Hussey Bank, GAR Building, print shop, dray office and livery, Holley, Mason and Marks Hardware Store (Spragpole Inn), confectioner and dry goods store, and the last building with the large balcony is the Palace Hotel with the flag pole out front.

⑲ Burton's Bakery

6276 Prichard Creek Rd. (Bedroom Gold Mine Bar)
Built in 1884 this building served as Burton's Bakery and then as a grocery store operated by Burton's daughter and her husband Walter Keaster. It has long been rumored that the best gold found in the valley is under the Murray town site so after buying the building in 1962, Chris Christopherson sank a shaft to bedrock in the back bedroom of this building in 1968. He also tunneled a drift to his property line and in the process he found a large gold nugget. In 1988 Leila Grebil took over and operated the mine and bar. The mine was closed after the 1996 flood knocked out mine timbers making it

unsafe but the bar remains
open.

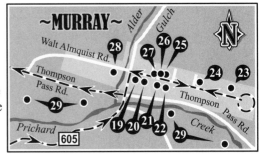

❷⓿ Masonic Lodge
6280 Prichard Creek Rd.
Built in Nov. 1886, this is the
second oldest Masonic Lodge
in Idaho. Coeur d'Alene
Lodge No. 20 meetings are
still held here on the second
floor. The room contains original furnishings and Masonic regalia.

❷⓵ Miller's Store & Post Office
6352 Prichard Creek Rd.
Built in 1884 this building housed the Miller's store, meat market and post
office. There was a trap door, above the gable end of the back of the house,
where ice was kept above the meat cooler during the building's meat market
days. The room had 16-inch thick walls that were filled with sawdust for
insulation. Mr. and Mrs. Floyd Culver lived here from 1959 to 1977 and Mrs.
Culver served as the postmaster. The home had three bedrooms upstairs and
a living room, kitchen and bathroom on the main floor. By the time the
Culver's lived there the meat cooler was remodeled into a bathroom. The
house had 12-foot ceilings and a heated front room, which served as the
lobby for the post office where there were mailboxes, a safe and an office.

❷❷ Post Office
6340 Prichard Creek Rd.
This log structure that now houses the Murray Post Office originally was
located behind the Murray Courthouse. In 2002 Dave Miller dismantled the
building and moved it to its present location.

At the hill turn around and go back through Murray

❷❸ Feehan House
On the right
This log structure with a rock foundation was built in 1884 with square nails.
It was one of the first homes in Murray. To the right of the Feehan house is
the grave of an unknown baby girl.

❷❹ Murray Courthouse 🏛
Prichard Creek Rd.
The Murray Courthouse, built in 1884 or 1885, collapsed under heavy snows

in the winter of 1996-1997 and was rebuilt using much of the original material. The courthouse is one of the last surviving courthouses dating from Idaho's territorial period and is a good example of frontier mining architecture from the 1880s. Many major mine claims disputes were settled here including Noah Kellogg's trial involving the ownership of the Bunker Hill, one of the world's largest lead-silver mines. Once called the Fuller Hall, it is being restored for use as a community hall.

㉕ Spragpole Steak and Rib House and Museum

6353 Prichard Creek Rd.
Children are welcome.
Built in 1884 this building served as the J.R. Marks Hardware store and later Holley, Mason and Marks Hardware which became the Coeur d'Alene Hardware Company. It then served as a stagecoach station and in 1933 as a carpenter shop. In 1968 Walt Almquist opened the museum with a large collection of artifacts, gems and rocks. In the early 1990s Lloyd Roath purchased the site, reorganized, and expanded the Museum.
Call 208-682-3901 for information.

㉖ Fire Hall

6343 Prichard Creek Rd.
The original building on this site was built in 1886 as a print shop. During the demolition of that building hundreds of pounds of broken glass and nails were uncovered. The fire station was built in the 1960s. The fire bell was located across the street on a tower in front of the original city hall and fire station, which are no longer there.

㉗ Adam Aulbach House

6325 Prichard Creek Rd.
Adam Aulbach lived in this 1884 house and at one time he owned half of the town. The Coeur d'Alene Sun newspaper operated from this building and the original safe is still inside.

At Walt Almquist Ave., turn left and then right on Thompson Pass Rd.
Set odometer to 0 at the stop sign

㉘ Murray School

On the right
This 1930s WPA project was built with little funds and was Murray's second school. As a one-room school (grades K-5) it served the communities of Prichard, Murray and Delta until the late 1970s. It was also the community center for Christmas and holiday programs.

🕖 Dredge Piles

Rock piles on the left for several miles
This is still part of the Yukon Gold Company floating dredge operation noted earlier on Prichard Creek.

Ⓐ The Settler's Grove of Ancient Cedars Side Trip

At 3.4 miles at Eagle follow Forest Service Road 152 and then Forest Service Road 805 for about 6 miles. The pavement ends after one mile and the single lane road forks to the left.
This area, set aside in 1970 as a National Forest Botanical Area, is an example of what the cedar bottoms looked like along the Coeur d'Alene River before they were logged.

Turn around and return to Forest Hwy 9, turn right and continue with the main tour.

🕥 Eagle Town Site

3.4 miles
Eagle was the first gold camp to appear during the gold rush of 1882-84. At its peak this tent city had a population of 3,500 but by the time frame structures were built the camp was already in decline. Many of the buildings were salvaged and used to build Murray. During the winter, supplies had to be brought in by dogsled from Prichard. Wyatt Earp and his brothers had a mining claim in Eagle and owned and operated the White Elephant Saloon in the spring and summer of 1884.

Several generations of sawmills operated at Eagle beginning with Joseph Avery and Herman Laumeister's Eagle Creek Pine Lumber Company in 1909. Avery also built and operated a short logging railroad along Eagle Creek and continued to log in the area until 1936. In 1920 Mountain Lumber Company built a band mill between the forks of Eagle Creek and then built several miles of logging railroad up the East Fork of Eagle Creek operating until 1929. In 1936 W.W. Powell took over operation until most of the available timber in the Eagle Creek area was logged in 1938. The plant was dismantled and moved to Weippe, Idaho. Just north of the highway, on the right, is the site of the Mountain States Lumber Company, which operated from 1939 to 1954. Burns-Yaak bought the company and operated a sawmill here from 1955 to 1965. The millpond is still visible north of the bridge that crosses Eagle Creek.

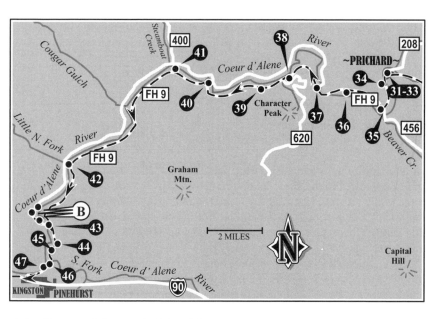

6.1 miles turn left onto Prichard St., over the Prichard Creek bridge and continue into Prichard

31 ~ Prichard ~

This site, known as Hummel's Landing from 1883 to 1901, served as jumping off point for prospectors camping along the Coeur d'Alene River. The town of Prichard was founded in 1908 and is named for Andrew J. Prichard who came to the Coeur d'Alenes in 1878 and discovered gold. City directories record a population of 150 during the early 1910s. Loggers, Forest Service employees and miners were the primary residents of the town which consisted of a post office, school, two grocery stores, warehouses, offices, OWR&N railroad depot, four hotel-restaurants, three bars and several homes. Winton Lumber Company headquarters warehouse and camp were located here during the Falls Creek and Shoshone Creek logging operations in the 1920s. The Prichard Resources Company of Boston, which owned most of the town, tore down all the buildings with the exception of two bars and three houses in 1985.

Across the river and a half-mile upstream from Prichard was the headquarters for the Prichard Ranger District. The ranger station opened in 1908 with access by a swinging suspension bridge across the river held together with suspended cables. Mule pack trains operated from here to supply the lookouts in the area. As many as eight pack trains left every day until the road was completed up the North Fork. The first Ranger's wife was very ambitious and landscaped the running stream behind the station with pools, rocks, flowers and holes to create riffles for her trout. The ranger station was very well kept. After being combined with the Wallace District in 1935, the site was abandoned and the improvements were removed.

㉜ Prichard Tavern
183 Prichard St., 6.1 miles
Built in the 1890s it served as a grocery store in the early 1900s. Walt Johnson bought the store and operated it as a grocery and hardware store with the family living upstairs. During the 1933 Flood, Walt's brother Jessie Johnson worked in the store continuing to sell staples such as beans, rice and flour, while wearing hip waders as water inundated the family store. Eventually they opened a tavern in the store. Later the tavern included a hotel with a lobby and as many as five rooms upstairs. A post office, located on the west side of the tavern, served the community from 1910 to 1943. Lizzie Backman was the first postmaster. A.J. Prichard served as postmaster followed by his son Jess with the family living in the back of the post office building. The Winton Lumber Company warehouse was located directly across the street.

㉝ Prichard School
6.2 miles on the right
This small building housed 14 students in 1928. It was purchased by the Stewart family and used as a residence until it was abandoned in the 1960s.

Go to the stop sign and turn left and continue on Forest Hwy 9 toward I-90 and Enaville. Set odometer to 0

Hauling supplies using bateaus pulled by horses on the Coeur d'Alene River above Prichard, 1923.

Transportation along the North Fork of the Coeur d'Alene River

Early travelers first poled up the river on flat bottom boats called bateaus. Later they used a wagon trail that can still be seen in places above the road further down river. Much of today's road along the North Fork of the Coeur d'Alene River was the OWR&N railroad grade built in 1908. To complete the railroad by year's end the railroad used 1,200 men. The railroad never carried much traffic especially after the U.S. Forest Service built roads into the area for logging trucks. After the December 1933 Flood washed out nearly all the track the railroad applied to abandon the line.

㉞ Prichard Bridge and Picnic Area

0.8 miles

An old wooden railroad bridge was converted for auto traffic by laying down planks. In the mid 1950s logging truck driver Chet Graybill hit the bridge but managed to make it across safely before the bridge collapsed. This accident was the end of that bridge but concrete abutments are still visible next to the picnic area.

㉟ Babins

21170 Coeur d'Alene River Rd., 1.5 miles (H & H Riverstop)

The OWR&N railroad extended up Beaver Creek to the Ray-Jefferson Mine at Carbon Center in February 1917. The mine failed to produce and in December 1917 a flood washed out the tracks. In the 1960s Lloyd Babin opened a service station and grocery on land homesteaded by his great grandfather.

㊱ Cedar Stumps

Starting at about 2.5 miles

The Winton Lumber Company staked timber claims at the mouths of all the creeks along the North Fork so other companies could not harvest the timber up those drainages. McGoldrick Lumber Company managed to log the valley floor of cedar timber in 1916-1918. However Winton's numerous claims blocked rival lumber companies from logging above the valley floor. Large cedar stumps with springboard cuts are visible along both sides of the highway.

㊲ Steel Bridge

4.4 miles

The Bureau of Public Roads built this bridge in 1958. From here to Cinnabar Creek the construction crew found railroad ties still in place. The old county road is on the other side of the river.

Cinnabar Creek and Oven

6.3 miles next to Forest Service FS Road 620
To access the oven site take FS Road 620 less than 0.25 miles to the first curve, park and walk over the log bridge across Cinnabar Creek and follow the abandoned wagon road for less than 200 feet. The oven, which looks like a mound of dirt, is located directly above the creek to the right of the roadbed.

The domed oven was built using local rock and two large gauge rails to support the roof. It is believed that the oven was built and used by Italian railroad workers to serve a large construction crew during the construction of the Idaho Northern Railroad, completed in December 1908. This railroad later became the Oregon Washington Railway & Navigation Company (OWR&N). The wagon road provided access to Murray, Eagle and Prichard along the upper Coeur d'Alene River area from the South Fork of the Coeur d'Alene River as early as the 1880s.

Graham Creek

8 miles look for a small bridge and trail head
Graham Creek Ranger Station was located on the right side of the road along with a large mule barn to house the pack mules. Nellie Baslington lived next to the ranger station and thought nothing of riding her bike the 13 miles to Enaville and then back. The Carter School was located on the south side of the road. The cliffs across the river are known as the Maple Cliffs because of their color, which comes from the iron rusting in the rock. Beginning at mile 8.7 between Graham and Coal creeks there were several log chutes that extended above the railroad grade dropping logs into the river. Chutes were used to transport logs from the hillside to the river where they were floated down to sawmills.

⑩ Castle Rock Formation

9.2 miles across the river to the right
Castle Rock is part of the Precambrian St. Regis Formation as are other cliffs along the river. This rock is made primarily of quartzite and, because of its hardness, has not eroded away.

⑪ Steamboat Rock and Steamboat Creek Pond

11.5 miles on the north side of the river just past the parking lot
Between 1883 and 1900 Coeur d'Alene Indians were seen hunting mule deer and gathering berries along the Little North Fork of the Coeur d'Alene River and on Grizzly Mountain. According to an old Blackfeet legend, the Blackfeet and the Coeur d'Alene fought for these hunting territories on Grizzly Mountain. They established a truce when the Blackfeet sent women

to marry the Coeur d'Alene men. Near Grizzly Mountain was a stream called "Quiet Water" or *Hnmiḻkwe'*.

The pond, operated by the Idaho Fish and Game, is open for fishing all year with a limit of six trout.

42▸ Linfor and the confluence of the Little North Fork and the North Fork rivers

17.2 miles

In 1911 a school was built here and in about 1912 Tuttle and Fay opened a general store. When they submitted the name Little North Fork for the post office, the department said it was too long. It was suggested that the first two letters of Little, the "n" from North and the first three letters of Fork were used to create the name Linfor. Archie Jacobson recalled: "About 1915 they ran a special "Fish Train" with 5 coaches on Sundays to Prichard. They let people off to picnic and fish. An old Finlander played the accordion at the Linfor station."

A siding for loading ore concentrate from the Empire Copper Mine and a Winton Lumber Company warehouse were located in this area.

43▸ Silver Bridge

20.4 miles

This single lane, plank-bottomed bridge was built in 1930 and has survived numerous floods. Under the bridge is a popular fishing and swimming hole. Archie Jacobson claimed he was the first person to jump from the top of the bridge and his sister was the first woman to do so. It is now illegal to jump off the bridge.

◆━━━━━━━━━━━━━━━━━━━━━━━━━━━━━━━━━━━━━━◆

Ⓑ▸ Old River Road Side Trip

Past the Silver Bridge turn left and the road swings around to go over the bridge

Ⓑ₁▸ Archie Jacobson's Log Cabin

Old River Rd. on the left

Archie Jacobson was born at Linfor in 1899, one of 10 children. His parent's house burned in 1919 and his father built a log home which was moved to this location from Linfor. The cabin did not have electricity or running water. The Forest Service hired Archie as a handy man and caretaker to shovel snow off the backcountry cabins. Archie was a logger who also ran trap lines with Frank McPherson. McPherson and Jacobson were both long time residents and colorful characters. Behind his cabin at Linfor were two very large sheds filled to the brim with tools, junk and odds-and-ends he picked up over the years from mines, dumps and logging camps.

(B2) Old Bearpaw Store
Old River Rd.
The store, built in 1949, was originally located across the North Fork of the Coeur d'Alene River. It was used in the 1997 film, Dante's Peak, in the role of a grocery store. After the flood of 1994 the Federal Emergency Management Agency planned to burn the store, but in 1998 Bert James had the building moved to this location. The 90,000-pound store was put on a large mover's dolly with 24 wheels and then pulled across the river with a bulldozer to this site.

(B3) Albert's Place
418 Old River Rd. (One Eye's Landing)
Roy Brickle recalled: "Albert's place was first run by a Finlander. He kept girls there . . . then the law shut 'er down. . . ."

The rough lumber and 2x4 structure was moved to this location in the late 1920s by Simeon Aro, a relative of the Aro family who homesteaded here in the early 1900s. When beer was legalized he was able to get a beer license and operate a beer parlor. About 1931 or 1932 Aro sold the beer parlor to Albert Legault, and the Aro family leased the land to Albert. After Albert acquired the beer parlor he hired a man named Koski to finish the interior of the building, added a cash register and put in a bar. Eventually Albert was able to purchase the land from the Aro family. In the 1950s Albert sold the business and moved to the Salmon River to placer mine for gold where he staked a few claims. The new owner had the bar for only two years when there was a bad shooting incident and he decided to sell it back to Albert. Albert moved back to the area and operated the beer parlor until his death in 1982. Harvey Legault, Albert's nephew, sold the bar shortly after Albert's death.

Turn around, go back over the bridge, turn left on the highway and continue down river.

(44) Enaville
21.2 miles
Enaville is located at the mouths of the North and South Forks of the Coeur d'Alene River. Many of the early residents were Finlanders including loggers

who came from the mid-west states after the timber there was logged out. The railroad station agent was asked to name this place. His wife's name was Ena so he added ville to it and got Enaville. Before the 1910 Fire, five taverns, a post office, store, sawmill and railroad station existed in Enaville.

45 Enaville Resort

1480 Coeur d'Alene River Rd.
The Enaville Resort, known over the years as the Snakepit, Josie's, Clark Hotel and many other names, has been a landmark for over 100 years. The resort has served as a boomtown bar, railroad layover, hotel and gaming house, and starting point for loggers and miners. When Josie Bates bought the hotel in 1953, she added the fireplace made of local rock and the twisted wood and moose and elk horns. The Enaville Resort serves food and drink.

46 Trail of the Coeur d'Alenes Trailhead

22.1 miles
This 71.4 non-motorized paved bike trail begins in Plummer and ends in Mullan. From Plummer, Enaville is at mile 47.3 of the trail. Parking and public restrooms are available.

47 Old River Road

The old river road can be seen about 100 feet above the highway along this stretch of the river. It was never paved.

Take I-90 west to return to Coeur d'Alene.

See page 7- 11 for Kingston

References listed here are for further reading and not intended as an inclusive list of all the references used in this work.

~ Bibliography ~

Aiken, Katherine G. *Idaho's Bunker Hill: Rise and Fall of a Great Mining Company, 1885-1981.* Norman: University of Oklahoma Press, 2005.

Allen, John Eliot and Marjorie Burns with Sam C. Sargent. *Cataclysms on the Columbia.* Portland, Oregon: Timber Press, 1986.

Alt, David D. *Glacial Lake Missoula and Its Humongous Floods.* Missoula, Montana: Mountain Press Publishing, 2001.

Alt, David D. and Donald W. Hyndman. *Roadside Geology of Idaho,* Missoula, Montana: Mountain Press Publishing, 1989.

Anderson, Augusta. *The Shadowy St. Joe.* circa 1906.

Anderton, Peg Gott. *Pleasant View.* Anderton Genealogy Services, 1986.

Anderton, Peg Gott. *800 Indian Horses and A Ghost Town Buried at Washington-Idaho Border and Interstate-Ninety.* Anderton Genealogy Services, 1986.

Asleson, David and Sandra Crowell. *Up the Swiftwater: A Pictorial History of the Colorful Upper St. Joe River Country.* Coeur d'Alene, Idaho: Museum of North Idaho, 1997.

Battien, Pauline. *The Gold Seekers: A 300 year History of Mining in Washington, Idaho, Montana & Lower British Columbia*, Colville, Washington: Statesman-Examiner, Inc., 1989.

Boone, Lalia. *Idaho Place Names: A Geographical Dictionary*, Moscow, Idaho: University of Idaho Press, 1988.

Brainard, Wendell and Ray Chapman. *Golden History Tales From Idaho's Coeur d'Alene Mining District.* Wallace, Idaho: Crow's Printing, April 1990.

Carbonneau-Kincaid, Simone, Carl Ritchie, and Diana Rigg. *Monument West, Monument West Addition and Handspike Helicopter Timber Sales Archaeological Surveys, Fernan Ranger District, Idaho Panhandle National Forests, Coeur d'Alene, Idaho.* Report on file at Idaho State Historic Preservation Office, Boise: October 1979.

Carbonneau-Kincaid, Simone. *Elk Ridge and Upper Cedar Creek Timber Sales Archaeological Surveys, Fernan Ranger District, Idaho Panhandle National Forests. Coeur d'Alene, Idaho.* Report on file at the Idaho State Historic Preservation Office, Boise: October 1980.

Carbonneau-Kincaid, Simone. *Cultural Resource Surveys of the Miller Can, Murray and The Break Timber Sales, Fernan Ranger Station, Idaho Panhandle National Forests, Coeur d'Alene, Idaho.* Report on file at the Idaho State Historic Preservation Office, Boise: October 1982.

Carbonneau-Kincaid, Simone. *Cultural Resource Surveys of the Halsey Creek Timber Sale, Fernan Ranger Station, Idaho Panhandle National Forests. Coeur d'Alene, Idaho.* Report on file at the Idaho State Historic Preservation Office, Boise: September 1981.

Chambertlain, V.E., Roy M. Breckenridge and Bill Bonnichsen, ed. *Guidebook to the Geology of Northern and Western Idaho and Surrounding Area*. Idaho Geological Survey, Bulletin #28, Moscow, Idaho: University of Idaho, 1989.

Chapman, Ray, *History of Idaho's Silver Valley 1878-2000*, Kellogg, Idaho: Chapman Publishing, 2000.

Chapman, Ray, *History of Kellogg, Idaho 1885-2002*, Kellogg, Idaho: Chapman Publishing, 2002.

Chapman, Ray. *Uncle Bunker: Memories in Words and Pictures*. Kellogg, Idaho: Chapman Publishing, 1994.

Cohen, Stan B. and A. Richard Guth. *A Pictorial History of the U.S. Forest Service 1891-1945 Northern Region*, Missoula, Montana: Pictorial Histories Publishing Company, 1991.

Cohen, Stan and Don Miller. *The Big Burn: Northwest's Forest Fire of 1910*. Missoula, Montana: Pictorial Histories Publishing Company, 1978.

Cohen, Stan. *The Tree Army: A Pictorial History of the Civilian Conservation Corps 1933-1942,* Missoula, Montana: Pictorial Histories Publishing Company, 1980.

Conley, Cort. *Idaho for the Curious,* Cambridge, Idaho: Backeddy Books, 1982.

Dahlgren, Dorothy and Simone Carbonneau Kincaid. *In All the West No Place Like This: A Pictorial History of the Coeur d'Alene Region.* Coeur d'Alene, Idaho: Museum of North Idaho, 1991.

Dolph, Jerry. *Fire in the Hole: Untold Story of Hardrock Miners*. Pullman, Washington: Washington State University, 1994.

Dolph, Jerry and Arthur Randall. *Wyatt Earp and Coeur d'Alene Gold! Stampede to Idaho Territory*. Eagle City Publications, 1999.

Fahey, John. *Inland Empire: D.C. Corbin and Spokane*. Seattle, Washington: University of Washington Press, 1965.

Fahey, John. *The Ballyhoo Bonanza, Charles Sweeny and the Idaho Mines.* Seattle and London: University of Washington Press, 1971.

Fahey, John. *The Days of the Hercules.* Seattle and London: University of Washington Press, 1978.

Fahey, John. *Saving The Reservation: Joe Garry and the Battle to Be Indian.* Seattle and London: University of Washington Press, 2001.

Fahey, John. *Shaping Spokane: Jay P. Graves and his Times*. Seattle and London: University of Washington Press, 1994.

Faust, Peggy and Ralph. *Wildflowers of the Inland Northwest: Idaho, Montana, Washington, Oregon, B.C. & Alberta*, Coeur d'Alene, Idaho: Museum of North Idaho, 1999.

Frey, Rodney, ed. *Stories That Make the World: Oral Literature of the Indian Peoples of the Inland Northwest as Told by Lawrence Aripa, Tom Yellowtail and other Elders.* Norman and London: University of Oklahoma Press, 1995.

Frey, Rodney. *Landscape Traveled By Coyote and Crane: World of the Schitsu'umsh (Coeur d'Alene Indians)*. Seattle and London: University of Washington Press, 2001.

Hahn, Margie E. *Montana's Mineral County in Retrospect.* 1997.

Hammes, Robert M. and E. Mark Justice. *The Way It Was,* St. Maries, Idaho: Western Historical, Inc. 1962.

Hanson, Donna M. ed. *Frontier Duty: The Army in Northern Idaho, 1853-1876.* Northwest Historical Manuscript Series, Moscow, Idaho: University of Idaho Library, 2005.

Hackbarth, Linda. *Bayview and Lakeview: And Other Early Settlements on Southern Lake Pend Oreille.* Coeur d'Alene, Idaho: Museum of North Idaho, 2003.

Hart, Patricia and Ivar Nelson. *Mining Town: The Photographic Record of T.N. Barnard and Nellie Stockbridge from the Coeur d'Alenes.* Seattle and London: University of Washington Press and Idaho State Historical Society, Boise, Idaho, 1984.

Hyde, Gene. *From Hell to Heaven: Death-Related Mining Accidents in North Idaho.* Coeur d'Alene, Idaho: Museum of North Idaho, 2003.

Johnson, Stanley W. *The Milwaukee Road in Idaho: A Guide to Sites and Locations Revised and Expanded Second Edition.* Coeur d'Alene, Idaho: Museum of North Idaho, 2003.

Kingston, Ceylon S. *The Inland Empire in the Pacific Northwest.* Fairfield, Washington: Ye Galleon Press, 1981.

Kowrach, Edward J. and Thomas E. Connolly, ed. *Saga of the Coeur d'Alene Indians: An Account of Chief Joseph Seltice,* Fairfield, Washington: Ye Galleon Press, 1990.

Kresek, Ray. *Fire Lookouts of the Northwest.* Fairfield, Washington: Ye Galleon Press, 1984, 1985, 1998.

Magnuson, Richard G. *Coeur d'Alene Diary: the First Ten Years of Hardrock Mining in North Idaho.* Portland, Oregon: Metropolitan Press, 1968.

Meeks, Harold A. *On the Road To Yellowstone: the Yellowstone Trail and the American Highways 1900-1930.* Missoula, Montana: Pictorial Histories Publishing Company, 2000.

Miss, Christian J. and Nancy Renk. *Cultural Resources Investigation for the Fernan Lake Road Saftey Improvement Project, Kootenai County, Idaho.* Prepared for David Evans and Associates, Inc. and Western Federal Lands Highway Division, Federal Highway Commission, Northwest Archaeological Associates, Seattle, Washington: December 2002.

Montgomery, James. *Liberated Woman: A Life of May Arkwright Hutton.* Fairfield, Washington: Ye Galleon Press, 1974.

Mullan, Captain John. *Miners' and Travelers' Guide.* Fairfield, Washington: Ye Galleon Press, 1991.

Mullan, Captain John. *Report on the Construction of a Military Road from Fort Walla-Walla to Fort Benton.* Originally published by U.S. Government Printing Office, Washington: 1863; reprinted by Ye Galleon Press, Fairfield, Washington: 1994.

Mueller, Marge and Ted. *Fire, Faults and Floods: A Road and Trail Guide Exploring the Origins of the Columbia River Basin.* Moscow, Idaho: University of Idaho Press, 1997.

Museum of North Idaho Library and Archive, Coeur d'Alene, Idaho.

Needham, Gordon. *Needham Family Memoirs.* Fairfield, Washington: Ye Galleon Press, 1988. Includes a reprint of: *The Official Map and Handbook of the Coeur d'Alene Mines, Idaho Territory* by Phil Markson, Portland, Oregon: Lewis and Dryden, 1884.

Otis, Alison T., William D. Honey, Thomas C. Hogg, and Kimberly K. Lakin. *The Forest Service and the Civilian Conservation Corps: 1933-42.* Pacific Crest Research and Services Corporation, Corvallis, Oregon: 1986.

Palmer, Gary B. Ph.D., prepared by Elder Grammarian Lawrence Nicodemus, and Lavina Felsman with the direction of Prof. Armando M. DaSilva. *Khwi' Khwe Hntmikhn'lumkhw, This is My Land: A Workbook in Coeur d'Alene Indian Geography*, Plummer, Idaho: Coeur d'Alene Tribe, 1987.

Peltier, Jerome. *Manners and Customs of the Coeur d'Alene Indians.* Spokane, Washington: Peltier Publications, 1975.

Peltier, Jerome. *A Brief History of the Coeur d'Alene Indians 1806-1909.* Fairfield, Washington: Ye Galleon Press, 1981.

Pyne, Stephen J. *Year of the Fires: The Story of the Great Fires of 1910.* New York: Viking, Penguin Putnam, 2001.

Ransome, Frederick Leslie and Frank Cathcart Calkins. *The Geology and Ore Deposits of the Coeur d'Alene District, Idaho.* Department of the Interior, United States Geological Survey, Professional Paper 62, Washington: Government Printing Office, 1908.

Ream, Lanny. *Idaho Minerals*, Coeur d'Alene, Idaho: Museum of North Idaho, 2004.

Reichard, Gladys. *An Analysis of Coeur d'Alene Indian Myths.* Memoirs of the American Folklore Society, Volume 41, Philadelphia: American Folklore Society, 1947.

Renk, Nancy F. *Driving Past: Tours of Historical and Geological Sites in Bonner County, Idaho.* Sandpoint, Idaho: Bonner County Centennial Committee, 1991.

Russell, Bert. *Calked Boots.* Harrison, Idaho: Lacon Publishers, 1967.

Russell, Bert. *Hardships and Happy Times.* Harrison, Idaho: Lacon Publishers, 1978.

Russell, Bert. *North Fork of the Coeur d'Alene River.* Harrison, Idaho: Lacon Publishers; Coeur d'Alene, Idaho: Museum of North Idaho, 1984.

Russell, Bert and Marie. *Rock Burst.* Moscow, Idaho: University of Idaho Press, 1998.

Russell, Bert. *Swiftwater People.* Harrison, Idaho: Lacon Publishers; Coeur d'Alene, Idaho: Museum of North Idaho, 1979.

Russell, Bert. *The Sawdust Dream.* Harrison, Idaho: Lacon Publishers, 1990.

Sandberg, Thomas and the Bonner County Historical Society Museum. *In the Wake of the Mary Moody: Historic Boat Tours on Lake Pend Oreille.* Idaho Panhandle National Forest, Sandpoint Ranger District, Sandpoint, Idaho: Northwest Interpretive Association, 1991.

Shiach, William S., Harry B. Averill and John M. Henderson. *An Illustrated History of North Idaho Embracing Nez Perce, Idaho, Latah, Kootenai and Shoshone Counties in the State of Idaho.* Western Historical Publishing Company, 1903.

Scott, Orland. *Pioneer Days on the Shadowy St. Joe,* Caldwell, Idaho: Caxton Printers, Ltd. 1967.

Shadduck, Louise. *At the Edge of the Ice: Where Lake Coeur d'Alene and Its People Meet.* Boise, Idaho: Tamarack Books, 1996.

Sims, Cort. *Ranger Stations on the Idaho Panhandle National Forests.* United States Department of Agriculture, Idaho Panhandle National Forests, Supervisor's Office, Coeur d'Alene, Idaho: 1986.

Singletary, Robert. *Kootenai Chronicles, Vol. 1.,* Coeur d'Alene, Idaho: Museum of North Idaho, 1997.

Smith, John E. *Pioneer Reminiscences.* Fairfield, Washington: Ye Galleon Press, 1996, originally published in the Washington Historical Quarterly, Vol. VII, 1916.

Smith, Robert Wayne. *The History of Placer and Quartz Gold Mining in the Coeur d'Alene District.* Fairfield, Washington: Ye Galleon Press, 1932.

Smith, Robert Wayne. *Coeur d'Alene, Mining War 1892.* Corvallis, Oregon: Oregon State University Press, 1961.

Spencer, Betty Goodwin. *The Big Blowup: The Northwest's Great Fire.* Caldwell, Idaho: Caxton Printers, Ltd., 1956.

Stoll, William T. *Silver Strike: The True Story of Silver Mining in the Coeur d'Alenes.* Moscow, Idaho: University of Idaho Press, 1991.

Stratton, David H., ed. *Spokane and the Inland Empire: An Interior Pacific Northwest Anthology.* Pullman, Washington: Washington University Press, 1991.

Strong, Clarence and Clyde Webb. *White Pine: King of Many Waters.* Missoula, Montana: Mountain Press Publishing Company, 1970.

James Teit. The Salish Tribes of the Western Plateaus: Coeur d'Alene, Flathead and Okanogan Indian. *45th Annual Report of the Bureau of American Ethnology for 1927-1928.* Smithsonian Institution, Washington: 1930.

Trimble, William Joseph. *The Mining Advance Into the Inland Empire.* Fairfield, Washington: Ye Galleon Press, 1986.

Umpley, Joseph B. *Geology and Ore Deposits of Shoshone County, Idaho.* Department of Interior, United States Geological Society Bulletin 732, Washington: Government Printing Office, 1923.

Unites States Forest Service. Coeur d'Alene National Forest Maps, Idaho. 1911, 1917, 1918, 1924, 1932, 1945, 1948, 1955, 1976.

United States Department of Interior. General Land Office and Master Title plat maps, and Historical Indexes on file at the Coeur d'Alene Bureau of Land Management District Office, Coeur d'Alene, Idaho.

Williams, Hill. *Restless Northwest: A Geologic Story.* Pullman, Washington: Washington State University Press, 2002.

Wood, John V. *Railroads Through the Coeur d'Alenes.* Caldwell, Idaho: Caxton Printers, Ltd., 1984.

Woodworth-Ney, Linda. *Mapping Identity: The Creation of the Coeur d'Alene Indian Reservation. 1805-1902.* Boulder, Colorado: University Press of Colorado, 2004.

~ Index ~

16 to 1 Saloon 7-36
3rd Generation Restaurant 7-11

~ A ~

AAUW 3-7
Acoustic Research Detachment 2-7
Adair 5-18, 5-25
Adair snow slide 5-25
Adams, Sam and Lenore 7-6
Addington, Winfield 4-12
Advance 1-5
Ahrs Creek 5-14
Airstrip, Magee 6-14
Akers, Cecil 4-25
Albert's Place 8-19
Albinola, Pete 7-47
Alder Creek 8-7
Alexander, Governor 4-14
Allen Ridge Trail 17 5-30
Allingson, Phyllis 7-19
Almond Farm 7-6
Almond, Herman 7-6
Almquist, Walt 8-12
Alpine Village 7-28
American Legion
  Plummer 4-22, 4-23
  Kellogg 7-35
American Trust Bank 3-14
Amwaco 4-27
Andrews Spring 4-23
Annis, A.B. 4-17
Antlers Tavern 5-23
Archer, Shorty 4-12
Argala 7-50
Argo, Clarence 2-12
Armstrong Garage 4-8
Arnhold Farm 7-6
Arnhold, Tony, Hannah, John, Frank
  and Frances Miller 7-6, 7-7
Aro Cabin 7-14
Aro, John and Alice 7-14, 7-15
Aro, Simeon 8-19
Arrow Point 4-5
Arvidson, Everett and Lois 7-16
ASARCO 7-16
Athol 1-24
Athol Community Center/City Hall

1-24
Atlas Building Center, Osburn 7-45
Atlas Tie Co. 7-45
Aulbach, Adam 8-12
Avery 5-22 to 5-24
  Historic Ranger Station 5-23
  Rail Yard Site 5-20, 5-21
  Ranger Station 5-19, 5-29
  Trading Post 5-23
  Joseph 8-13
Avista, see Washington Water Power
Avondale
  Barn 2-15
  Cottages 2-16
  Farm 2-15
  Golf and Tennis Club 2-15
  Lake 2-15, 2-16

~ B ~

B.R. Lewis/Blackwell logging
  railroad 4-27
Babins 8-16
Backman, Lizzie 8-15
Baker Clothing Co. 7-31
Bank of Spirit Lake 1-21
Barclay House 3-16
Barclay, Alexander Dr. 3-16
Barclay, Gedney 3-8
Barker Sawmill 6-12, 6-13
Barker, R.C. "Bob" 6-12, 6-13
Barrel 7-45, 7-47
Baseball 3-10
Baslington, Nellie 8-17
Bateaus 8-15, 8-16
Bates, Josie 8-20
Bates, Randy 3-18
Bayview 2-5 to 2-9
  Inn 2-6, 2-7
  Memorial Garden 2-9
Beatty, James 3-7
Beauchamp 5-16
Beauty Bay 4-4, 4-5, 6-3
  Campground 4-4
  Seed Orchard 4-5
  Viewpoint 4-5
Beaver Creek 8-6, 8-7, 8-16
Beaver Station 8-6

Bedroom Gold Mine Bar 8-10
Belle, Guy and Velma 7-38, 7-39
Bellows Dairy 5-17
Bellows, Harris and Annetta 5-17
Belmont 2-10
Ben Hur 8-4
Benewah Lake 4-19 to 4-21
Benham, Arthur Mellville 'Mel' 1-8
Bennet Bay 4-2
Bennett Family 4-14
Bennett's Photo Studio 4-14
Benoit 4-19
Bentley, Elton and Doris 6-8
Berges Block 1-14
Berges, A.A. 1-14
Bernard Peak 2-10
Big Creek Mining Co. 7-41, 7-42
Big Creek, Coeur d'Alene NF 6-16,
   7-40 to 7-43, 7-46
Big Creek, St. Joe NF 5-8, 5-14, 5-18
Big Creek West Fork 5-16
Big Dick Creek 5-26
Big Eddy 5-14
Big Hank Meadows and Campground
   6-15
Big Meadow Ranch 4-19
Biinwa 4-19
Bi-Metallic Building 7-52, 7-53
Bitter End Marina 2-8
Bitterroot Divide 5-28
Bitterroot Mercantile 7-33
Bjorklund, Eric 3-7
Bjorklund, Mary 3-15
Black Cat 7-18
Black Cloud 8-4
Blackfeet Indians 8-17
Blackwell Houses
   Coeur d'Alene 3-15
   Spirit Lake 1-22
Blackwell Lumber Co. 5-16
Blackwell Reminder Printing Co.
   7-29
Blackwell, Frederick 1-16, 1-18,
   1-21, 1-22, 3-9, 3-15
Blackwell, Russell 3-15
Blake, Dennis and True 7-42
Blankenship, Tom 8-9
Bloem, Sandi 3-14

Blue Creek Bay 4-4
Blue Lagoon Saloon 5-5
Bluff Creek 5-31
Boat Restaurant 7-17
Bockstruck, Larry 2-9
Bodine's 7-10
Boise Statesman 7-53
Bond Creek 5-11
Bonham, Emil 7-31
Bootjack Creek 6-12
Borax Mine 5-28
Boxing 8-4
Boy Scout Jamborees 2-2
Boy Scouts 4-5, 7-35, 7-36, 8-7
Bozanta Tavern Resort 2-13, 2-15,
   2-16, 2-17
Bozanta Tavern Resort golf course
   2-16
Brack Motor Supply 7-38
Brass, Gustav 4-11
Brawl, Frank 7-50
Brayer Bakery 7-31, 7-32
Brayer, John 7-32
Breakwater 6-11
Brickle, Roy 8-19
Bridgeman Building 4-10
Bridgeman, Wayne 4-10
Brig Museum 2-4
Broughton, Joseph 4-5
Brown 5-13
Brown, Harry and Vi 7-17 to 7-19
Brown, Kate 7-12
Brown, Oscar 4-19
Brown, Rose 5-2
Brownawell, H.D. 4-10
Brownlee, Scott and Pam 1-8
Bruher, Alice and Louis 6-6
Buell Memorial Bridge 5-14
Buell Sawmill Site 5-15
Buell, Lloyd and Glen 5-14, 5-15
Bull Pen 4-14, 7-36
Bull Run Lake 5-3, 5-4
Bullion Mine 5-27
Bunker Hill and Sullivan Mine 7-26,
   7-28, 7-34
   Assay Office 7-19, 7-23
   Company 6-15, 7-21 to 7-24, 7-34
   to 7-36, 7-42, 8-6, 8-7, 8-12

Main Office 7-23
Crusher Plant 7-23
Fertilizer plant 7-20
management housing 7-22
Mine Dump Station 7-23
Mine yard 7-22
slag pile 7-20, 7-21
Smelter 7-17, 7-20 to 7-22
Smoke Stacks 7-22
Warehouse and Engineering 7-23
Zinc Plant 7-20 to 7-22
Bureau of Land Management (BLM)
7-45
Bureau of Public Roads 8-16
Burke 7-21
Burleigh's store 4-11
Burlington Northern Railroad
Overpass 1-9
Burlington Northern Santa Fe
Railroad 1-9, 1-25, 3-4
Burmeister, Doug 7-19
Burns, Jim 7-44
Burns, John 7-10
Burns-Yaak River Lumber Co. 7-44,
8-13
Burnt Cabin Creek Railroad 6-9
Buroker, Herb and Gladys 2-10,
2-11, 3-3
Burton's Bakery 8-10
Buster Brown and the Curly Heads
7-31
Butler, Walter 2-2
Butte local 5-27
Buttonhook Group Camp 2-3

~ C ~

C Sly Meat Co. 4-18
Cahoots 7-25
Caladay Mine 7-50
Calder 5-14, 5-15
Calder Bridge 5-15
Calder General Store 5-15
Callis Creek 6-14
Camas Fields 5-10
Cameron apartments 7-45
Camp Coeur d'Alene, see Ft. Sherman
Camp Fire Girls 3-8
Camps
44 5-21

Arrow Boys 4-5
Blister Rust Control (BRC)
4-5, 5-30, 6-12, 6-13
Easton 4-5
Ferguson 8-6, 8-7
Outdoor Education 6-13
Rock City CCC 6-15
Shoshone Base 6-16
Tin Can Flat CCC 5-30
Turner Flat, CCC 5-30
Waldron 2-2
Winton 22 6-12
Youth Conservation Corps 6-13
Canfield Mountain 2-21, 3-3
Canfield, Oscar 2-20, 2-21
Canyon Creek 6-11, 7-11, 7-51
Canyon Garage 7-5
Canyon Store 7-5, 7-6
Cape Horn 2-7, 2-9
Captain Billy's Whiz Bang 4-11
Carbon Center 8-16
Carey, J.M. 3-7
Carfagno, Brother Achilles 7-8
Carlin Creek and Bay 4-6
Carlin, William Col. 4-6
Caron Machine Shop 8-4
Carroll, James 3-14
Cassedy Funeral Home 1-12
Cassedy, Constance 1-12
Cassedy, Louise 1-12
Castle Rock Formation 8-17
Cataldo 7-8, 7-9, 7-10
Beer Parlor 7-10
Cataldo Mission 4-23, 7-8
Cataldo, Father Joseph 7-9
Cathcart 6-12
Cathella Mine 8-3
Cattle Crossing 6-3
CCC (Civilian Conservation Corp)
4-4, 4-5, 4-21, 5-13, 5-14, 5-16,
5-17, 5-19, 5-21 to 5-23, 5-26,
5-30, 5-32, 6-3 to 6-5, 6-9, 6-12,
6- 13, 6-15, 6-16
CCC (Civilian Conservation Corp)
Bridge,
Avery/St. Joe River 5-21
Cedar Mountain 2-10, 5-19
Cedar Stumps 7-16, 8-18

Cemeteries
  Day's 7-45
  Evergreen 1-10
  Greek 1-17
  Harrison 4-10
  Lane 5-5
  Medimont 5-8
  Mountain View 1-23
  Murray GAR 8-9
  Nine Mile 5-28, 8-3
  Pine Grove 1-17
  Pleasant View 1-8
  Rose Lake 5-2
  St. Thomas 3-18
  Wallace 8-6
  Woodlawn Historical Fire Ring
    4-18, 4-19, 5-20
Central Shoe Shop 7-33
Cerny, Elma 4-12
Chaffee family 7-38
Chain Lakes 5-2
Chapen Home 8-7
Chapen, John and Nelda Lorenzi 8-7
Chapin Drug 1-5, 1-6
Chapin, Walter 1-5
Chase family 1-9
Chatcolet Lake 4-20, 4-21
Chatcolet Trestle 4-19
Chatfield, Harry and Wilma 5-5
Chicago Milwaukee & Puget Sound
  Railway see Milwaukee Road
Chilco 2-12
Chilco Falls 2-12
Chinese 1-17
Chisholm, Dan 7-27
Christopherson, Chris 8-10
Churches
  American Lutheran, Kellogg 7-38
  Little White, Athol 1-24
  Community Baptist, Harrison 4-9
  Community Presbyterian, Post Falls
    1-16
  Episcopalian, Spirit Lake 1-22
  Federated, Kellogg 7-29
  Lutheran, Spirit Lake 1-19
  McGuire Wesleyan, Post Falls 1-9
  Methodist, Harrison 4-9
  Methodist, Kellogg 7-29

  Old Church Post Falls 1-6
  Omega Gospel & Hall 5-9
  Our Lady of Perpetual Help
    Catholic, Harrison 4-9
  Our Savior Lutheran, Pinehurst 7-38
  Community Baptist, Pine Creek 7-15
  Pleasant View 1-8
  Plymouth Congregational,
    Kellogg 7-29
  Presbyterian, Harrison 4-9
  Presbyterian, Spirit Lake 1-19
  St. Joseph's Catholic, Spirit Lake
    1-19
  St. Stanislaus Catholic, Rathdrum
    1-15
  St. Thomas Catholic, Coeur d'Alene
    3-15, 3-16
  United Methodist, Rathdrum 1-16
Circling Raven 7-7
Cinnabar 7-19
Cinnabar Creek 8-16, 8-17
City Bakery and Confectionery 7-32
City Halls
  Coeur d'Alene 3-5, 3-14
  Harrison 4-9
  St. Maries 4-14
City Meat Co. 8-4
Clark Hotel 8-20
Clark House, Hayden Lake 2-18, 2-19
Clark House, St. Maries 4-16
Clark, Ernest and Lillian 4-15, 4-16
Clark, Mr. and Mrs. F. Lewis 2-18 to
  2-20
Clark, William A. Jr. 7-4
Clement, Sister 3-18
Coal Creek 8-17
Coeur d'Alene & Pend Oreille
  Railway 2-7, 2-10
Coeur d'Alene & Spokane electric line
  1-5, 1-9, 2-13, 2-16, to 2-18, 2-
  20, 2-21, 3-2, 3-9 to 3-12, 3-15
Coeur d'Alene 3-2 to 3-18
  3rd St. Dock 3-12
  Airport 4-4
  Dike 3-6, 3-9
  Hardware 7-41, 8-12
  Jr. College 3-5
  Library 3-13, 3-14

Lumber Co. 3-13
Press 3-7
Resort 3-12
Resort Golf Course 4-2
Senior Recreation Center 3-17
waterfront 3-11, 3-12
Coeur d'Alene Indian Reservation 4-7, 4-21 to 4-27
Coeur d'Alene Indians 1-2, 1-7, 1-8, 1-17, 1-19, 2-13, 3-2, 3-4, 4-5, 4-7, 4-13, 4-19, 4-20, 4-21, 4-23, 4-24, 4-27, 4-28, 5-2, 5-7 to 5-10, 5-12, 5-28, 5-29, 5-31, 6-6, 6-8, 7-7 to 7-9, 7-26, 7-43, 7-51, 8-17, 8-18
Coeur d'Alene Mine dredge 7-7
Coeur d'Alene Mining District 3-12, 4-7, 7-14, 7-22, 8-2 to 8-20
Coeur d'Alene name 3-2
Coeur d'Alene National Forest 6-8, 7-11
Coeur d'Alene Railway & Navigation Co. 7-36, 7-37
Coeur d'Alene River 4-6, 4-7, 5-3, 5-5, 5-8, 6-8, 6-11, 6-14, 7-11, 7-12, 8-6, 8-10, 8-13
    Little North Fork 6-4, 6-8, 6-12, 6-14 to 6-16, 8-17, 8-18
    Road (Old) 7-12, 8-17, 8-20
    North Fork 7-14, 7-44, 8-10, 8-14, 8-16, 8-18, 8-19
    South Fork 7-14, 7-24, 7-44, 7-51, 8-17, 8-19
Coeur d'Alene St. Joe Divide Trail 16 5-28
Coeur d'Alene Sun 8-12
Coeur Mine 7-46, 7-48
Colonial Tavern 7-28
Colton 1-24
Columbian 5-27
Community Building Partners 1-6
Connolly, Mrs. 7-19
Consolidated Silver Corporation 7-44
Constitution Mine 7-14
Cook, Fulton and Charles 4-19
Cooper, Jake 2-18
Cooperative Supply 3-11
Coopers Bay 2-18
Copper Creek 6-11

Corbeill, Ike and Vance 7-17
Corbin
    D.C. 1-9, 1-11, 2-11
    Ditch 1-2, 1-3
    Junction 2-11
    Ranch 2-11
Corkhill, Brad 7-8
Corliss Steam Engine 3-11
Corrigan Group 7-16
Corskie Building 4-10
Corskie, John 4-10
Costello, John 3-18
Cougar Creek 5-2
Cougar Gulch 4-28
Cougher, Harry 7-41
Courthouses
    Benewah County 4-15
    Kootenai County 3-14
    Murray 8-11, 8-12
Craik, Charles 3-8
Crane family 4-7, 4-11
Crane House 4-11
Crane, Edwin 4-11
Crane, Silas W. 4-11
Crane, William 4-11
Crawford, A.W. 5-5
Crenshaw Block 1-14
Crescent Ore Chute 7-41
Crown Electric 7-15
Crowley, M.M. 1-11
Crystal Creek 5-16
Crystal Gold Mine 7-39, 7-40
Cullum residence 6-6
Cultural Arts Center 1-6
Culver, Mr. and Mrs. Frank 8-11
Cutter, Kirtland 1-16, 1-22, 2-16

~ **D** ~

Dahlgren homestead 4-6
Dalton Gardens, City of 2-20, 2-2
Daly Gulch 7-50
Daly, Father T.A. 4-9
Dance Hall Flat 4-27
Dancewana 3-8
Danner, Monty 2-19
Dante's Peak 8-19
Dave Smith Motors 7-37
Davenport Hotel 2-20
Day Mines 8-5

Day, Eugene, Harry and Jerome 7-43
Day, family 8-5
Day, Harry 7-45
Day, Henry 7-8, 8-5
Dayrock Mine 8-4, 8-5
Dayrock Mining Co. 8-4, 8-5
Deadwood Gulch 7-22
DeArmond Stud Mill 3-4, 3-9
Debitt, Ralph, Jessie and Marie 5-20, 5-23
Deception Creek 6-4, 6-8, 6-9, 6-11
  Experimental Forest 6-8
Deerfoot Ridge 6-7
Delaney Creek Splash Dam 6-11
Delta 8-6 to 8-8, 8-12
Depot Grocery 7-36
Depots
  Avery 5-20 to 5-23
  Bayview 2-7, 2-8
  Coeur d'Alene 3-11
  Dalton Gardens 2-21
  Hayden Lake 2-17
  Kellogg-Wardner 7-25
  Marble Creek 5-17, 5-18
  Rathdrum 1-16
  Rose Lake/Bull Run 5-3
  Wallace 7-53
DeSmet 1-7, 4-23, 4-24, 7-8
  Hill 4-23
  Mission 4-23, 4-24
DeSmet, Father 2-13, 4-24, 7-7
Devil's Elbow Campground 6-15
Dighton 5-13
Dingle Building 3-14
Dingle, T. Hedley 3-14
Diomedi, Father 4-24
Dittman 5-16, 5-17
Dittman, Henry and Mamie 5-11
Dobson Pass 7-50, 8-2, 8-61
Dobson, William 8-6
Dollar, William 3-13
Dose, David 7-24
Douglas, Bob 7-36
Down By The Depot RV Park 8-2
Downey, Glen and Marian 7-9
Dream Gulch 8-8
Dredge Piles 6-16, 8-9, 8-13
Drennan, D.D. and Blanche 3-8

Ducommun, Emile 5-9, 5-10
Dudley Bridge 5-3
Dudley Creek 8-6
Dunn Peak Lookout 5-19
Durning, Frank 7-5

~ E ~

Eagle City 7-43, 8-7
Eagle Creek 8-13
Eagle Creek Pine Lumber Co. 8-13
Eagle Town Site 8-13
Eagles 4-4
Eagles Lodge, Smelterville 7-19
Earp, Wyatt 7-43, 8-13
Easton House 3-17
Easton, Stanly 3-17, 4-5
Easton, Stanly and Estelle 7-23, 7-24
Edelblute, W.H. 1-15
Ed's Rexall Drug 7-32
Electric line railroad, see Coeur
  d'Alene & Spokane
Elgin Creamery Co. Ice Cream 7-32
Elk Creek Swimming Hole 7-40
Elk 7-41
Elk Prairie 5-14
Elks
  Kellogg 7-25, 7-34
  Wallace 7-25
Eller, E.W. 3-15
Ellett, Iola 4-16
Empire Copper Mine 8-18
Enaville 7-14, 8-17, 8-19, 8-20
Enaville Resort 8-20
English Point 2-20
Environmental Protection Agency
  (EPA) 7-40
Erickson 6-12
Erling Moe Mill Site 5-17
Etherton, Dan 7-15
Evenden, James and Ella 3-7
Evolution
  Claim 7-43
  Trail 7-43, 8-7
Ewing's
  General Store 7-11
  Inn 7-10, 7-11
Excelsior Cycle 7-36
Exchange National Bank Building
  3-13

Experimental Forest 6-4
Export Lumber Co. 4-8
Eye Opener 7-30

~ F ~

Fairgrounds
  Kootenai County 3-3, 3-13
  Plummer 4-23
Falls Club 1-10
Falls Creek 5-10, 5-13, 8-14
Farragut
  Admiral David 2-3
  buildings 1-10, 1-24, 3-18, 4-26, 5-15
  College & Technical Institute 2-3
  Naval Training Station 2-2 to 2-4, 2-7, 2-10, 3-13
  sailors 7-35
  Visitors Center 2-3
Fay 8-18
FBI 7-25
Federal Emergency Management Agency 8-19
Federal Mining and Smelting Co. 7-16, 7-21
Federal troops 7-36
Feehan House 8-11
Fellin, Gene 7-50
Ferguson, Charles 5-29
Ferguson, John "Lon" and Zoe 8-6
Ferguson, Lodge 8-6
Fernan Creek 6-6
Fernan Lake 6-2, 6-4, 6-5
  bridge site 6-5
  Road 6-4, 6-5
  Ranger Station 6-2, 6-3
Fernan
  John and Mary Jane 6-3
  Saddle 6-7
  Village 6-3
Fernwood Lake 2-15
Ferrell 5-10
Ferrell, William 5-10, 5-13
Fields, Merrill 7-47
Fighting Creek Store and Tavern 4-27
Finney, Capt. John and Thelma 3-8
Finney, Dr. John 4-12
Finucane, Charles and Marion 2-20
Finucane Ranch 2-20

Fire
  1881 4-24
  1884 1-11
  1889 5-33
  1890 1-13
  1910 2-10, 4-19, 5-16 to 5-18, 5-20, 5-21, 5-24, 5-27, 5-28, 5-33, 6-11, 8-4, 8-20
  1919 6-11
  1924 1-12, 1-13, 1-16
  1928 5-28
  1929 5-14
  1934 5-21, 5-26
  1953 5-15
  Bullion 5-27
  Rathdrum 1-11
  Setzer Creek 5-20
  Sunshine Mine 1972 7-43
  Trout Creek 5-16
Fireside Lodge 1-20
First and Last Chance 1-9
First Bank
  of Harrison 4-12
  of St. Maries 4-12
First National Bank
  Coeur d'Alene 3-14
  Kellogg 7-33
Fish Train 8-18
Fish traps 5-8, 5-9
Fisher, Joe 4-19
Fisher, William, John and Jesse 4-13
Fishpond, Avery 5-23
Five Finger Saddle 6-7
Flash Peak 5-19
Flathead Indians 3-4
Flathead Reservation 4-24
Fleming, Leo and Shirley 4-26
Flewelling's Mill 5-11, 5-12
Flood
  1917 5-3, 5-5
  1933 3-6, 5-3, 5-5, 5-10, 5-25, 5-17, 7-8, 7-9, 7-15, 8-15, 8-16
  1938 5-17
  1974 3-6, 7-11
  1994 8-19
  1996 3-6, 7-11
  1997 3-6
  Missoula 1-9, 1-19, 1-23, 2-12

Spokane Flood 1-23
Folkins, Bert 4-25
Ford 4-27
Fort Grounds Neighborhood 3-6 to
  3-9
Fort Grounds Tavern 3-4
Fort Hemenway Manor 4-15, 4-16
Fort Sherman 2-20, 2-21, 3-2, 3-4 to
3-10, 4-5, 4-6, 5-29, 7-4
  Chapel 3-6
  Hospital 3-18
  Officers' Quarters 3-6
  Powder Magazine 3-5
Fortin, "Blackie" 3-10
Fossum, Andrew 4-6
Fourth of July Pass 7-2, 7-4, 7-8
Frank, Angelo 7-50
Franklin Mine 5-19
Frazey family 1-10
French 3-2
Fritzche's 1-15
Fritze, F.W. 4-5
Frost Peak 7-7
Fruechtl, Frank 3-18
Fuller Hall 8-12

~ G ~

Gaby, John H. News Store 7-29
Galbreath, Tex 7-17
Galena Mine 7-49, 7-50
Gambling 7-25
Garwood 2-12
Gem State Bar and Cafè 4-17
Geology 2-12, 5-8, 8-17
George family 7-47
George, John 7-26
George, Lee 7-44
Georgetown 7-44
Giants 8-8
Gibbs 3-3, 3-4
Glacier Lake Missoula 1-23
Gold Creek 5-31
Golf, first 18 hole course 2-16
Good Samaritan Nursing Center 7-49
Goodrow, Mrs. 5-14
Gookstetter, Jennifer 6-6
Goose Heaven Lake 5-9
Gotham Bay 4-6
Gouyd 5-26

Government Gulch 7-19 to 7-21, 7-23
Graham Creek 8-17
  Ranger Station 8-17
Graham, James 3-18
Graham, Theresa 3-16 to 3-18
Grain Elevator, Setters 4-27
GAR (Grand Army of the Republic),
  Murray 8-10
Grange 422, Harrison 4-4, 4-11
Granite Creek 8-9
Grant Lumber Co. 4-7
Graue, Clarence and Lulu 3-7, 3-9
Graves, Forty-Nine Gulch 5-25
Gray & Knight 3-8
Gray, Wyatt, Red and Ruth 3-4
Graybill, Chet 8-16
Gray's Grocery 3-4
Greater St. Joe Development
  Foundation 4-18
Grebil, Leila 8-10
Grist Mill 1-2
Grizzly Mountain 8-17, 8-18
GTE (General Telephone and
  Electronics) 4-27
Guggenheims 8-9

~ H ~

H & H Riverstop 8-16
Hagadone, Burl 3-7
Hagadone Corporation 3-12, 4-2
Hager, John 2-13, 2-15, 2-16
Halfway Hill 5-31
Hall, Ross 4-6
Halsey, Homer 6-12
Halsey Homestead 6-12
Ham, David 3-6, 3-9
Hamer, Robert, June, Karen 7-47
Hamilton, C.J. and Bill 3-15
Hammond Creek 5-26
Hammrich, Henry and Opal 3-18
Hanging Gardens 5-12
Hanley, Lew 8-4
Hardy Loop 7-7
Harrison 4-7 to 4-12
  Flats 4-12
  Old Timers Picnic 4-10
Harry's Grocery 7-17, 7-18
Hart
  Block 1-13

Drug Store 3-13
  Warren 1-13, 1-16
Harvey Creek 5-31
Hauser Junction 1-9, 1-11
Hay and Sons Grain Elevator 4-8
Hayden Creek 2-10
Hayden Lake 2-12 to 2-20, 3-18
  Country Club 2-13, 2-15, 2-16,
  2-17
  Dike 2-19, 2-20
  Improvement Co. 2-16
Hayden Loop 7-7
Hayden Village 2-13
Hayden, Mathew 2-13, 2-19, 3-18,
  7-7, 7-10
Haynes, Ranger 6-8
Healy, Ellen 3-17, 3-18
Hecla Mining Co. 7-46, 8-5
Heimark Building 4-18
Heimark Jewelry 4-18
Hell's Gulch Creek 5-8, 5-9
Hemenway, Frank and Lucinda 4-15,
  4-16
Hemminger, Benjamin 8-6
Hendrickson, Blackie, Sam and Ray
  7-50
Henley Aerodrome 2-10, 2-11
Henley, Clay and Nadine 2-10, 2-11
Hercules Mill 7-43, 7-49, 7-51, 7-52
Herrick 5-14, 5-16
Herrick, Fred 4-16
Heyburn, Weldon B. 4-21, 7-43, 7-44
Hickey, John 2-13, 2-15
Hicks, Gwin 3-3
Hidden Lake 4-21
Higgens Point 1-5
Highland Surprise Mine 7-14
Highways
  10 7-2, 7-38, to 7-40
  54 2-2
  95 1-25, 1-26
  95 Bridge 1-25
  95, south 4-23 to 4-28
Historic Silver Valley Chamber of
  Commerce 7-25
Historic Wallace Tour 7-2, 7-51
Hiway 10 Motel 3-18
Hoag, Charles 4-25

Hobo Creek 4-18
Holley, Mason and Marks Hardware
  Store 8-10, 8-12
Holt, Ray 4-25
Honeysuckle
  Beach 2-18
  Creek 6-12
  Hill 2-20
  Ranger Station Site 6-9
Hood, Mrs. 7-26
Hopper, Bob 7-23
Horseracing 3-13
Hotel Idaho 3-12
Howard, E. Viet 7-41
Howard, Needles, Tannem and
  Bergendoff 4-2
Hoyt, Charlie 5-19
Hoyt Creek Bridge 5-19, 5-20
Hoyts Flat 5-19, 5-20, 5-23
Huckleberry Finn 8-9
Huckleberry
  Lookout 5-13
  Mountain 6-4 to 6-7
  Mountain Trail 28 6-7, 6-8
  Hudlow Peak 6-7
Hughes
  Florist Greenhouses 1-7
  House Historical Museum 4-14
  Father Martin 4-9
  Howard and Marcia 1-7
  Raleigh 4-14
Hull, Jack 7-50
Hummel's Landing 8-14
Hump Creek 6-12
Humphries 1-8
Hunter Claim 7-11, 7-51
Hydraulic mining 8-8

~ I ~

Icebox 1-17
Idaho
  and Washington Northern Railroad
  1-16, 1-17, 1-22
  First National Bank 3-14
  Fish and Game 3-12, 6-13, 7-41,
  8-18
  Mercantile Co. 3-14
  National Guard 1-15, 4-14
  Northern Railroad 8-10, 8-17

Panhandle Council 4-5
Idlewild Bay 2-3
IHM (Immaculate Heart of Mary)
   3-18
Independence Creek 6-14
Independence Point 3-11, 3-12
IWW (Industrial Workers of the
   World) 4-13, 4-14
   St. Maries 4-14
   Spirit Lake 4-14
Inland Empire Railroad, see Coeur
   d'Alene & Spokane electric line
Inland Lounge 7-35
Inland Northwest Lutheran Ministries
   6-16
I.O.O.F. (International Order of Odd
Fellows) Hall
   Harrison 4-9, 4-11
   Kellogg 7-29, 7-30
   Plummer 4-22
   Spirit Lake 1-21, 1-23
Internet 7-27, 7-28, 7-38
Interstate 8-6
   90 1-8, 1-9, 7-2, 7-7, 7-17, 7-38,
   7-40,7-52, 7-53
Interstate Co. 5-23
Interstate Utilities Telephone Building
   1-13, 1-16
Interstate-Callahan Mine 8-5
Iroquois 3-2
Irwin, Tom 7-39, 8-6
Ives, Red 5-32
IXL Clothing Store 3-7

~ J ~

J.C. Penney 3-7, 7-34
J.R. Marks Hardware 8-12
Jackass Ski Bowl 7-28
Jackass Trail 8-7
Jacobson, Archie 8-18, 8-19
Jacots 5-10
Jails
   Kootenai County 1-15, 3-14
   St. Maries 4-14
James, Bert 8-19
James, Dale and Barbara 1-7
Japanese
   in Avery 5-21
   railroad workers 2-11

tourists 7-28
Jesuits 3-4, 4-24
Jewett, Fritz 3-17
Jewett, George Frederick 3-17
Jewett House 3-17
John Creek 6-11
Johnson, Henry 7-47
Johnson, Lady Bird 2-5
Johnson, Oscar and Hazel 7-18
Johnson, Walt and Jessie 8-15
Johnson, W.J. 5-5
Johnson's Cafe 7-18
Johnson's Store 1-25
Johnston, Ben E. 7-45
Jokuthlaup Point 2-4
Jones, Honey Thomas 5-13
Jones, J.E. Brokerage Corp. 7-31
Jones, Thomas 5-13
Jo's Hole Bar 1-21
Josie's 8-20
Justin, Mr. 2-20

~ K ~

Kalispell Indians 3-4
K-Bar Ranch 6-3, 6-5
Keaster, Walter 8-10
Keesey 7-22
Kelley Creek 5-23
Kellogg 7-17, 7-22 to 7-39
   Auto Center 7-33
   Bowling Alley 7-35
   By-Pass 7-38
   Hardware Co. 7-32
   News 7-28
   Noah 8-12
   Noah and Dora 7-26
   Rio Hotel 7-34
   School District 7-22
   Tunnel 7-23, 7-26, 7-27
Kellogg-Wardner Business College
   7-29
Kellogg-Wardner News 7-28
Kelly Dude Ranch 6-6
Kelly Homestead 6-5, 6-6
Kelly, John 6-6
Kelly, William 6-5, 6-6
Kentuck 7-26
Kerl, Thomas and Lola 3-10
Kerl, Thomas T. 3-6, 3-9

Kerns, Delmar 7-6
Kiln, Washington Brick & Lime Co. 2-8
King, Clement 2-15
King, Homer 2-15, 2-16
Kings Inn 7-11, 7-12
Kings Pass 7-50, 8-2, 8-9
Kingston 7-11 to 7-13
Kingston Ranger District 6-9, 7-11
Kit Price Campground 6-15
K Klub 7-30
Klein Homestead 5-7
Knight, Harry and Orene 3-8
Kootenai Cabins 7-9
Kootenai County 3-2, 4-15
Kopper Keg 7-25
Korner Klub 7-31
Koski 8-19
Krech Building 1-21
Kreig, E.M. 3-15
Kuisti family 7-15

~ L ~

Lacey's Gardens 2-13
Lacon 4-12
Lafferty Transportation Co. 4-4
Lagow, Marge 4-26
Laird, Captain Eli 4-16
Lake Coeur d'Alene 4-2, 4-3, 6-11
Lake Creek 4-27
Lake View, Arrow Point 4-5
Lakeshore Development Co. 3-13
Lakeside
  Drug 3-14
  Drug and Book Co. 3-14
  Pharmacy 3-14
Lakeview 2-7, 6-14
Lane 5-5
Lane, Bill and Judy 7-40
Lane, R.D. 7-36
Lang's Grocery 7-38
Larsen Brothers 1-14
Latour Baldy 7-7
Laumeister, Herman 8-13
Laverne Creek 6-11
Lee's Grocery 7-15
Lee's Lodge 7-2, 7-3
Legault, Harvey and Albert 8-19
Leiberg

Creek 6-11, 6-12
  John B. 6-11
  Saddle 6-12, 6-13
Leinwebber Spur 4-19
Lemonade Peak 5-14
Leo's 4-26
Lewellyn Creek 2-10
Lewis, Zach 1-11
Liberty Billiards 7-30
Liberty Theater 7-29
Lilypad Bay and Wetlands 6-5
Limber Limb Lumber Co. 5-15
Limestone 2-8, 2-9
Lindow, Ruth 5-22
Lindstrom, Alfred 4-19
Linfor 8-18, 8-19
Linn, Art and Margaret 7-50
Linville 7-17
Lions Club 1-17, 4-5
Little, Ewing 7-32
Little Falls 1-2
Little Plummer Creek, Culvert 4-21, 4-22
Loch Haven Farm 2-20
Log Cabin
  Spirit Lake 1-23
  Wallace 7-50
Log chute/flume 4-12, 6-9 to 6-12, 5-16, 8-17
Log House, Smelterville 7-19
Logging 4-12, 5-16, 6-8 to 6-14, 8-13, 8-14
Logging railroads 4-6, 4-27, 5-16, 6-9
Long, J. Grier 2-7
Longshot Saloon 7-36
Lookout Pass 7-50, 7-53
Lookouts 5-19, 6-4, 6-7
Lorenzi, Nelda, Pete, Laura and Mike 8-7
Lost Block 6-11
Lucky Swede Mine 5-27
Lumberjack Booster Club 4-18
Lumberjacks 4-18
Lumberman's State Bank 4-14, 4-17
Lunceford, June Kelly 6-6

~ M ~

MacAsslin Store 4-22
Magee

Ranger District 6-13
Ranger Station 6-14
Charlie 6-14
Mahoneys Tavern 5-23
Main Exchange 7-31
Mann's Variety Store 7-30
Maple Cliffs 8-17
Marble Creek 5-15, 5-17
    Bridge 5-18
    Interpretive Center 5-18
    Store 5-14, 5-18
Markwell's Dairy 7-49
Marler and Brass Meat Market 4-11
Marler, F.E. 4-11
Martial Law 7-36
Martin, Fletcher 7-26
Martins 7-46
Mary Immaculate, convent 4-24
Mascot Gold Mining Co. 8-7, 8-8
Mason, Thomas 7-14
Masonic Hall/Temple
    Coeur d'Alene 3-14, 3-15
    Harrison 4-8, 4-9
    Kellogg 7-29, 7-34
    Murray 8-11
    Rathdrum 1-15
    Spirit Lake 1-22
    St. Maries 4-15
Mastodon Mine 5-19
Mastodon Mountain 5-28
Mattmiller Agency 7-33
Mattson, Gunnar and Enar 7-50
McBride, T.E. 2-15
McCarty, Edward and May 3-16
McCauley, Doctor 1-5
McClain, Hoyt 7-14
McClain, Lee and Nettie 7-15, 7-16
McConnell Hotel 7-28, 7-31
McCormick, Eldred and Mary 1-7
McCormick, Ferrell and Lillian 1-7
McEuen Field 3-13
McEuen, Mae 3-13
McFadden's law office 4-23
McGillivray, Dorothy 7-11
McGoldrick Lumber Co. 6-8, 6-15,
    8-16
McGregor Billiards 7-30
McGuire, Stanley "Hook" 5-24

McKinley Inn Hotel 7-34
McKinney, William 7-29
McKinnon, Jerry 8-2, 8-3
McKinnon Mural 8-2
McKivers, Judy 7-6
McManam, Phillip and Deborah 3-15
McMillan, Anna 4-16
McMillan's Store 4-22, 4-23
McPherson, Frank 6-14, 6-15, 8-18
McPherson Meadows 6-14, 6-15
McQuade 5-18
Medicine Mountain 5-8
Medimont 5-7, 5-8
    Mercantile 5-8
Meister Burger 7-33
Melody Lane 7-35
Memorial Field 3-10
Meredith's Repair 4-26
Merriam Block 3-14
Merriam, Dr. 3-14
Mica Bay 4-27
Mica Creek 5-15, 5-16
Mica Flats Grange 4-28
Mica Meadows 5-15
Miles House 2-15
Mill Executive Houses, Spirit Lake
    1-22
Miller, Dave 8-11
Miller, Frances 7-6
Miller, Jim and Dorothy McvGillivray
    7-11
Miller, Joseph and Harriet 7-11
Miller, Virgil 7-11
Miller, Wilson 7-50
Miller's Store 8-11
Millsap, Rev. Jesse 1-8
Milo 7-22
Milwaukee Land Co. Sawmill 5-11,
    5-12
Milwaukee Mill workers 4-16
Milwaukee Road Railroad 1-16, 2-12,
    3-2, 3-12, 4-13, 4-20, 4-21, 4-25,
    4-27, 5-10 to 5-14, 5-16 to 5-27, 5-29
    1933 Train Wreck 5-25
    Bridge, St. Joe River 5-13
    Grade 5-19
    Roundhouse 5-21, 5-26
    Substation 14 5-22

Mine Rescue 7-26
Mineral Creek 6-11
Mineral Ridge Scenic Trail 4-4
Miner's Hat 7-39
Miner's Hat Realty 7-39
Miners' Memorial Statue 7-43
Mining 4-4, 5-19, 6-15, 7-4, 7-16,
    7-17, 7-19 to 7-22, 7-39 to 7-44, 7-46,
    7-49, 7-50 to 7-52, 8-3 to 8-5, 8-7 to
    8-10, 8-13, 8-14
Mining Heritage Exhibition 7-51
Mining War 7-19, 7-23, 7-36
Mission
    Flats 7-7
    Inn 7-10
    Point 5-9
Moate Lake House 6-3
Moate, Tom and Robert 6-3
Modern Woodmen of America 4-17
Modine, Emil "Swede" 4-27
Moe, Bud 7-30
Moe, Erling 5-14
Moe, Joseph and Iver 5-7, 5-8
Moe, Melissa Anderson 5-7
Mohr's Service Station 7-45
Molly B'Damn 8-9
Molly B'Damm Motel 7-50
Monaghan, James 2-20
Monarch Timber Co. 5-12
Monard's Ranch 6-3
Montana Trail 5-31
Montandon 5-10
Monteith 7-9
Montgomery Gulch 7-39
Montgomery, James 5-17
Moon
    Creek 7-40
    Gulch 7-40, 7-41
    Pass 5-24
Moore, Bill 6-9
Moose Lodge, Rathdrum 1-13, 1-15
Morbeck Grocery 7-15
Morbeck, Walter and Vivian 7-15
Morning Mine Shop 7-7
Morrison, John 8-6
Morrows Department Store 3-14,
    7-31
Moscow 7-25

Mountain Lumber Co. 8-13
Mountain Park Hotel 5-21
Mountain States Lumber Co. 8-13
Mullan 1-13
    Captain John 1-2, 4-4, 5-9, 7-2
    to 7-4, 7-14, 7-44
    Field 3-13
    Road 1-2, 5-9, 5-28, 7-2, 7-10,
    7-52
    Tree Historic Site 7-3
Mullan Statues
    Coeur d'Alene 7-4
    Fourth of July Pass 7-4
    Kellogg 7-26, 7-4
    Mullan 7-4
    Post Falls 1-2, 7-4
    St. Maries 4-18, 7-4
    Wallace 7-52, 7-4
Murray 6-15, 7-44, 7-51, 8-7 to 8-12
    Fire Hall 8-12
    George 8-9
    Molly and Jean 7-19
Museum of North Idaho 3-11, 7-3
Museum of North Idaho, Ft.
Sherman 3-5, 6-15
Musgrove, Mark and Flora Belle
    1-15
Musick, Dana 7-26
Myles' Motel 7-50

~ N ~

Native Americans, see specific tribe
    4-28
National Democratic Committee
    3-17
National Exchange Bank 3-13, 3-16
National Forest Botanical Area 8-14
National Register of Historic Places
    (NRHP) 1-2 to 1-4, 1-6, 1-7, 1-10,
    1-15,1-20, 2-8 to 2-10, 2-18, 2-19,
    3-5 to 3-7, 3-10, 3-11, 3-14 to 3-16,
    4-15, 4-18, 4-19, 4-21, 5-5, 5-8,
    5-32, 6-14, 7-7, 7-8, 7-15, 7-26,
    7-52, 7-53, 8-11, 8-12
Nautical Loop 1-18
Needham, Jack 6-14
Neely 5-15
Nelson, A.B. 1-12
Nelson, Virginia 1-12

Nettleton Gulch 2-21
Nettleton, John 2-21
Nevers, Anna Laurie 3-7
New York Stocks 7-31
Newcomb, George 5-13
Newton, Kate 3-7
Nine Mile Creek 8-4
Niscot Club 3-9
Nitkey, John 4-8
Noble, Frank 4-16
No Name Dam 6-12
Nordburgh compressor 7-23
Nordstrom, Carl and Evelyn 7-6
Nordstrom Logging Co. 7-6
Norris, Art 7-10
Northern Pacific Railroad 1-9, 1-10,
    1-11, 1-24, 2-8, 2-10, 3-12, 5-26,
    5-28, 7-36, 8-4
    Bridge 1-26
    Depot Museum 7-53
    Sunset Branch 8-4
North Idaho Centennial Trail, Post
    Falls 1-4, 1-5
North Idaho (Junior) College 3-4 to
    3-6, 3-14
North Shore Motel 3-12
North West Fur Trading Co. 3-2
Northwest Timber Co. 3-2, 3-4, 3-5
Norton, Gary 2-11
Norton, Wayne 2-11
Noyen, Bill, Gary and Hazel 7-19

~ O ~

Oasis Bordello Museum 7-52, 7-53
O'Brien House 3-15
O'Brien, Jimmy 5-29
O'Brien, Major John 3-15
Occupation of 1918 4-13
O'Dwyer's Hardware 4-17
Office of Price Administration (OPA)
    7-33
O'Gara Bay 4-12
O'Gara, Annie 4-12
Ogilvie, Morris 7-50
Ohio Match
    Company 2-12, 2-13, 6-11
    Road 2-12, 6-9
    Railroad 2-12, 6-9
O.K. Rubber Welders 7-38

Old Bearpaw Store 8-19
Old Pioneer Hotel 7-11
Olmstead, J.C. 2-16
Olson, Mr. 3-7
Olympian 5-25 to 5-27
One Eye's Landing 8-19
One Shot Charlie's 4-11
On the Hill Bed and Breakfast 7-26
Orchards 2-20, 2-21
Oregon Railway & Navigation Co.
    4-7, 4-27, 7-10, 7-36
Oregon Washington Railroad Co. 7-37
Oregon-Washington Rwy & Navigation
    Co. 4-21, 5-2 to 5-5, 5-8, 7-10, 7-17,
    7-25, 7-36, 7-37, 8-10, 8-14, 8-16 to
    8-18
O'Reilly, Mr. and Mrs. James 4-2
Osburn 7-43 to 7-48, 8-48
    Fault 7-48
    Locker Plant 7-46
    Lumber Co. 7-45
Osburn, S.V. William 7-44
Osprey Inn 4-8
Owens & Atkins 7-25
Owl Tavern 7-10

~ P ~

Pabst Brothers 7-50
Pacific Fruit Warehouse 8-2
Pacific Hotel 1-24
Pack River Co. 7-44
Packsaddle Campground 5-29
Page, L.B. and Etta 7-17, 7-39
Page Mine 7-16, 7-17
Page Pond 7-17
Palace Hotel 8-10
Panhandle Lumber Co. 1-18 to 1-22
Papesh Meat Co. 7-32, 7-33
Paragon 8-10
Parish House 7-8
Parks
    Blackwell, Coeur d'Alene 3-9
    Coeur d'Alene City 3-9
    Conklin 4-12
    Falls 1-2
    Farragut State 2-2 to 2-5
    Gene Day County 7-43
    Harrison City 4-10
    Heyburn State 4-21

Mullan, Coeur d'Alene 3-13
Mullan Fourth of July Pass 7-4
Mullan Trail, St. Maries 4-18
Old Mission State 7-7
Q'emlin Riverside 1-7
Rathdrum City 1-16
Ruth Lindow 5-22
Treaty Rock Park 1-10
Vic Camm, St. Maries 4-19
Parsons Building 4-26
Parsons, "Wid" Willard 4-27
Passon, Edgar 7-4
Patano's Men's Wear 7-31
Pat's Grocery 7-32
Paul Bunyan Statue 4-18
Paulsen Grocery Store 4-11
Pears, Bud and Doris 5-23, 5-25
Pearson brothers 5-27
Pearson, Eric Pete 6-15
Pearson Trailhead 5-27
Peg Leg Pete 7-18
Pend d'Oreille City 2-3, 2-4
Pend Oreille Indians 3-4, 5-28, 5-29
Penman, Dick and Virginia 1-12
Pennaluna & Co. 7-31
Penney, J.C. 3-7
Penney, John 7-17
Perkins, C.H. 7-45
Peters, Kate 1-6
Peterson, Chuck 7-27, 7-28
Peterson, Dr. 2-15
Petroglyph 1-10
Picnic Creek 6-11
Pierce, Jon 7-32
Pik Kwik Grocery 7-38
Pinchot Ranger Station site 5-20
Pine Creek 7-13, 7-14
Pine Creek Lumber Co. 7-14
Pine Creek, West Fork 7-14
Pine Prairie 7-14
Pinehurst 7-13 to 7-16
Pioneer Market 1-14
Pix Theater 7-19
Placer Center 7-51
Placer Creek 7-50
Placer Creek, West Fork 5-28
Platt, Dr. Owen 4-14
Playland Pier Amusement Park 3-11

Pleasant Homes 7-26
Pleasant View 1-7, 1-8
Pleasant View Cemetery 1-8
Pleasant View Community
  Association 1-8
Plonske, William 1-7
Plummer 4-21 to 4-24
Plummer Forest Products Mill 4-23
Plummer Junction 4-22
Pocono siding 5-17
Polar Bear Club 3-17
Polaris Mill 7-43, 7-44
Pole Mountain Ranger District 5-32
Poleson Building 1-14
Poleson, Walter and Julia 1-14
Polio Pond 7-40
Porrett 5-10
Portland International Cement Co.
  2-7
Post Falls 1-2 to 1-10
Post Falls Dam 1-5, 7-7
Post Falls Historical Society 1-2
Post Offices
  Athol 1-25
  Carlin Bay 4-6
  Cataldo 7-10, 7-11
  Chilco 2-12
  Enaville 8-20
  Harrison 4-11
  Hayden Lake 2-13
  Kellogg 7-26
  Linfor 8-18
  Marble Creek 5-18
  Medimont 5-7, 5-8
  Mica Creek 5-16
  Murray 8-9, 8-11
  Pinehurst 7-15, 7-16
  Plummer 4-22, 4-23
  Prichard 8-14, 8-15
  Rathdrum 1-11, 1-14
  Rose Lake 5-2, 5-3
  St. Maries 4-17
  Silverton 7-48
  Smelterville 7-17, 7-18, 7-19
  Spirit Lake 1-19, 1-23
  Tensed 4-23
  Wallace 7-51
  Worley 4-25

Post, Fredrick 1-2, 1-7, 1-10, 1-16
Potlatch Corp., Avery 5-21
Potlatch Corporation St. Maries
Prichard 8-14, 8-15
   Rathdrum 1-11, 1-14
   Rose Lake 5-2, 5-3
   St. Maries 4-17
   Silverton 7-48
   Smelterville 7-17, 7-18, 7-19
   Spirit Lake 1-19, 1-23
   Tensed 4-23
   Wallace 7-51
   Worley 4-25
Post, Fredrick 1-2, 1-7, 1-10, 1-16
Potlatch Corp., Avery 5-21
Potlatch Corporation St. Maries
   Complex 4-13
Potlatch Forest see Rutledge Timber Co.
Potlatch Log Landing 5-21
Potter, Alice 3-16
Powderhorn Bay 4-6
Powell, Glenn and Marguerite 3-9
Powell, W.W. 8-13
Prairie Development Co 2-6
Preston, Mary 3-16
Price, Kid 6-15
Prichard 8-12 to 8-14, 8-18
   Bridge and Picnic Area 8-16
   Creek 6-15, 6-16, 7-11, 8-9, 8-10,
    8-13
   Ranger District 8-14, 8-15
   Resources Co. 8-14
   Tavern 8-15
Prichard, Andrew J. 7-43, 8-9, 8-14,
   8-15
Prichard, Jess 8-15
Princess Theater
   Harrison 4-8
   Kellogg 7-31
Prindle, Earl S. 1-19
Prindle Hospital 1-19, 1-20
Prisoners 2-4
Progressive Printing 7-29
Propane By Lane 7-38
Prospect Gulch 7-43
Prostitution 7-25, 7-52, 7-53, 8-9
Providence Academy of Sacred Heart
   4-24

Pulaski, Ed 5-28
Pulaski Interpretive Sign 5-28
Pulaski Tunnel 8-4
Purcell, Father 3-18

~ Q ~
Quarles Peak 5-29
Quarry, Washington Brick & Lime Co.
   2-8, 2-9
Quin-Ne-Mo-See 1-8

~ R ~
Ragan's Musical Museum 5-17
Railroads
   B.R. Lewis/Blackwell logging 4-27
   Burlington Northern Overpass 1-9
   Burlington Northern Santa Fe 1-9,
    1-25, 3-4
   Burnt Cabin Creek 6-9
   Coeur d'Alene & Pend Oreille
    Railway 2-7, 2-10
   Coeur d'Alene & Spokane Railway
    (electric line) 1-5, 1-9, 2-13, 2-16,
    to 2-18, 2-20, 2-21, 3-2, 3-9 to 3-12,
    3-15
   Idaho and Washington Northern 1-16,
    1-17, 1-22
   Idaho Northern Railroad 8-10, 8-17
   Milwaukee Road 1-16, 2-12, 3-2,
    3-12, 4-13, 4-20, 4-21, 4-25, 4-27,
    5-10 to 5-14, 5-16 to 5-27, 5-29
    1933 Train Wreck 5-25
    Bridge, St. Joe River 5-13
    Columbian 5-27
    Grade 5-19
    Hiawatha 5-27
    Olympian 5-25 to 5-27
    Roundhouse 5-21, 5-26
    St. Paul Pass (Taft) Tunnel 5-27
    Substation 14 5-22
   Northern Pacific Railroad 1-9, 1-10,
    1-11, 1-24, 2-8, 2-10, 3-12, 5-26,
    5-28, 7-36, 8-4
    Bridge 1-26
    Depot Museum 7-53
    Sunset Branch 8-4
   Oregon Railway & Navigation Co.
    4-7, 4-27, 7-10, 7-36

Oregon Washington Railroad Co. 7-37

Oregon-Washington Rwy & Navigation Co. 4-21, 5-2 to 5-5, 5-8, 7-10, 7-17, 7-25, 7-36, 7-37, 8-10, 8-14, 8-16 to 8-18

St. Maries Railroad 4-20

Spokane Falls & Idaho Railroad 1-9

Union Pacific Railroad 1-25, 4-7, 4-8, 4-12, 4-20, 5-2 to 5-4, 7-25, 7-36, 7-37, 7-44, 7-45
  Swing Bridge 4-20

Rathdrum 1-11 to 1-17
  Iron Works 1-14
  Prairie 1-1, 1-11, 2-12
  Tribune 1-13

Ravalli, Father 7-8

Ray-Jefferson Mine 8-16

Red Collar Line 3-7, 3-12, 3-15, 4-4, 4-8

Red Cross Drug 4-17

Red House 2-16

Red Ives
  Creek 5-33
  Generator Plant 5-33
  Ranger District 5-19
  Ranger Station 5-31 to 5-33

Red Men's Hall 7-27

Redemptorist Mission House 3-16

Red's Place 8-6

Reeds Baldy 5-12

Reiman, Oscar 7-31

Reiniger Brothers 1-14

Remnant Basalt 5-8

Rena Theatre 7-38

Rex Mine 8-6

Rex, Ronnie and Donna Nordstrom 7-6

Reynolds, Oscar 1-6

Reynolds, Ted 7-39

Reynolds, Walt 7-18

Rhodebeck, Pete 1-19

Rice's Bakery 7-52

Rickel, Jerry and Bob 2-11

Rickel Ranch 2-11

Rimrock 2-12

Rimrock Golf Course 2-12

Rio Club 7-34

Riordan, G.C. 3-16

Road Curve 7-9

Roath, Lloyd 8-12

Robinson Motors 7-35

Robinson, A.B. 1-9

Rochat Creek 5-9, 5-10

Rochat Ranch and Barn 5-9

Rochat, Henri, Paul and William 5-9

Rock Waste Pile 7-45, 7-46

Rockefeller, Avery and William 5-22

Rockford Bay 4-27

Rockin' B Ranch 1-8

Rocky Beach 1-18

Rocky Point 4-21

Rodell, C.E. 2-18

Rodeo 3-13, 6-3

Rogers, A.H. 1-9

Rondeau Farmstead 6-6

Rondeau, Charlie 6-6

Rondo Creek 6-6

Rooney and Stritesky Architects 3-15

Roosevelt, Franklin 2-3

Rories 5-3

Rose Creek 5-2

Rose Lake 5-2 to 5-4, 7-5
  Bridge 5-3
  Historical Society 5-3
  Lumber Co. 5-2
  Lumber Co. 1 5-5
  Lumber Co. office building 5-3

Rosenberry Drive 3-6, 3-9

Rosenberry, Walter 3-8, 3-15, 5-3, 5-4

Rossi, Herman 8-4

Ross Oil 7-22

Rostead Dance Hall and Apartments 7-19

Rothrock, F.M. 8-5

Roundhouse Complex 5-21

Round Lake 4-20

Route of Hiawatha Rail Trail 5-27, 7-53

Rumple, Don 7-39

Russell and Pugh Lumber Co. 4-6, 4-7, 4-9, 4-12

Russell, Bert and Marie 4-12

Russell, Howard and Evelyn 4-11

Rutledge Timber Co. 3-7, 3-9, 3-11, 3-17, 4-2

~ **S** ~

Sacred Heart Mission 4-23, 4-24
Sage, Mr. 2-10
Saginaw Lumber Co. 3-13
Sailor Boy Mine 5-19
St. Gertrude Sisters 4-16
St. Joe Baldy 5-12
St. Joe City 5-10 to 5-12
  bank vault 5-11
  photo display 5-11
St. Joe Lodge 5-17
St. Joe Quartz Mine 5-31
St. Joe River 4-13, 4-20, 5-8 to 5-22, 5-28 to 5-32
  North Fork 5-24 to 5-26
St. Joe River Road 5-13
  bridge 5-13
  Old 5-19
St. Joseph Indian Mission 5-8
St. Maries 4-13 to 4-19
  Brick Works 4-18
  Lumber Co. 4-13
  Murals 4-18
  Outdoor Art Gallery 4-18
  Railroad 4-20
  Ranger District 5-19
  School District 4-16
  waterfront 4-16
St. Mary's Academy 4-16
St. Paul Pass (Taft) Tunnel 5-27
St. Regis 5-31
St. Vincent de Paul 7-38
Sala, Anna 4-11
Sala, Mr. and Mrs. George 7-17
Salmon 3-4, 4-4
Sand Creek 6-8
Sand, Isaac and Mary 6-8
Sanders, V.W. 3-14
Sass Jewelry 7-30, 7-32
Sather Field 7-48
Sather, Norman 7-48
Scenic Bay 2-7
Schee-Chu-Umsh 3-2
Scheffy's General Store and Motel 5-24

Schini, Forrest, Arlene and Robert 3-8
Schmalhorst, Sophie Margaret 5-29
Schmidt Brothers 4-21
Schools
  Athol 1-24
  Atlas Elementary 2-18
  Avery 5-21 to 5-24
  Bayview 34 2-9
  Calder 5-14
  Canyon 7-5, 7-6
  Carter 8-17
  Cedar Mountain 74 2-10
  Elk Creek 7-40
  Green 7-5
  Harrison 4-9, 4-10, 5-3
  Hayden Lake Elementary 2-18
  Heyburn Elementary 4-18
  Indian Springs 5-8
  Kingston 7-12, 7-13
  Lane 5-5
  Lincoln 7-24
  Mica Creek 5-16
  Mica Flats 4-28
  Murray 8-12
  Pinehurst 7-15
  Pleasant View 1-7
  Plummer 4-22
  Prichard 8-15
  Rathdrum High 1-14
  Rose Lake 5-2, 5-3, 5-5
  St. Maries 4-14
  Silver Hill 7-46
  Silver King 7-20
  Silver Valley Alternative 7-32
  Spirit Lake 1-19
  Wallace 8-3
  Worley 4-25, 4-26
School Bell, Bayview 2-9
Schrieber Barn 3-3
Schrieber, Susan 3-8
Sciuchetti, Henry 7-46
Scott, Frank and Walter 5-13
Scott homestead 5-13
Scout House 7-35
Sears Store 7-29
Season's Hill 1-17, 1-18
Seelig Block 7-31
Seelig Grocery 7-31

Seely family 7-31
Seeweewana 3-8
Seiter, Edgar and Gladys 1-10
Seiter's Cannery 1-10
Sellers, Bert and Sylvia 5-4
Seltice, Andrew 1-7
Seltice, Moses 1-7
Seneaquoteen Trail 1-23
Senior Center, Kellogg 7-34
Senior Citizen's building, Harrison 4-9
Setters 4-27
Setters, Anne 4-27
Settler's Grove of Ancient Cedars 8-13
Seyforth, William and Evelyn 1-7
Seyforth's Grocery 1-6, 1-7
Shady Lady Saloon 7-28
Shamel, Art 4-14
Shamel, Georgene Bennett 4-14
Shapiro, Dr. Stan 7-13
Sheep Corral Site 5-18
Shelton, John and Florence 3-8
Sherman Park Addition 3-6 to 3-9
Sherman, General William T. 2-20,
    2-21, 3-4 to 3-6, 7-4
Shewmaker, Billie 7-12, 7-19, 7-21
Shiplett and Sons Gas Station 7-13
Shiplett, Jack 7-13
Shoshone County 5-24, 5-25, 7-51
    Council of Boy Scouts 4-5
    Food Bank 7-29
    Infirmary 7-48
    Jail 7-48
    Mining & Smelting Museum 7-23,
    7-24
    seat 8-9
    Sheriff 7-25, 7-41, 7-50
Shoshone Creek 8-14
Shoshone News Press 7-28
Shoshone Work Center 6-15, 6-16
Sidney Mine 7-14
Sierra Silver Mine Tour 8-3
Silver Bridge 7-14, 8-18
Silver Capital of the World 7-51
Silver Creek 7-16
Silver Mountain Ski Resort 7-28
Silver Needle 7-29
Silver Valley 7-14
Silver Valley Appliance and Mercantile

7-29
Silver Valley Lab 7-19
Silverton 7-45, 7-46, 7-48, 7-49
Silverwood Theme Park 2-10, 2-11
Simon's Amusement Co. 7-38
Simpson, Howard 7-15
Sims, George and Nellie 2-20
Singletary, Robert and Connie 3-16
Sisters' Building 4-24
Skating Rink, Kellogg 7-30
Skindlov, A.M. 1-19
Skinner, Stewart Service Station 1-13
Skippy motorboat taxi 3-9
Skitwish Peak 6-7
Skookum Creek 6-9 to 6-11
Slab and Knot Hole Lumber Co. 5-15
Slab Inn 1-9
Slate Creek 5-20, 5-26
Slate Creek Road 225 5-28
Slate Peak 5-14
Slaughterhouse Gulch 7-27
Smelterville 7-17 to 7-19, 7-49
    Feed Store 7-18
Smith, Arch 5-29
Smith, Frank and Elizabeth 7-13
Smith House 7-13
Smith, Yellow Dog 6-15
Snakepit 8-20
Snyder, George 7-10
Snyder, Ted and Cleo 7-11
Snyder, Tom 7-10
Snyder's Grocery 7-11
Sondahl's Pottery 1-20
Sourdough Club 6-3
Spaceships 8-2, 8-3
Spades Mountain Lookout 6-7
Spear Home 2-8, 2-9
Spear, Joseph Home 2-9
Speck, Clay 8-6
Sperry, Lyman 5-12
Spirit Lake 1-17 to 1-23
    Historic Business District 1-20
    Land Co. 1-18
    Real Estate Office 1-20
Spokane Aquifer 1-11, 2-4
Spokane Bridge 1-8, 1-9
Spokane Falls & Idaho Railroad 1-9
Spokane Idaho Mine 7-14

Spokane International Railway 1-25, 1-26, 2-6 to 2-12, 3-2
Spokane Iron Works 4-17
Spokane Irrigation Canal see Corbin Ditch
Spokane Reservation 4-24
Spokane River 1-2, 1-4, 1-8 3-6
 Bridge 1-8
Spores 5-25
Spragpole Inn 8-10
Spragpole Museum 8-12
Spring Creek Cabins 5-17
Springston 4-6, 4-7
Spruce Tree Campground 5-31, 5-32
Squaw Bay, Lake Pend Oreille 2-5
Squaw Bay Resort Marina and Store 4-5
Stack-Gibbs Lumber Co. 3-4
Staff House 7-23, 7-24
Stanley, Al 5-19
Stanley Ranch 5-19
Star Lodging 4-12
State Creek 6-5
Stauffer 5-10
Stauffer, Bobby 5-31
Steam Donkey 4-18
Steamboat Creek Pond 8-17
Steamboat Landing 2-3
Steamboat Rock 8-17
Steamboats 3-11, 3-12, 4-3, 4-4, 4-27, 7-11
 Flyer 4-16
 Mary Moody 2-3, 2-4
 Miss Spokane 4-8
 Rustler 2-9
Steel Bridge, Coeur d'Alene River 8-16
Stein, Ed 7-32, 7-33
Stein's Grocery 7-32, 7-33
Sterling silver 7-41
Stetson Trestle 5-26
Stevens, Governor 4-4
Stevens Peak 5-28
Steven's Ranch 7-43
Stewart family 8-15
Stone, Herb 6-14
Stone's Grocery 7-30
Storm Creek 5-20, 5-26

Storm Mountain 5-19
Strahorn, Mr. 2-13
Stratton Mines 8-5
Strobel, John 5-4
Strobel Mill 5-4
Sturgeon 1-17
Submarines 2-7
Substation, electric line railroad 3-10
Sugar beets 2-11
Sunnyside 7-37
Sunset 8-4
Sunset Peak 8-6
Sunset Stage 8-6
Sunshine Mine 7-8
 miners' strike 7-41
 General Manager's House 7-41
 Silver refinery 7-41
Surface Plant 7-42
Superfund Site 7-20
Sverdsten, Terry 7-6
Swedes 2-20
Sweeney, Charles 7-21
Sweeney
 Heights 7-20
 Mill 7-21
Swiftwater 5-17
Switzerland 5-30

~ T ~

Taft Tunnel 5-27, 7-53
Tall Pine Drive-In 7-16
Tamarack 8-6
 Mine 8-5
Taylor House 3-17
Taylor, Huntington 3-17
Taylor, Marshall and Edith Hubbard 3-17
Taylor, S.M. 5-27
Teeters Field 7-35
TeleSystems 7-38
Templin, Robert 3-12
Tendall, Lars 3-7
Tensed 4-23
Tepee Summit, Creek 6-12, 6-14
Tesemini 1-18
Texaco Gas Station, Fighting Creek 4-27
The Pub 5-23
Theis, Sam 6-3

Theriault 5-31
Thompson, David 3-2
Thompson Falls Pass 8-9
Thompson, G.S. "Doc" 4-14
Thompson, John 4-16
Thompson Slough 4-6
Thomson, George 3-16
Thomson House 3-16
Thornhill, Mr. 7-31, 7-32
Three Toots 7-17
Thunder Peak 5-19
Tip Top Bar 7-36
Tobler Marina 2-18
Tom Wright 6-12
Toncray, Addison 8-9
Tourtellotte and Hummel, Architects 7-15
Town brothers 7-16
Trail 186 5-29
Trail Creek 6-12, 6-14, 8-7, 8-8
  Work Camp Site 6-13
Trail of the Coeur d'Alenes 4-7, 4-12, 4-20, 5-3, 5-4, 5-8, 7-2, 7-10, 7-36, 7-37, 7-41, 8-20
Transporting Logs by Water 6-11
Trapping 6-14
Triangle Trucking 8-4
Triplett, Allen and Kay 5-5
Triplett Ranch Site 5-5
Trout Creek 5-8
Truss Bridge, Marble Creek 5-17 to 5-19
Tubbs Hill 3-12, 3-13
Tubbs, Tony 3-13
Turner Bay 4-6
Turner Campground 5-29, 5-30
Turner, Mary Elizabeth, Eugene and Jessie 5-30
Turner, Sherman 4-6
Tuttle 8-18
Twain, Mark 8-9
Twentieth Century Reading Circle 1-16
Twin City 7-27, 7-36
Twin City Fuel 7-27
Twin City Furniture 7-27, 7-32
Twin City Hardware 7-27, 7-33
Twin Lakes 1-17

Two Mile Creek 7-44
Two-Mile Stage Route 8-6
Two Mile Wagon Road 7-44
Two Yay Yays Grocery Store 4-25
Typhoid Epidemic 5-20

~ U ~

Union Legion Building 7-35
Union Pacific Railroad 1-25, 4-7, 4-8, 4-12, 4-20, 5-2 to 5-4, 7-25, 7-36, 7-37, 7-44, 7-45
  Swing Bridge 4-20
Upper Log Landing 5-29
Uptown Hair Studio 7-31
USAMedia 7-38
U.S. Army Corp of Engineers 6-14
U.S. Forest Service 2-21, 4-19, 5-14, 5-16, 5-18 to 5-25, 5-29, 5-32, 5-33, 6-3, 6-4, 6-6, 6-8, 6-9, 6-12 to 6-16, 7-11, 7-12, 7-49, 8-14 to 8-16, 8-18
U.S. Hwy 10 see Yellowstone Trail
U.S. War Department 3-6

~ V ~

Van Dorn, Nancy 1-7
Van Rena 7-18
Vang, Lloyd 7-33
Vang, Ole Martin 7-33
Vang's Shoe Shop 7-33
Veterans Memorial 1-10
Veterans Memorial Centennial Bridge 4-2
VFW (Veterans of Foreign Wars) Hall
  Kellogg 7-31
  Kingston 7-13
  Spirit Lake 1-22
  St. Maries 4-13
Villa Glendalough 3-16, 3-17
Vollmeck, J.W. and Grace 3-8
Voltolini, Faust 7-50
Von Luertzer, Baron Feodar 3-17
Vork, Vernon and Calvin 7-15

~ W ~

Waggoner, Allene 7-18
Waggoner, Mike 7-29
Wah Hing Chinese Restaurant 7-35
Wall, Darrell 7-6
Wallace 7-51 to 7-53

District Mining Museum 7-52
Lew 8-4
Meat Co. 8-4
Oscar 8-4
Parade 7-32
Ranger District 7-48, 8-15
to Murray stage route 8-6
Visitor's Center 7-51
William and Lucy 7-51
William R. 7-11
Wall's Service Station 7-6
Ward Peak 5-31, 5-32
Ward Peak Ranger Station 5-29, 5-32
Wardner 7-22, 7-23, 7-25 to 7-28, 7-36, 7-38
Gift Shop and Museum 7-27, 7-28
Hospital 7-22, 7-31
Industrial Union 7-35
News 7-28
Parade 7-27
Wardner, James 7-26
Wardner-Kellogg News 7-28
Warren Hussey Bank 8-10
Warren, James House 4-13
Washington Brick & Lime Co. 2-6 to 2-9
Washington Post 8-9
Washington Trust Co. 2-7
Washington Water Power (Avista) 1-3, 1-4, 3-7, 3-8, 3-11, 4-18, 7-16, 7-21
Bridge 1-3, 1-4
Watts, Sherman and Lawanna 7-16
Waverly, Washington 2-11
Wayside Market 7-18
Weeks Field 3-3
Weippe, Idaho 8-13
Wellman, Albert and Charlie 7-37
Wendler Brothers Confectionary 1-14
Wendt, F.W. and Constance 4-11
Wenz, Dr. Frank 1-14, 1-15
Wenz Drug Store 1-14
West Wallace 7-48
Wester, Frank 3-18
Western Rooming House 4-18
Westwood Historical Society 1-15
Westwood, see Rathdrum
Weyerhaeuser, J.P. "Phil" Jr. and Helen
3-8, 3-9
Whalen Hotel 7-10
Whalen, Patrick J. 7-9, 7-10
White Creek 8-7
White Elephant Saloon 8-13
White Horse Saloon 1-20
White, J.C. 3-15
White Star Navigation Co. 4-4
Whitehouse Apartments 1-19
Whiteman Lumber Co. 7-8
Whiteman, Wesley, Harry, Laddie and Keith 7-8
White's Shoes 7-33
Whitman Massacre 2-21
Wiggett Building 3-14
Wiggett, J.W. 3-14
Wigwam Club House 2-16
Wilbur, Rusty and James 7-15
Wilbur's Grocery 7-15
Wildflowers 6-12
Wildhorse Trail 2-4
Wildlife Federation 3-12
Williams, George 3-10, 3-15
Williams, Oscar 7-11
Williams, Sam "49" 5-22, 5-31
Wilson, Bob 4-19
Wilson Drug 3-14
Wilson, Mr. 7-41
Wilson, Ralph, Clayton and Victor 3-14
Windy Bay 4-27
Windy Ridge 6-7
Wine's Auto Court 7-50
Wingover Café 2-11
Winton, Charles and David 5-3
Winton, Charles and Henrietta 3-8
Winton, David and Katherine 3-8, 3-9
Winton Lumber Co. 3-4 to 3-6, 3-8, 5-2 to 5-5, 6-9 to 6-12, 6-14, 6-16, 8-14 to 8-16, 8-18
Winton Mansion 5-4
Winton Mill Site 5-3
Winton-Rosenberry Lumber Co. 5-12
Winton Row House 5-5
Winton Store 5-3
Wolf Lodge 4-4, 7-3
Wolf Lodge Saddle 6-7
Wolfe, Rodney 5-14